SHELLFISH COOKERY

Shellfish Cookery

ABSOLUTELY
DELICIOUS
RECIPES
FROM THE
WEST COAST

BY JOHN DOERPER

Pacific Search Press

To Victoria

Pacific Search Press, 222 Dexter Avenue North,
    Seattle, Washington 98109
© 1985 by John Doerper. All rights reserved
Printed in the United States of America

Edited by Margaret Foster-Finan
Designed by Judy Petry

Cover: Photographs by Fred Milkie

LIBRARY OF CONGRESS CATALOGING-IN-PUBLICATION DATA

Doerper, John.
    Shellfish cookery.

    Includes index.
    1. Cookery (Shellfish)   I. Title.
TX753.D64 1985   641.6′94   85-17031
ISBN 0-931397-01-4

CONTENTS

INTRODUCTION

Why a book on shellfish? Because I love shellfish. True, you may say, so does just about everyone else. There are very few people out there who do not like shrimp, scallops, or crab and lobster, or even squid (calamari), abalone, and octopus. But I start losing some of my fellow shellfish aficionados as soon as I serve oysters raw, on the half shell, and I have a lot of culinary friends who refuse to eat such delightful marine delicacies as limpets, sea urchin roe, and sea cucumber. I have noticed two main reasons for this reluctance to eat some of the stranger of our shellfish: appearance and freshness.

The eating of even the best and freshest of shellfish may be an acquired art, since many shellfish look outlandish, to say the least. To those of us who are used to eating our meats in the form of tidy steaks or fillets, who partake of clams mostly in the form of chowders, and know scallops only as roundish little white things, shellfish in the rough appear rather formidable. But once any shellfish is cleaned and readied for the table, it looks considerably less scurrilous.

Shellfish is at its best, and presents us with its true taste, only when eaten perfectly fresh, preferably just after it has been removed from the water. (This is not to say that some shellfish is not palatable when eaten a day or so after it has been collected. It is simply not as good.) This exquisitely fresh taste lasts for only a brief, fleeting moment. Once that moment has passed, the shellfish will still be edible for a while, but it will not possess that special flavor of true freshness. I relate this evanescent beauty of taste to the evanescent beauty of nature.

The Japanese have expressed the evanescence of natural beauty through the symbol of the morning glory, which opens in the morning, fully charged with life and yet becomes but a memory of its glory by nightfall. I think of it as the evanescent beauty of an oyster's aroma, taste, and texture. Once you open an oyster, its beauty fades even more quickly than that of the morning glory. You must get the oyster fresh from its native waters, and you must eat it right away, while its plump little body still lies quivering on the shell. Else you will taste only a faded memory of its toothsome glory.

This too holds true for mussels and clams, for crayfish and shrimp, and for lobsters and crabs. Shellfish must be eaten perfectly fresh, or they will lose their special beauty.

Yet life is full of compromises. It is not always possible to get shellfish fresh from the water, no matter how much energy we put into the effort. We must then settle for the best we can get, that is, for shellfish that is fresh enough and has been handled well to preserve as much of that evanescent flavor as possible.

I overcome this problem in a simple fashion, by adjusting my methods of preparation to take advantage of the best shellfish has to offer at each stage of edibility: very fresh shellfish I like to eat raw. Just-caught shrimp may be eaten just as they come from the shell, still quiveringly alive. Oysters, mussels, cockles, clams, and scallops may be shucked in situ and slurped from the shell. These should be served with no condiments but a few drops of fresh lemon, lime, or limón juice.

Large mollusks such as squid or geoduck clams may be cleaned and sliced and enjoyed as sashimi. Others are better if they are lightly cooked. Crayfish, crabs, octopi, and spiny lobsters can be steamed, boiled, or quickly grilled after they are captured and may be accompanied by simple, taste-enhancing dipping sauces. None of these seafoods should ever be overcooked, lest they lose their delicate flavors.

Once shellfish have lost that special fresh flavor edge, they are still perfectly acceptable in dishes that require longer cooking. Oysters are very good in stews and pies. Scallops, crabs, and shrimp do very well in all sorts of sauced dishes. Clams and mussels lend themselves to spiced pasta sauces, and squid do well in stewed dishes. Octopus keeps well in the freezer once it has been cooked.

If you cannot find perfectly fresh shellfish at your fish-monger's, you are better off eating high-quality frozen shell-fish. Unfortunately, not all shellfish freeze well. I avoid frozen oysters, mussels, clams, crayfish, and crabs. (Though these may be all right if they are made into a dish and then frozen.) But frozen scallops and shrimp can be truly excellent (much better than a product that has been "fresh" for several days). Spiny lobster also freezes exceptionally well, as do squid, octopus, limpet, and abalone. Buy only the best brand of frozen shellfish (you may have to spend a few pennies more, but it is well worth it) and take care in defrosting it. Follow package instructions precisely and never defrost shellfish in hot water or you will lose all of its flavor. Defrost only as much as you will use for one meal.

FORTUNATELY, FRESH SHELLFISH, just hours from the water, is readily available to West Coast cooks today. For this, we must thank a handful of determined aquaculturists — or "sea farmers," as they like to be called. Shellfish farms assure a reliable supply of this tasty food, because sea farmers "seed" their shellfish beds and harvest only enough to meet the daily needs of the market. Aquaculture thus is aloof from the feast or famine approach that characterizes the plucking and dig-ging of wild shellfish.

In nonfarm shellfish collecting, every man is on his own and must gather his allotted share of the wild stocks quickly, before another collector harvests it. Often the shellfish is then stored out of the water (a method not known to improve its palatability), while the gatherer searches for a buyer. Rapa-cious exploitation of wild stocks led to the decline and final collapse of native oyster stocks in San Francisco Bay, Willapa Bay, and Puget Sound, and it has driven the Pismo clam and the razor clam to the brink of commercial extinction.

As shellfish farms increase their capacity, they more than keep up with market demand. And, since shellfish release their spawn (in uncounted millions) into the water, where it is picked up and distributed by ocean currents, the stable breeding population of shellfish living on farms helps restock depleted shellfish beds along the entire West Coast. In this fashion several desirable introduced species, particularly the Pacific (or Japanese) oyster, the Japanese littleneck (Manila) clam, the ribbed horse mussel, and a Korean brackish-water shrimp have established themselves over a wide range. The introduction of these species has not only benefited man, but has also been quite fortuitous for other animals: seabirds just dote on the ribbed mussel, and the small Korean shrimp are now an important food for fish in the Sacramento River delta and in the San Francisco Bay region.

The introduced cultivated species have taken commercial harvesting pressure off domestic species as well. The Pacific oyster and the European flat oyster have replaced the embattled native (Olympia) oyster in the seafood trade, and the Japanese littleneck clam is now more popular with both shellfish growers and consumers than native littleneck and butter clams.

Shellfish culture has had other benefits as well. Sea farmers have long been in the forefront of the fight to maintain clean waters, and they deserve much of the credit for keeping bays and estuaries up and down the West Coast clean. Thanks largely to their efforts, the water quality along the coast is now better than it was thirty or forty years ago.

The selective processes of aquaculture have also led to a most remarkable improvement in the flavor of our shellfish. Forty years ago, marine biologist Ed Ricketts could say of the Pacific oyster that it "is about as appetizing to a gourmet as a blob of mucus." No longer. As these oysters have adapted themselves to West Coast growing conditions, they have undergone an evolution in flavor. The best now surpass the much touted East Coast oyster (which grows wild in some of our bays and sounds) in flavor. There is even some suspicion that the Pacific oyster may have hybridized here and there with the Atlantic oyster to produce a flavorful superspecies. (The Atlantic oyster was farmed on the West Coast for a few decades early in the century.)

West Coast oysters received their due at a seafood extravaganza held in March of 1985 at the Seattle aquarium in conjunction with a convention of the International Association of Cooking Schools where knowledgeable food professionals were given an opportunity to taste our shellfish at its best and freshest. Earlier that day I had moderated a shellfish seminar at which several shellfish growers lovingly described their products and handed out samples to an eager audience of food writers, cooking teachers, and *bec fins*. The response exceeded our expectations. Even such unusual (to Americans) offerings as raw mussels on the half shell were devoured with gusto. Everybody just loved the oysters, whether native Olympias, Pacifics, hybrids, or European flats. The response was the same, though on a larger scale, at the seafood extravaganza. That evening, during dinner, I asked food authorities Julia Child and Ann Willan about their response to our West Coast oysters. They loved them. I told them about Ricketts's "blob of mucus" statement. They did not think it applied. West Coast oysters have finally arrived.

What holds true for oysters applies to other shellfish as well. Dungeness crab received its due a few years back when a famous New York food critic, who had called this delectable crab "inferior," finally visited the West Coast and tried it fresh. Among other shellfish, our sea snails are now receiving the critical attention they deserve. West Coast octopus and squid are becoming increasingly popular, and our small, farm-raised steamer clams delight gourmets everywhere. And even the most hard-boiled critics now admit that West Coast scallops are at least as good — if not better — than East Coast scallops. Especially when they are prepared whole, in the shell (a method we have learned from the French).

OYSTERS ARE THE MOST PLENTIFUL of our farmed shellfish. They have been farmed on the West Coast for a hundred-odd years now. About six types of oysters are raised on the coast: the native (Olympia) oyster, the Pacific oyster, the Kumamoto oyster (a sport of the Pacific oyster), a hybrid oyster (Pacific Kumamoto), and the European flat oyster.

In the simplest form of oyster culture, the grower cleans an intertidal beach and "seeds" it with cultch (old oyster shells to which young oysters have become attached). Then he tends the oysters (keeping away predators, such as starfish and cleaning them of suffocating silt) until they reach a harvestable size. Native (Olympia) oysters demand a slightly different treatment. They are raised on diked tideflats that turn into shallow pools when the tide goes out, so the oysters are never exposed. This native oyster is surprisingly tender and easily killed by extremes of heat or cold. Stake culture is slightly more advanced: the cultch is attached to short upright stakes. This exposes more of the oysters to tidal currents (and nutrients).

In rack culture, young oysters laid out in heavy plastic mesh bags are placed onto low racks raised above tideflats. Here they are completely protected from predators, and they can grow fat on nutrients carried by the water surrounding them on all sides during high tide.

In longline culture, the spat is attached to long lines suspended in deep water. These oysters are very tender, because they are never exposed to the stresses of low tide. Since they are always surrounded by nutrient-rich waters, they grow plump and fat very quickly. They are the crème de la crème of commercial oysterdom.

Manila clams are raised on beaches prepared with a sand/gravel mixture of just the consistency these clams like best. The beaches are then covered with fine-meshed fishnet (to keep out predators) and seeded with tiny clamlings. When the clams have reached harvestable size (in a year or two), they are plowed up and the beach is readied for the next crop.

Commercially raised mussels are the greatest contribution made by sea farmers to our cuisine. More tender and more flavorful than wild mussels, cultivated mussels are among our most exquisite shellfish. They have taken the West by storm. All but unknown a mere decade ago, mussels are now to be found just about everywhere in fish markets and first-rate restaurants.

There is more to come. Right now, sea farmers in Southern California and on Vancouver Island are already raising abalone to marketable size. In the near future, the shrimp we eat will come increasingly from sea farms, and at least one aquaculturist is experimenting with such tasty species as rock scallops.

We can say with confidence that there has never been a period in West Coast culinary history when shellfish were more popular than they are now. The reasons for this are simple. Besides the remarkable improvement in flavor, the quality of the shellfish available to the consumer is better than ever before. Modern storage, cooling, and transportation methods make it possible to carry the shellfish from the farm to the consumer in so short a time that it is still fresh when it reaches the table. There is quite a difference between native oysters gathered at Willapa Bay and taken to San Francisco by slow sailing schooner (as in the middle of the nineteenth century) and native Olympia oysters plucked off the tideflats on the first low tide of the morning and airfreighted to the city in time for dinner. Crab landed in Noyo or Eureka in the morning are taken by truck to San Francisco the same day, and shrimp from the Sea of Cortez can reach markets in Los Angeles the next day.

These twentieth century advances in handling, storage, and transportation apply to other seafoods as well. But what makes shellfish unique is the way it is eaten, what we might call its "cultural diversity."

FEW FOODS SPAN AS MANY CULTURAL gaps as shellfish. Oysters, for example, are collected on the tideflats by (often low-income) families and either eaten on the spot or taken home to enrich the family larder. They are served as fritters in fast-food eateries, and they are presented, freshly shucked and on the half shell on a bed of crushed ice (commonly atop a silver platter) in the fanciest restaurants. The same kind of shrimp trapped by sportfishermen in Puget Sound or along the California coast and cooked or roasted over a campfire are rushed by commercial fishermen to sushi bars and other restaurants (where they command a high price). Crabs, clams, abalones, and sea snails, free for the taking, are plentiful along our coast, yet the very same species are among the fancy offerings at seafood markets and restaurants.

Shellfish may be enjoyed in its most simple form, raw, fresh from the shell, or in the most fanciful of preparations. A fresh oyster, shucked and eaten on the beach where it has spent its entire lifetime is an inimitable treat. Yet that same oyster is equally good enhanced by a few drops of lemon or limón, or by a mignonette or soy dipping sauce. It becomes sublime when topped with fresh sturgeon caviar. It is eminently delectable with a tomato sauce and herbed bread crumbs, or in a lightly seasoned creamy stew. Crayfish, spiny lobster, and prawns are superb barbecued just after they come from the water, or broiled, boiled, or steamed. They are delicious served with a simple lemon butter or with a fancy cream or wine reduction sauce over which a skilled chef has slaved for hours. They make perfect eating by the light of a beach fire and by the subdued candlelight of a snooty eatery. They are as enhanced by paper plates and plastic forks as they are by *Shino* dishes and ivory chopsticks or Spode china and silver.

Shellfish are the most democratic of foods, since they are equally available to both the very rich and the very poor — though the very poor may have the advantage here since they collect their shellfish at the source. There is nothing fresher than an abalone, limpet, mussel, or oyster plucked off the rocks; a crab, shrimp, spiny lobster, or crayfish freshly trapped; or clams and cockles freshly dug.

THERE ARE, HOWEVER, A FEW PROBLEMS with collecting your own shellfish that must be mentioned here. The first of these is that you must be absolutely sure the beach is unpolluted by raw sewage or by industrial effluents. Check with a local fish store, tackle shop, or health department. You cannot always see, smell, or taste pollutants.

I must also add a word of caution about a peculiar, and potentially deadly, phenomenon that protects bivalves from warm-blooded predators during much of the spawning months: the notorious red tide. At certain times of the year, usually in summer, when combinations of water temperature, light, salinity, nutrients, and minerals reach the proper concentration, rapid multiplication of a tiny dinoflagellate, a free-swimming microscopic sea creature, may occur. These organisms may then appear in such great numbers that they dye the ocean water red. Thus, "red" tide. This "bloom," as it is called by the specialists, is good news for bivalves, who eagerly filter this increased food source into their digestive tracts, and bad news for humans and other warm-blooded animals to whom these dinoflagellates are toxic. Bivalves absorb the toxin into their body tissues in varying concentrations and for unpredictable lengths of time as they digest the dinoflagellates.

The toxin seems to have no effect whatsoever on the bivalves, but it severely affects human nerve impulses. If ingested in large enough quantities by humans (the amount of tolerance, or lack thereof, seems to vary in different individuals and is little understood by medical doctors and scientists), the paralytic shellfish toxin may cause, at first, numbness and tingling of the lips, tongue, face, fingers, and toes. More severe cases may cause difficulty in speaking, an inability to swallow, and muscle incoordination. Very extreme cases may cause death. There is no known antidote for the toxin; treatment consists of emptying the stomach and the use of a quick-acting laxative. Artificial respiration should be applied if breathing becomes difficult.

Now that all that unpleasant stuff has been said, I must point out that very few people are ever affected by paralytic shellfish poisoning (PSP), that there have been even fewer severe cases, and only a couple of fatalities. Ever. There is even some speculation that longtime residents of the coast, who were raised on local shellfish, may be immune to the toxin to a greater or lesser extent (but don't tempt your luck!).

In California, all wild bivalves are quarantined from 1 May to 1 October. In the Northwest things are not as simple. There are no blanket closures, but all along the northern coasts local health departments keep an eye out for possible outbreaks of PSP, test potentially affected mollusks regularly, and close beaches where clams, oysters, and mussels may be affected for the duration of an outbreak. You must use a bit more caution in Mexico and Canada, where the health departments are not quite as vigilant (due mainly to staffing and access problems). Be sure, too, that any clams, oysters, or mussels you collect in the wild come from *unpolluted* waters. Such dangerous pollutants as coliform bacteria affect mussels as well as other shellfish — after all, the mollusks spent their entire life in the water and cannot help picking up free-floating organisms as they strain their food from the marine broth encompassing them.

There is a reassuring note, however: all the shellfish you buy from a commercial producer should be safe, the health department makes sure of that.

Crabs and other crustaceans are not affected by this red tide (though you should discard all of their internal organs at such times as a precaution: the crabs may have been feeding on clams). Grazing mollusks, like abalones, limpets, and other snails are also unaffected, since they do not filter their sustenance from the water. This means that even during the height of the summer tourist season (when seaside weather is at its most pleasant), there should be enough shellfish out there to make a collecting trip worthwhile.

Even if you have access to the best fish market with the best and freshest seafood in the world, you should plan an occasional trip to the coast to collect shellfish for yourself. There is no other way to truly experience its magnificent taste (though a few oyster bars and sushi places may come close). Besides, what better excuse for a vacation! Fortunately almost everyone on the West Coast lives within a few hours' — or at most a day's — drive of the coast. Bring your shovel, bucket, and oyster knife and enjoy yourself. And keep in mind, as you sit on a beach, eating freshly shucked oysters from the shell, or as you recline by the campfire eating crab, shrimp, or crayfish you have just caught and cooked that no one else, anywhere, is eating better than you at that very moment.

SAUCES

Béchamel Sauce
(BASIC WHITE SAUCE)

MAKES ABOUT 1½ CUPS

4 tablespoons butter
4 tablespoons all-purpose flour
Salt and freshly ground
 white pepper to taste
1 cup milk
1 cup cream

Nouvelle cuisine abandoned the roux for basic sauces. But a well-done roux can do things for a sauce like nothing else. It possesses an amazing thickening power, because the little flour granules swell up and gain the ability to soak up moisture like microsponges. Make sure the flour is cooked for several minutes, or the roux (and thus the sauce) may taste of raw flour forevermore. Unsalted butter adds a good flavor to the sauce (from the butter solids). Clarified butter (melted butter from which the butter solids have been skimmed and strained) is easier to use if you have problems with browning or burning the roux. It acts much like an oil. Béchamel Sauce goes very well with most shellfish, including barnacles, scallops, and mussels.

1. Melt butter in heavy saucepan over low heat. Stir in flour to make a roux. Add salt and pepper. Keep heat low so roux will not turn brown (or even burn), and stir constantly so it will not be lumpy (or stick to the pan). Cook for several minutes.
2. Slowly stir in milk, then cream. Cook, stirring, until sauce is smooth and creamy.

Herb Sauce

MAKES 1 CUP

1 cup Béchamel Sauce
 (see p. 18)
1 tablespoon chopped fresh
 herbs or ½ tablespoon
 dried herbs

To the basic Béchamel Sauce, add fresh or dried herbs of your choice: dill, parsley, chives, chervil, rosemary, basil, celery, lovage, or whatever tastes good to you and strikes your fancy. Restaurant chefs often like to veil their herb sauces in mystery, but this is all there is to it. Like the basic Béchamel Sauce, this Herb Sauce enhances most shellfish. Try it with abalone, mussels, crab, crayfish, and barnacles.

1. Blend sauce and herbs.

3 egg yolks
6 tablespoons unsalted butter
¼ cup boiling water
2 tablespoons freshly squeezed
    lemon juice
¼ teaspoon salt
    Sprinkle cayenne

Hollandaise Sauce

This is one of the most popular sauces for shellfish. It is quite delicate and really brings out the delightful flavors of the seafood. It enhances crab, spiny lobster, crayfish, abalone, oysters, and scallops.

1. In top of double boiler, heat egg yolks, whisking until smooth. Slowly add butter 1 tablespoon at a time and stir constantly.
2. Cook over hot water (boiling water will curdle the sauce) until thickened, stirring constantly. Gradually stir in water and lemon juice, then salt and cayenne. Use immediately.

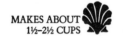

4 tablespoons butter
4 tablespoons all-purpose flour
    Salt and freshly ground
        white pepper to taste
1–2 cups dry white wine
        (depending on desired
        thickness of sauce)
1 cup cream (optional)

White Wine Sauce

This is a very simple recipe. It does not have the finesse of a wine reduction sauce, but, nevertheless, it performs many admirable workhorse functions in the culinary repertoire. It is particularly good with mussels.

1. Melt butter in heavy saucepan over low heat. Stir in flour to make a roux. Add salt and pepper. Keep heat low so roux will not turn brown (or burn), and stir constantly so it will not be lumpy (or stick to the pan). Cook for several minutes.
2. Slowly stir in wine. I also like to add cream at this point to make a richer sauce, but cream is not absolutely necessary for this sauce. Do not overheat sauce, or cream may curdle. Cook, stirring, until sauce is smooth and creamy.

MAKES 1½ CUPS

¼ cup vinegar
¼ cup dry white wine
1 tablespoon finely chopped
    fresh tarragon
1 tablespoon minced shallot
1 tablespoon finely chopped
    chervil or parsley
¼ bay leaf (California laurel
    or Oregon myrtle)
¼ teaspoon freshly ground
    pepper
3 egg yolks, beaten
¼ teaspoon salt
½ cup melted unsalted butter
    Dash of cayenne

Béarnaise Sauce

This sauce is basically a tangier version of Hollandaise Sauce, flavored with onion and tarragon. Use it with crab, shrimp, crayfish, barnacles, mud shrimp, mussels, oysters, clams, cockles, and scallops.

1. Combine vinegar, wine, tarragon, shallot, chervil, bay leaf, and pepper in saucepan. Cook over low heat until reduced by ½. Strain mixture into top of double boiler.
2. With wire whisk or rotary beater, beat in egg yolks and salt. Cook over hot water until thickened. Beat in butter 1 tablespoon at a time. Sharpen with a little cayenne. Beat over heat until creamy, about 1 minute.

MAKES ABOUT 1–1½ CUPS

4 tablespoons butter
4 tablespoons all-purpose flour
    Salt and freshly ground
    white pepper to taste
1 cup milk
1 cup cream
½ cup grated hard Sonoma
    Jack, Gruyère, or
    Parmesan cheese
1 egg yolk, lightly beaten

Mornay Sauce

This is basically a Béarnaise Sauce to which grated cheese and an egg yolk have been added. Try this sauce with crab, shrimp, scallops, and abalone.

1. Melt butter in heavy saucepan over low heat. Stir in flour to make a roux. Add salt and pepper. Keep heat low so roux will not turn brown (or burn), and stir constantly so it will not be lumpy (or stick to the pan). Cook for several minutes.
2. Slowly stir in milk, then cream. Add grated cheese; blend in. Cook, stirring all the time, until sauce is smooth and creamy.
3. Just before serving, add egg yolk, stir to blend well (be sure sauce is not too hot, or egg yolk will cook before it is integrated into the sauce).

Oyster Mushroom Sauce

4 tablespoons butter
4 tablespoons all-purpose flour
Salt and freshly ground
   white pepper to taste
1–2 cups dry white wine
   (depending on desired
   thickness of sauce)
½ cup finely chopped oyster
   mushrooms, lightly
   sautéed in butter
1 cup cream (optional)

I like to use oyster mushrooms for shellfish sauces because their flavor is more delicate and has an affinity for mollusks and crustaceans. Fresh oyster mushrooms are available in ethnic markets, gourmet supermarkets, and in the wild (from California north). This sauce is a variation on the wine sauce. Try it with mussels, oysters, scallops, crab, and crayfish.

1. Melt butter in heavy saucepan over low heat. Stir in flour to make a roux. Add salt and pepper. Keep heat low so roux will not turn brown (or burn), and stir constantly so it will not be lumpy (or stick to the pan). Cook for several minutes.
2. Slowly stir in wine. Add mushrooms; blend in well. After the oyster mushrooms have been blended in, I like to add cream to make a richer sauce, but cream is not absolutely necessary for this sauce. Do not overheat sauce, or cream may curdle. Cook for a few minutes more, stirring constantly, until sauce is smooth and creamy.

Velouté Sauce

4 tablespoons unsalted butter
4 tablespoons all-purpose flour
Salt and freshly ground
   white pepper to taste
2 cups fish fumet, mild chicken
   stock, or dashi
1 cup cream

Velouté Sauce can be made with different stocks. But you should use a fish fumet, mild chicken stock, or Japanese dashi stock if you plan to use the velouté with shellfish.

1. Melt butter in heavy saucepan. Stir in flour, salt, and pepper, making sure no lumps form. Cook for about 1 minute over low heat. Slowly stir in fish fumet. Simmer for 15 minutes; occasionally skim off scum. Add cream and stir until thick and smooth.

MAKES 1½ CUPS

½ cup unsalted butter
2 tablespoons chopped parsley
1 teaspoon fresh tarragon or
    ½ teaspoon dried
¼ teaspoon salt
    A few grinds pepper
1 tablespoon freshly squeezed
    lemon juice
1 cup Velouté Sauce
    (see p. 21)

Maître d'Hôtel Sauce

To make a maître d'hôtel butter, omit the final step and leave out the Velouté Sauce. Serve the butter as soon as the lemon juice has been stirred in. This sauce goes very well with shrimp, crab, barnacles, abalone, limpets, and scallops.

1. Melt butter in stainless steel or enamel saucepan over low heat. Stir in parsley, tarragon, salt, and pepper. Beat in lemon juice, drop by drop.
2. Mix butter with Velouté Sauce. Use at once.

MAKES ABOUT ¼ CUP

4 shallots, finely chopped
2 tablespoons white wine
1 teaspoon red wine vinegar
    (or to taste)
    Several grinds pepper to taste

Mignonette Sauce

This sauce is commonly served with oysters on the half shell, but it also may be used as a dipping sauce for other shellfish.

1. Combine all ingredients. Serve at room temperature.

MAKES ABOUT 3 CUPS

½ cup minced shallots
2 tablespoons fresh basil or
    1 tablespoon dried
2 tablespoons butter
1 tablespoon olive oil
1½ cups sour cream
¾ cup homemade mayonnaise
⅓ cup horseradish

Horseradish Sauce
(RAIFORT SAUCE)

This sauce is served at the Rhododendron Cafe with smoked shellfish, a superb combination.

1. Sauté shallots and basil in butter and oil for 5 minutes over low heat. Cook and blend with sour cream, mayonnaise, and horseradish. Serve as a dipping sauce.

MAKES ABOUT 2 CUPS

8 chiles serranos or 3–4 chiles
    verdes (Anaheim or
    New Mexico)
½ cup ground dried shrimp,
    unsoaked
3 red onions, coarsely chopped
1 (or more) clove(s) garlic,
    minced
¾ cup almost boiling hot water
    Salt and freshly ground
    white pepper to taste
1 teaspoon fresh gingerroot
¼ cup mission olive oil
2–4 tablespoons white sesame
    seeds (optional)

Shrimp Sauce

If you like your shrimp au naturel, *you may want to accompany
them with this easily prepared very shrimpy hot dipping sauce.*

1. Place chiles, shrimp, onions, garlic, water, salt, pepper,
   and gingerroot in large *molcajete*; crush and blend
   thoroughly with *tejolote,* or put in bowl of food
   processor and process until well blended.
2. Heat oil and add to mixture (scoop mixture into
   heat-proof bowl if using food processor). Stir in well.
   Serve hot or cold (for beach picnic). If served cold, stir
   in sesame seeds to taste.

MAKES 1 CUP

2 eggs
½ teaspoon salt
2 teaspoons dry mustard
1 teaspoon honey
4 tablespoons lemon juice
¾ cup olive oil
1 tablespoon minced parsley
1 tablespoon minced green
    onions
½ teaspoon horseradish
½ teaspoon freshly ground
    pepper
    Dash cayenne
½ teaspoon fresh tarragon,
    chopped

Shrimp Dip

This recipe comes from Lila Gault's The Northwest Cookbook. *"This dip is fine for crab too."*

1. In a blender combine eggs, salt, mustard, honey, and
   lemon juice, and whirl until well blended. Drizzle in
   oil while blending at medium-high speed until
   mixture begins to thicken.
2. Transfer to a bowl, add remaining ingredients, and
   blend thoroughly.

MAKES 1½–2 CUPS

2 tablespoons olive oil
4–6 shallots, chopped
1 clove garlic, chopped
1 cup of chile pulp
        (reconstituted from dried
        chiles that have been
        soaked)
½ teaspoon salt
¼ teaspoon oregano
⅛ teaspoon dried cumin, ground
        Water as needed

Basic California Chile Sauce

This spicy sauce works quite well with all sorts of mild-flavored shellfish (if you like your food hot). Try it with shrimp, crab, crayfish, clams, scallops, oysters, and sea snails.

1. Heat oil in frying pan. Fry shallots and garlic until transparent; add chile pulp, salt, oregano, and cumin.
2. Add enough water to make a thin gravy and boil for about 20 minutes or until sauce thickens. If sauce thickens too quickly, add more liquid. You may use ½ water and ½ simple red country wine.

MAKES ABOUT 2–3 CUPS

1 pound tomatillos, husks
        removed and coarsely
        chopped
6 chiles serranos, chopped
        Water
4 tablespoons cooking oil
¼ medium onion, chopped
        Salt to taste

Salsa Chile Verde I

For a special treat, if you can find fresh green chiles in the fishing port wilderness where you buy your shrimp fresh off the boat, serve shrimp with this chile verde dipping sauce.

1. Place tomatillos in pot with just enough water to cook them; add chiles, simmer until tender. Carefully strain off excess water (if any). Mash and blend until smooth.
2. Heat oil in heavy skillet, add onion and fry until translucent (do not brown). Add tomatillo/chile mixture and cook over high heat until sauce has reduced a little, about 5 minutes. Be careful not to burn it. When sauce seems thick enough, add salt and serve.

MAKES ABOUT 2 CUPS

1 clove garlic
6 green chiles (mild or hot),
    roasted, peeled, and
    seeded*
1 medium-sized onion,
    chopped
4 ripe tomatoes, roasted
    and peeled
  Salt and freshly ground
    black pepper to taste
1 teaspoon white wine
    vinegar

Salsa Chile Verde II

Raw or sautéed shellfish may be served with salsa de chile verde as a dipping sauce. This spicy salsa goes with a surprising variety of mild-flavored shellfish: clams, mussels, oysters, scallops, abalone, sea snails, limpets, cockles, shrimp, crab, barnacles, and crayfish.

1. Mash garlic in a wooden salad bowl. Add chiles and onion. Cut tomato into small pieces; add to bowl with salt, pepper, and vinegar. Mix well and serve.

* To roast and peel peppers: wash peppers well and dry them. Place on hot grill over gas or charcoal (or under broiler in gas or electric oven) until skins blister. Carefully pull off skin. Slice pepper open and remove veins and seeds. If you have sensitive skin, wear thin rubber gloves. In any case, wash hands thoroughly afterwards; do not rub eyes.

MAKES 1 CUP

1 teaspoon curry powder
    (see p. 233)
1 cup Béchamel Sauce
    (see p. 18)

Curry Sauce

This mild curry sauce goes particularly well with crab, shrimp, mud shrimp, barnacles, and crayfish.

1. Make Béchamel Sauce. Before adding milk and cream, stir in curry powder. Cook for a couple of minutes. Then proceed with recipe.

MAKES ABOUT 1¼ CUPS

2 teaspoons almond or apricot
    oil
1 clove garlic, minced
1 teaspoon curry powder
    (see p. 233)
1 cup shellfish, fish, or unsalted
    chicken stock
¼ teaspoon salt
½ teaspoon sugar
1 teaspoon minced fresh
    gingerroot
1 chile poblano or chile verde,
    roasted, peeled, and
    coarsely diced into
    ¼-inch squares (see p. 25)
Cornstarch paste as needed
    (see p. 37)

Chinese Curry Sauce

Chinese Curry sauce, like French Curry Sauce, is much milder than the hot curries of India and southeast Asia. It goes very well with crab, crayfish, shrimp, cockles, and clams.

1. Heat oil in saucepan. Sauté garlic until fragrant. Add curry powder. Stir over medium heat for about 1 minute (avoid burning powder).
2. Add stock, salt, sugar and gingerroot; bring to boil and cook for 1 minute. Add chile; stir in enough thin cornstarch paste to slightly thicken. As soon as sauce thickens, remove from heat.

3 ripe avocados
1 cup virgin olive oil
½ cup white wine vinegar
1 clove garlic, finely chopped
    Lettuce or chicory leaves as
        needed
    Dressing

Basic Aguacate
(AVOCADO)

This is more of a side dish or garnish than a sauce, but it is nice to have around when the spiciness of a sauce becomes overpowering. Nothing cools the palate as nicely as avocado.

1. Peel and slice avocados. Place in shallow bowl or deep platter.
2. Blend olive oil and vinegar; add garlic. Pour over avocado slices. Let marinate overnight.
3. Drain and reserve marinade. Serve on lettuce or chicory leaves. Sprinkle with dressing.

Reserved oil and vinegar
marinade (from
avocado mixture)
¼ *teaspoon salt*
¼ *teaspoon hot paprika*

MAKES ABOUT 2 CUPS

3 *ripe avocados*
Pulp of 1 red chile or
1 teaspoon chili powder
1 *large ripe tomato*
1 *cup chopped celery*
½ *teaspoon salt*
1 *tablespoon finely chopped*
onion or shallot
1 *(or more) clove(s) garlic,*
finely chopped
1 *teaspoon lemon or lime juice*
or ½ teaspoon lemon
and ½ teaspoon lime
Lettuce or chicory leaves
as needed

MAKES ABOUT ½ CUP

½ *cup unsalted butter*
1 *teaspoon freshly squeezed*
lemon juice
Salt and freshly ground
white pepper to taste

DRESSING

1. Blend ingredients in mixing jar; shake vigorously.

Guacamole

Guacamole is one of those sauces that seems to go well with just about anything, especially shellfish cooked in spicy sauces.

1. Coarsely mash avocados and chile pulp; add next 6 ingredients and blend well. Serve on lettuce or chicory leaves.

Beurre Noir

This sauce is best when quickly made in the same pan in which the shellfish has been sautéed. Be sure to use some of the remaining cooking fat for extra flavor. It is good with pan-fried scallops, abalone, and barnacles.

1. Melt butter in small pan. Cook over low heat until brown. Stir in lemon juice and season with salt and pepper. Use at once.

MAKES ABOUT ¾ CUP

¾ cup homemade mayonnaise
1 teaspoon finely chopped
    shallot
1 teaspoon finely chopped
    sweet pickles
1 teaspoon chopped capers
1 teaspoon finely chopped
    stuffed green olives
1 teaspoon chopped parsley,
    and/or chervil and other
    herbs to taste

Tartar Sauce

Homemade Tartar Sauce is a must for deep-fried shrimp, scallops, and clams.

1. Blend together well. Serve as dipping sauce for breaded and deep-fried shellfish.

ABALONES

and

LIMPETS

ABALONE SASHIMI IN GARLIC SAUCE

ABALONE WITH A CALVADOS AND
MAJORCA ROSEMARY SAUCE

OYSTER MUSHROOM AND ABALONE SOUP

ABALONE SALAD

COLD ABALONE AND FETTUCINE SALAD

LIMPET, MUSSEL, AND BELGIAN ENDIVE SALAD
WITH A GINGER-MUSTARD VINAIGRETTE

ABALONE WITH OYSTER MUSHROOMS

ABALONE WITH GREEN FETTUCINE

ABALONE IN RED WINE

BASIC ABALONE STEAK

CLAMLIKE ABALONE

PIA CARROLL'S ABALONE SAUTÉED WITH HAZELNUT
AND LIME BUTTER SAUCE

GINGERED ABALONE WITH PEPPERS AND HOT SAUCE

BARBECUED LIMPETS IN THE SHELL

LIMPETS AU BEURRE NOIR

LIMPET FRITTERS

STIR-FRIED ABALONE AND ASPARAGUS

STIR-FRIED ABALONE WITH BOK CHOY

COMMON NAME	
Red Abalone *(California to Washington)*	This is the largest of our abalones (to ten inches across). It is most common, and larger, in the southern part of its range. This excellent tasting abalone is sufficiently tender for sushi and sashimi.
Pink Abalone *(Baja California to* *Point Conception, California)*	This large abalone (to eight inches across) is very common in southern California. It has a very good taste.
White Abalone *(Baja California to* *southern California)*	This uncommon, large abalone (to seven inches across) is found primarily in the Channel Islands, California. It may well be the tastiest and tenderest of all abalones.
Green Abalone *(California to Juan de Fuca* *Strait, Washington)*	This uncommon abalone is harvested only occasionally. Although they can grow to seven inches across, most green abalones reaching the market are quite small — about four or five inches across. Good taste.
Northern Green Abalone *(California to Juan de Fuca* *Strait, Washington)*	This very small abalone (to four inches across) is moderately common and good to eat.
Pinto Abalone *(Northern Abalone)* *(central California to* *southeastern Alaska)*	This small abalone (to five inches across) is the commercial abalone of British Columbia and Alaska. It is fairly common. It is good to eat, though not as good for sushi and sashimi as the southern species.
Black Abalone *(Baja California to Oregon)*	The black abalone is our only smooth-shelled abalone. It is quite common in intertidal waters, but mostly quite small (can grow to seven inches across), about the size of a very large limpet. Its taste is not as fine as other abalones.
Threaded Abalone *(Baja California to* *southern California)*	This pretty and rather rare deep-water abalone is occasionally dredged up or brought up by divers. Small (to five inches across), it is still good to eat.
Rough Keyhole Limpet *(Baja California to* *southeastern Alaska)*	This small (to one inch across), purplish limpet has a shell marked by numerous rough radial riblets. Common on tidal rocks. Very good to eat.

Volcano Limpet
(entire Pacific Coast of
the United States)

This small limpet (to one inch across) has weak ribs, but pronounced dark purplish rays on a grayish background. Very common in the intertidal zones. Good to eat.

Great Keyhole Limpet
(Baja California to
central California)

Once common in the lower tidal zone, the great keyhole limpet is becoming increasingly rare. It generally grows to three inches across, though very old ones can reach up to six inches across. It is a most delectable limpet with a flavor surpassing that of abalones. It is so tasty, it is just hard to pass up.

Giant Owl Limpet
(Baja California to California)

This large limpet (to four inches across) is common on rocks at the high tide line. It has a most delicious foot. Prepare it like abalone.

Shield Limpet
(Baja California to Bering Sea)

This is one of several limpets, which all look pretty much alike (to one inch across) and are all very good to eat. It is ubiquitous on tidal rocks.

DESCRIPTION

Abalones and limpets are sea snails with low, asymmetrical, flattened shells. Abalone shells have several "breathing" holes in the shell; keyhole limpets have one, in the very top of the shell; and limpets have none.

All have a strong muscular foot used for clinging to rocks and crawling. This is the part commonly eaten.

HABITAT

Abalones and limpets graze on algae-covered rocks. They move about mostly at night. Limpets, with a few exceptions (like the white cap limpet) occur primarily in the upper tide zones. Except for remote areas of the coast, abalones have become scarce in the upper tidal areas (mainly due to overharvesting). Most now live in subtidal waters down to about one hundred feet.

METHODS OF
CATCHING

Collecting abalones and limpets is simple (once you have found them). Search for larger animals in crevices or on the less accessible underside of boulders and rock overhangs.

When threatened by predators, abalones and limpets pull the shell down to the rock with the help of powerful foot muscles while expelling air from the cavity, creating a virtual vacuum. This makes it difficult to remove the large abalones from rocks. Bring a crowbar and a bucket (or gunnysack). Be sure to wear nonslip shoes as you climb about the tidal rocks.

Pluck limpets off the rocks with your fingers (before they have a chance to hunker down), or remove from the substrate by slipping a thin, sharp knife between the shell and rock. (I use the honed tip of my oyster knife.)

Setting captured abalones and limpets onto a flat surface where they can hunker down will preserve precious body moisture. You will be rewarded by a better flavor.

AVAILABILITY IN FISH MARKETS AND RESTAURANTS

Fresh abalones can be bought in better fish markets (particularly in southern California). Look for them in Oriental seafood markets. Most of the commercial harvest on the West Coast is in California, but it is illegal to export abalones from the Golden State. A large share of the abalones sold throughout the country comes from Mexico, British Columbia, and Alaska. Watch out for bootleg abalones.

Abalones are also available frozen and canned. Restaurants serve primarily frozen or canned abalone, though occasionally it is possible to find fresh abalone on the menu. Sushi bars are the great exception here. Look for it in the glass case. It is best if it is still in the shell.

Limpets are sometimes available in sushi shops and Chinese seafood markets.

SEASONS

Abalones are good to eat year-round, but their harvest is strictly regulated in all western states.

Be sure to check on the latest regulations from your state fish and game department. If you are in doubt, inquire at a seaside bait and tackle shop.

HOW TO CLEAN

Flip abalone on its back. Sprinkle foot with coarse salt. This will kill the abalone and draw excess moisture from the foot. Let abalone rest for about five minutes. Remove abalone from its shell by running a thin sharp knife between the shell and body. Cut off foot.

Scrub foot with a stiff brush. Trim off all black matter and cut foot into thin slices. Cut slices lengthwise for abalone "steaks"; at the diagonal, against the grain, for abalone sushi or sashimi pieces.

Limpets may be eaten whole, straight from the shell. Or they can be cleaned by picking up the animal by the shell and running the tip of a sharp knife along the inside of the shell. Limpets must be shucked when fresh, but they may be frozen for later use. The guts and the green liver may be scraped off, but this is not necessary. Rinse well in cold running water. Pound the oval tidbits gently with the flat side of a cleaver to tenderize. Stop pounding when the meat looks limp.

HOW TO PREPARE

Use cleaned limpets in any recipes calling for escargots or clams. Slice the foot of abalone and serve it as sushi and sashimi. If it is cooked, it should not be cooked more than about 30 seconds on each side, or it will toughen beyond redemption. Abalones and limpets are also good in chowders and seafood stews. They should be added at the very end.

SERVES 4–6
AS AN APPETIZER

Abalone Sashimi in Garlic Sauce

2 cups fresh abalone meat,
    thinly sliced across the
    grain
2 tablespoons almond or
    apricot oil
2 teaspoons minced garlic
1 teaspoon soy sauce
2 tablespoons clam broth

There seems to be a mistaken belief among abalone fanciers that raw abalone is tough. Processors believe that it must be left lying around for hours until it relaxes enough to be prepared. From my own experience, fresh raw abalone, eaten shortly after it comes from the shell, is not at all tough and chewy; very crunchy, perhaps, but not tough. Try it. Accompany this dish with a first-rate lager beer.

1. Arrange abalone in overlapping slices on serving platter.
2. Heat oil in wok until smoking. Turn off heat. Quickly stir in garlic. Leave in hot oil until garlic turns golden brown. Add soy sauce and clam broth. Stir well to blend. (If sauce seems too thin, turn heat to high and cook until sauce is reduced to desired consistency.) Let cool.
3. Pour garlic sauce over abalone and serve.

1¼ cups fish stock or ½ clam
   nectar and ½ water
½ teaspoon finely minced garlic
½ cup whipping cream
1 tablespoon Calvados or
   brandy
1 tablespoon finely minced
   fresh Majorca rosemary
2 tablespoons clarified butter
   or unsalted butter
4 medium-sized abalones,
   sliced
4 small sprigs rosemary for
   garnish
1 apple, cored and cut into
   thin slices

Abalone with a Calvados and Majorca Rosemary Sauce

The kitchen garden at the Sooke Harbour House is something to behold. All sorts of rare and common herbs grow there in profusion the year-round. The nearby ocean waters teem with a different kind of bounty: common and uncommon marine animals for the inn's table. Sinclair Philip, who runs the place and dives to gather some of the seafood, loves abalone. He warns that it cooks very quickly. Be sure to watch it closely. This dish calls for a nice sauvignon blanc, pinot blanc, or lesser chardonnay.

1. In a small saucepan, bring 1 cup stock and garlic to a boil and reduce by ½. Add whipping cream and reduce until thick. Add Calvados and rosemary. Boil 1 minute and remove from heat.
2. Warm 4 attractive appetizer plates.
3. In a small saucepan, heat butter over high heat; add sliced abalone. Add the reserved ¼ cup stock and continue to cook, shaking the pan back and forth for a maximum of 2 minutes.
4. Gently reheat sauce and divide between 4 warmed plates. Arrange abalone slices in center and garnish with rosemary sprigs. Sauté apple in butter and arrange around rosemary sprigs.

1 cup fresh oyster mushrooms
1 tablespoon almond or apricot
   oil
3 cups unsalted chicken stock
½ cup clam stock (the stronger,

Oyster Mushroom and Abalone Soup

I have never eaten an "oyster" mushroom that actually tastes like an oyster (whoever came up with the name must have had strange taste buds). But the delicate flavor of oyster mushrooms goes very well with all sorts of seafood. If you cannot find fresh oyster mushrooms, use fresh shiitake.

*the better, you might want
to use cockle stock)*
½ *tablespoon sake (use a good
brand like Shirayuki)*
12 *snow peas, ends broken off*
12 *sprigs fresh watercress
Salt and freshly ground
white pepper to taste*
1 *cup thinly sliced fresh raw
abalone meat*

1. Cut mushrooms into thin slices.
2. Heat oil in saucepan over medium heat, add mushrooms; cook until soft.
3. Add chicken and clam stock, sake, snow peas, and watercress; season with salt and pepper. Cook for a couple of minutes until the snow peas are almost done.
4. Add abalone; cook for 1 minute longer (overcooking will toughen the abalone beyond redemption).

SERVES 4

Abalone Salad

4 *abalone steaks, cooked and
sliced into ¼-inch strips*
½ *cup red pepper, roasted,
peeled, and cut into ⅛- to
¼-inch strips (see p. 25)*
2 *mild green chiles (chiles
poblanos or chiles verdes),
roasted, peeled, cut into
⅛- to ¼-inch strips
(see p. 25)*
¼ *cup red onion (sliced, slices
cut crosswise in half),
blanched*
1 *teaspoon chopped fresh basil*
2 *tablespoons rice vinegar*
¼ *cup olive oil
Juice of 1 lemon*

Leftover abalone should not be reheated, that is paramount to overcooking. Use it in a refreshing seafood salad. If you cannot find abalone (or if you think the price is too high), you may use geoduck instead in this recipe. One rule that holds true for geoduck as well as abalone: do not overcook it, or it will become abominably tough. This salad may be chilled before serving.

1. Toss abalone, red pepper, chiles, onion, and basil in ceramic bowl.
2. Blend together vinegar, oil, and lemon juice. Pour over abalone salad. Toss well and serve.

SERVES 4

2 tablespoons oyster sauce
1 teaspoon soy sauce
⅛ teaspoon hot Chinese chili
    sauce
1 teaspoon minced pickled
    ginger
1 teaspoon honey
1 tablespoon rice vinegar
1 tablespoon minced garlic
4 pinto abalones, cut into thin
    julienne strips
1 cup fish stock or clam
    nectar
    Cooked spinach fettucine
    for 4
1 bunch green onions, cut on
    the bias into slivers
    Nasturtium flowers or other
    edible flowers for garnish

Cold Abalone and Fettucine Salad

This dish comes from the Sooke Harbour House on southern Vancouver Island where abalone is always in plentiful supply, and where the kitchen staff knows how to prepare it properly. Accompany this flavorful dish with an off-dry sauvignon blanc or muscat.

1. In a saucepan, bring oyster sauce, soy sauce, chili sauce, ginger, honey, vinegar, and garlic to boil. Simmer for 5 minutes. Remove from heat and let cool.
2. Poach abalones 2 to 3 minutes in fish stock. Drain and let cool.
3. In a large bowl, combine the marinade mixture, abalone, pasta, and green onions; toss well. Let marinate for at least 1 hour.
4. Drain abalone salad and garnish with nasturtium flowers.

SERVES 4

20 very fresh raw limpets
8–16 California (sea) mussels
4 average-sized Belgian
    endives, washed and cut
    into bite-sized pieces
1 red-skinned apple, cut into
    cubes (do not peel)
1 cup broken (small pieces)
    hazelnuts or walnuts

Limpet, Mussel, and Belgian Endive Salad with a Ginger-Mustard Vinaigrette

I collect and eat a lot of seafood, but I am always amazed by the interesting dishes Sinclair Philip and the staff at the Sooke Harbour House invent. I tried this dish with both a Guenoc chardonnay and a Charles Lefranc sauvignon blanc, and both worked beautifully in bringing out and enhancing different aspects of the dish.

1. Remove meat from limpet shells. Cut off guts and small

¾ cup cubed Pleasant Valley
   gouda or Gruyère
2 tablespoons Dijon mustard
1 tablespoon grated young
   gingerroot
2 tablespoons red wine vinegar
½ cup olive oil
   Petals from 8 calendula
   flowers or edible
   chrysanthemum petals

head. Steam open mussels. Remove from shell. If using
large mussels, cut into smaller pieces.
2. Mix endive, apple, hazelnuts, cheese, limpets, and
   mussels in a salad bowl.
3. Make a vinaigrette by placing mustard, gingerroot,
   and vinegar in mixing bowl. Begin beating with a
   wire whisk; gradually add oil until the sauce becomes
   emulsified and incorporates the mustard completely.
4. Pour vinaigrette evenly over salad and sprinkle calendula
   petals over top.

SERVES 4

Abalone with Oyster Mushrooms

*I really get excited about cooking whenever I find a good
quantity of mushrooms in the woods. This dish came about when
I was lucky both in the forest and on the shore. Try it with a very
dry northwest riesling.*

4 tablespoons olive oil
6 medium garlic cloves, finely
   chopped
5 large fresh oyster mushrooms
   or fresh shiitake, sliced
   and cut into thin strips
1 pound abalone meat,
   pounded, thinly sliced,
   and cut across the grain
   into julienne strips
1 pound thin-stalked
   asparagus, cut into 2-inch
   pieces
1 cup unsalted chicken stock
4 green onions, cut diagonally
   into ⅛-inch slices
1 tablespoon light soy sauce
1 tablespoon dry sherry or
   Shaoxing wine
   Cornstarch paste as needed*
   Steamed rice for 4
¼ cup very finely chopped,
   loosely packed cilantro or
   chervil

1. Heat oil in deep, heavy skillet. Sauté garlic until soft.
   Add mushrooms. Cook for a couple of minutes until
   soft. Add abalone. Cook for a maximum of 2 minutes.
   Set aside.
2. Add asparagus pieces to pan. Sauté until just barely
   tender. Remove to abalone platter.
3. Add stock, onions, soy sauce, and sherry. Cook over
   high heat for 5 minutes. Return garlic, mushrooms,
   abalone, and asparagus to skillet. Heat through. Add
   just enough cornstarch paste to thicken sauce. Stir until
   sauce is clear. Serve at once with steamed rice.
   Sprinkle with cilantro.

★ To make cornstarch paste, thoroughly mix together
3 tablespoons cold water and 1 tablespoon cornstarch.
Always stir mixture again just before using because the
cornstarch settles. For a thick paste, reduce water and
cornstarch by ⅓.

SERVES 6

1½ pounds cooked spinach
  fettucine
2 cups thinly sliced fresh
  abalone
2 tablespoons almond oil
2 green onions cut diagonally
  into ½-inch pieces
¾ cup abalone stock or clam
  broth
1 tablespoon dry sherry or
  Shaoxing wine
½ teaspoon salt (or to taste)
  Cornstarch paste (see p. 37)
¼ teaspoon Chinese sesame oil
6 tablespoons very finely
  minced fresh cilantro or
  chervil
6 center slices from ripe
  tomatoes
6 teaspoons crème fraîche
3 teaspoons salmon caviar or
  golden whitefish caviar,
  drained

Abalone with Green Fettucine

I love both the look and taste of this dish. Fresh abalone and fresh pasta are just made for each other. This dish calls for an unpretentious little white wine.

1. Heat oil in wok. Quickly stir fry abalone for a maximum of 1 to 2 minutes (no longer or abalone will become tough). Set abalone aside.
2. When oil has returned to full heat, stir fry green onions until soft. Discard green onions or save for another dish.
3. Add stock, wine, and salt to oil. Bring to boil. Stir in just enough cornstarch paste to lightly thicken sauce.
4. Add abalone slices; toss to coat. Add sesame oil; stir. Remove from heat.
5. Divide fettucine onto 6 plates. Pour a little sauce over fettucine. Arrange abalone slices on top in concentric circles. (You should end up with smooth rounded mounds.) Pour remaining sauce over abalone. Sprinkle each serving with 1 tablespoon cilantro. Set a tomato slice onto each mound. Top with 1 teaspoon crème fraîche and ½ teaspoon salmon or whitefish caviar.

SERVES 2

1 large red or pink abalone,
  sliced
  Coarse (kosher) salt as
  needed
2 chiles poblanos or chiles
  verdes, roasted, peeled,
  and seeded (see p. 25)
2 tablespoons olive oil

Abalone in Red Wine

We have Italian friends who insist on drinking red wine with all their meals, even when they are eating seafood. Here is a dish that lets you. Try it with either a Martini barbera or a Parducci zinfandel.

1. Lightly pound abalone slices with side of cleaver, then cut into thin julienne strips.

¼ cup dry red wine
¼ teaspoon freshly squeezed
    lemon juice
    Salt and freshly ground
        black pepper to taste
½ pound cooked linguine
1 tablespoon finely chopped
    chervil

2. Cut chiles into thin strips.
3. Heat oil in heavy skillet. Sauté abalone over medium heat for about 1 minute. Remove abalone to warm platter.
4. Add wine and lemon juice to skillet. Stir until well blended. Add chile strips. Cook over high heat until reduced by ½. Season with salt and pepper. Add linguine to skillet (time cooking, so linguine has just finished draining at this point and is still hot). Toss to coat well with sauce. Return abalone to skillet. Mix with pasta. Divide onto 2 serving plates. Sprinkle with chervil. Serve immediately.

SERVES 4

Basic Abalone Steak

12 abalone slices (about 1½
    pounds)
2 eggs, beaten
    Salt and freshly ground
        black pepper to taste
    Dash cayenne
    Sifted all-purpose flour as
        needed
4 tablespoons olive oil or
    ½ butter and ½ almond or
    apricot oil
1 lemon, cut into 6 wedges

This is an old standby that has been popular almost forever and will always be in vogue. Like many old standbys, it is best accompanied by a good beer, a first-rate lager, or perhaps an ale or porter.

1. Pound abalone slices with wooden mallet or handle of Chinese cleaver between 2 sheets of wax paper until they become limp.
2. Beat eggs, salt, pepper, and cayenne together. One at a time, dip abalone slices in egg mixture, then coat with flour. Lay onto a sheet of wax paper; let dry for about 5 to 10 minutes. Turn over once (lay onto new sheet of wax paper if necessary).
3. Heat oil in skillet until quite hot. Cook abalone slices very quickly until golden brown on both sides. Oil should be hot enough to brown abalone in 1 minute per side.
4. Remove cooked slices to heated serving platter; keep hot while cooking remaining abalone. Garnish with lemon wedges. Serve hot.

SERVES 4

6 medium abalone slices
1 egg white
2 tablespoons cornstarch
6 fresh water chestnuts, peeled
      and halved horizontally
12 pieces ham, cut into chunks
12 strips lean bacon
12 medium-sized fresh
      mushroom caps
      Cooking oil as needed
1 tablespoon Chinese oyster
      sauce
2 tablespoons sugar (optional)
1 teaspoon dry sherry
      Dash freshly ground black
      pepper
1 tablespoon light soy sauce
4 tablespoons clam broth or
      unsalted chicken stock
1 teaspoon cornstarch dissolved
      in water (or more, as
      needed)
      Cooked rice for 4
      Steamed vegetables for 4

Clamlike Abalone
(WEN HA BAO YU)

The Chinese, who like clams very much, do not seem to be able to get enough of them, as the following dish attests. Who else would try to make abalone taste like clam? Enjoy this dish in the company of a first-rate fine sherry.

1. Trim abalone slices well, cut each slice crosswise into quarters. Pound to tenderize. Cut a checkerboard pattern on the inside surface of each piece. Cut as deeply as you dare, but make sure not to cut all the way through the meat.
2. Blend egg white and cornstarch into a smooth batter.
3. Dip abalone, water chestnuts, ham, and bacon into batter. Top ½ the abalone slices with a slice of water chestnut, a piece of ham, and another slice of water chestnut. Top with the remaining abalone slices. Wrap each packet with a strip of bacon. The contraptions should be held together by the cornstarch batter. If that seems too flimsy, skewer them together with toothpicks.
4. Stir fry the clamlike abalones in wok until they turn golden. Remove from wok and keep warm.
5. Quickly sauté mushrooms in hot oil, sugar, sherry, pepper, soy sauce, and clam broth. Toss mushrooms in sauce. Remove mushrooms to platter; arrange around clamlike abalone pieces.
6. Thicken sauce with cornstarch solution. Pour over abalone and mushrooms. Serve with rice and steamed vegetables.

Pia Carroll's Abalone Sautéed with Hazelnut and Lime Butter Sauce

SERVES 4

2–4 abalones in the shell
2 shallots, chopped
1 clove garlic, chopped
¼ cup pure apple cider vinegar
½ cup fish stock
½ cup dry sauvignon blanc
   (I found Guenoc worked
   best for this)
½ pound cold unsalted butter,
   cut into small pieces
   Juice from ½ lime
⅓ cup ground toasted hazelnuts
   Thinly shredded red pickled
   gingerroot for garnish
   (optional)

This recipe comes from Pia Carroll, head chef at the Sooke Harbour House on Vancouver Island. Pia uses the small local abalone — one or two of the larger red or pink abalones may be substituted. Accompany this dish with a dry California sauvignon blanc or northwest riesling.

1. The abalone may be frozen first to tenderize the muscles. If abalone is frozen, thaw to remove from shell (a large spoon is helpful). Discard viscerae. Wash and scrub abalone to remove black coating from foot. Cut meat into ⅛-inch-wide *vertical* slices (not steaks).
2. Over high heat, reduce shallots, garlic, vinegar, fish stock, and wine to ½ cup. Strain.
3. Over very low heat, add butter bit by bit, whisking it in. Then add lime juice and hazelnuts and stir to blend for a few seconds and spoon onto heated plates.
4. When sauce is ready, heat 1 tablespoon clarified butter in sauté pan. Add abalone slices and cook very briefly for 30 seconds on each side. Arrange in sauce by overlapping abalone slices.
5. Garnish each plate with a few shreds of red pickled gingerroot.

SERVES 4

Gingered Abalone with Peppers and Hot Sauce

2 tablespoons clarified butter
½ teaspoon hot chile sauce
    (add more, if a hotter
    sauce is desired)
¾ teaspoon minced garlic
1 teaspoon minced gingerroot
1 red bell pepper, seeded and
    cut into julienne strips
1 green bell pepper, seeded and
    cut into julienne strips
¼ cup white wine
⅓ cup fish stock or ½ clam
    nectar and ½ water
½ pound thinly sliced abalone
¼ cup chopped fresh cilantro

Here is another creation by Pia Carroll, head chef at the Sooke Harbour House on southern Vancouver Island. Abalones are particularly plentiful on Vancouver Island and may be obtained fresh throughout much of the year. Pia recommends serving steamed vegetables to complement this dish. Accompany it with a dry or off-dry sauvignon blanc.

1. In a heavy skillet, heat butter over medium heat, add chile sauce, garlic, gingerroot, and peppers. Sauté briefly.
2. Raise heat to high. Add wine and stock; stir to mix well.
3. Add abalone and cook 2 to 3 minutes until abalone is tender. Sprinkle in cilantro and serve immediately.

SERVES 4-6

Barbecued Limpets in the Shell

24–36 assorted limpets
    Fresh lemon juice to taste

One day on the beach, we sent out a boat party to gather shellfish for our barbecue. The only edibles the boat party found were rather small limpets, but that did not matter much. We had cooked a surfeit of hamburgers and hot dogs on the barbecue grill. We now simply sat the limpets onto the grill, shell side down, and cooked them until the body curled away from the shell. As soon as they were done, we slurped them from the shell. They turned out very delicious, and even finicky eaters ate their share. The recipe is very simple.

1. Wash limpets in clean, unpolluted sea water and place upside down on barbecue grill (about 4 to 6 inches above a bed of white coals).
2. Cook limpets until they curl away from side of shell.
3. Sprinkle limpets with lemon juice and serve in shell.

SERVES 2

Limpets au Beurre Noir

1 pound limpet meat
  Salt and freshly ground
    white pepper to taste
1 tablespoon olive oil
½ cup butter
1 teaspoon freshly squeezed
    lemon juice
1 pound cooked pasta

At first glance, it may seem as though it will take you a long time to gather one pound of limpet meat, but that is not necessarily so. Occasionally I have stumbled upon dense colonies of very large limpets. Such finds make collecting a pound an almost effortless task.

1. Season limpet meat with salt and pepper. Sauté in olive oil over high heat for a maximum of 1 minute on each side. Remove from pan.
2. Add butter to olive oil. Cook over low heat until dark brown. Blend in lemon juice.
3. Add limpets. Toss to coat. Pour over pasta. Serve at once.

SERVES 4–6

Limpet Fritters

24 (or more) large limpets
   Coarse salt as needed
   Salt and freshly ground
     black pepper to taste
 2 eggs (preferably duck eggs)
⅔ cup (approximately)
     all-purpose flour
 1 cup milk
   Almond or apricot oil for
     deep frying as needed
 1 lemon cut into 6 wedges for
     garnish

Limpets are exceedingly common all along our rocky shores, but they are among our most underutilized shellfish. They are delicious by themselves, or they may be used in most oyster and snail recipes. Large limpets may be treated like abalone. Here is an old oyster recipe I have adapted to limpets.

1. Wash limpets and place upside down on a bed of coarse salt in a flat oven-proof dish.
2. Broil until limpets curl and pull away from side of shell. Remove from oven; season with salt and pepper.
3. Break eggs into bowl; mix in flour, then gradually add milk. If batter is too thin to coat a spoon, add a little more flour.
4. Dip limpets in batter and fry in deep, boiling oil (375°) until brown and crisp.
5. Remove with slotted spoon and serve immediately with lemon wedges.

SERVES 4–6

Stir-Fried Abalone and Asparagus

½ pound fresh thin-stalked
   asparagus
½ cup abalone stock or clam
   broth
   Dash freshly ground white
   pepper
½ tablespoon unsalted mirin
   (sweetened rice wine)
½ tablespoon soy sauce
1 tablespoon cornstarch
1 teaspoon Chinese sesame oil
1 tablespoon almond or apricot
   oil
½ teaspoon minced fresh
   gingerroot
½ cup unsalted chicken stock
1 cup thinly sliced fresh raw
   abalone
1 tablespoon minced country
   ham
1 tablespoon finely chopped
   fresh cilantro

This dish is very easy to prepare; it takes only a couple of minutes cooking time. Yet it can be a very elegant dish. Be sure to cut the ingredients as evenly as you can: it will help the eye appeal of the food. Drink a light, dry muscat or a sauvignon blanc with this abalone.

1. Snap off tough ends of asparagus stalks (save for soup). Rinse asparagus well; set into colander to drain.
2. Cut asparagus diagonally into 2-inch pieces.
3. In a small bowl combine abalone stock, pepper, mirin, soy sauce, cornstarch, and sesame oil (be sure cornstarch does not form lumps).
4. Heat cooking oil in wok over high heat, add gingerroot, drop in asparagus, and toss for 15 seconds. Pour in chicken stock and cover; cook for 1 minute. Uncover, stir in mixture from bowl; cook only until sauce begins to thicken.
5. Stir in abalone and cook for 1 minute. Transfer to serving platter and sprinkle with ham and cilantro. Serve immediately.

SERVES 4

Stir-Fried Abalone with Bok Choy

1½ pounds fresh abalone meat,
    cut into thin slices
1 teaspoon minced fresh
    gingerroot
1 tablespoon light soy sauce
1 tablespoon ground white
    pepper (or to taste)
½ tablespoon cornstarch
¼ teaspoon mirin
1 teaspoon Chinese sesame oil
3 tablespoons apricot or
    almond oil
3 slices peeled fresh gingerroot
3 cups shredded bok choy
1 teaspoon minced garlic
1 tablespoon sake

You must use the baby bok choy available in Oriental groceries for this, not the coarse, ugly things sold in supermarkets. If you can get only supermarket bok choy, cut out large midrib, reserve for other dishes. Try this dish with a dry California gewürztraminer.

1. Lightly pound abalone slices with side of cleaver, then cut into thin julienne strips.
2. Mix abalone strips with gingerroot and set aside.
3. In a small bowl, combine soy sauce, pepper, cornstarch, mirin, and sesame oil. Set aside.
4. Set wok over high heat. When it begins to smoke, pour 1 tablespoon oil down sides. Add gingerroot slices and bok choy; stir fry for 1 minute and transfer to a plate.
5. Clean wok. Set over high heat again. When wok begins to smoke, add remaining oil, garlic, and abalone. Stir; add sake. Stir for another minute. Add sauce mixture. When thickened, add bok choy and toss. (The whole process should take less than 2 minutes.) Transfer contents of wok to serving platter and serve.

SEA SNAILS
and
ESCARGOTS

PERIWINKLE APPETIZERS

FORAGER'S SITKA PERIWINKLE SALAD
WITH WATERCRESS DRESSING

LEAFY HORNMOUTH SNAILS IN SEA URCHIN BUTTER

TURBAN SNAILS AND OYSTER MUSHROOMS IN HERB BUTTER

ESCARGOTS WITH HAZELNUT BUTTER

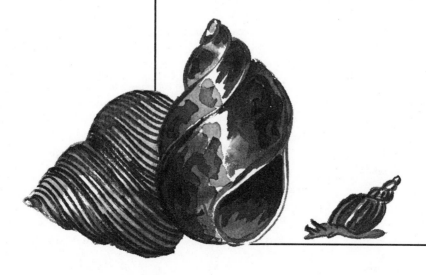

COMMON NAME

Black Top-Shell
(Baja California to
British Columbia)

This snail is distinguished by a purplish black shell (one inch across) in the form of a low, rounded cone. They are very common on rocky shores. This snail is very good to eat; compares favorably with British winkles.

Dusky Turban
(Baja California to
southeastern Alaska)

A brown-shelled snail (one and one-half inches across) that looks much like the black turban but is slightly larger. It lives lower in the littoral zone on rocky shores. This snail is quite common and very good to eat.

Speckled Tegula
(Baja California to California)

A snail with a large (one and one-half inches across) grayish green shell marked by narrow whitish zigzag stripes. It is common among intertidal rocks. It is easily gathered and good to eat.

Brown Tegula
(California to Oregon)

Common among subtidal rocks. Similar in appearance to the black top-shell (one inch across). Good to eat.

Blue Top-Shell
(Ribbed Top-Shell)
(southern California to Alaska)

You will not see the beautiful blue color of this shell (one inch across) unless you remove the brown periostracum. This snail is also common in the shallow water of rocky shores. It, too, is good to eat.

Gem Top-Shell
(Mexico to California)

Despite its small size (one-half inch across), this common snail is worth gathering. It is common on rocky shores.

Ringed Top-Shell
(southern California to Alaska)

This large (to one and one-half inches across) top-shell lives on offshore kelp. It is worth the extra collecting effort.

Channeled Top-Shell
(southern California to Alaska)

This large (one and one-half inches across) top-shell is common in offshore kelp beds. It is meaty and very good to eat.

Smooth Turban Shell
(Baja California to California)

A large (one and one-half inches across) meaty snail with rounded, glossy black whorls. This snail is common from the shore into the kelp beds and makes for very good eating.

Margarite Shells
(California to Alaska)

These small (one-half inch across) snails are quite common on rocky beaches. Despite their small size, they are perfectly edible.

Red Turban
(California to British Columbia)

The shell of this snail is large (to three inches by two and one-fourth inches), squat, and wide. The red turban snail is fairly common on protected rocky shores. It makes for excellent eating.

Wavy Turban
(Baja California to southern California)

A very large (to six inches across) snail common among algae and rocks of protected shores. It has a lot of meat in its foot; large ones may be served like abalone.

Periwinkles
(Baja California to Alaska)

A number of small (one-half to three-fourths inch across) snail species living on rocks high in the intertidal zone. They are difficult to tell apart even for experts (with some of these snails the coloring of the shell seems to be determined by the color of the rocks they frequent). All may be cooked. Extract the meat with a toothpick.

Slipper Shells
(Baja California to Alaska)

These are peculiar-looking, small to medium-sized (one to one and one-half inches across) snails, which baffle even experts. Slipper shells look remotely like limpets, but have a shelf inside their shell extending about halfway across the opening. They are fairly common on rocks in shallow water. All are good to eat. The Atlantic slipper shell has been introduced to France and to the Puget Sound. In France it is becoming a gourmet item.

Moon Snails
(Baja California to Alaska)

Three species of large (two and one-half to four inches across) yellowish brown globose snails that look pretty much alike. These marine snails look like small apples. They are common in sandy/muddy areas, where they feed on clams. Moon snails have a very large, fleshy foot that is exceptionally good to eat. Do yourself and the clams a favor and eat a lot of moon snails.

Oregon Hairy Triton
(California to Alaska)

A predacious snail with a large (three to five inches by two inches) spindle-shaped shell. It is common on sandy or rocky bottoms, usually in the subtidal zone but may be close to shore on rocky coasts. It is quite good to eat; just make sure to remove the bitter, greenish bile sac after cooking.

California Frog Shell
(Baja California to Monterey Bay, California)

This snail with a heavy knobbed shell (three inches across) is common among offshore rocks. It is quite good to eat.

Dire Whelk
(California to Alaska)

A predacious snail with spindle-shaped shell (one and one-half inches across), which is common on rocky beaches at the low tide level or below. It, too, is edible.

Northwest Neptune
(Washington to Arctic Ocean)

A predacious snail with a large (five inches across) dingy brown shell. It is common in the sublittoral zone and may be trapped with bait like crabs or shrimps.

Kellet's Whelk
(Mexico to California)

A large (four inches across) whelk that is common on sandy or rocky bottoms of the sublittoral zone. Good to eat.

Channeled Dog Whelk
(California to British Columbia)

This scavenger snail (one to one and one-half inches across) is edible, as are a number of smaller related snails. They can be trapped with bait like crabs or shrimps.

Oyster Drills and Dwarf Tritons
(California to Alaska)

A number of small (three-fourths to one inch across) snails, which prey on oysters and other shellfish and may do considerable damage. Luckily they are good to eat and easy to collect. Cook them and pull the meat from the shell with a toothpick.

Petit Gris
(Garden Snail)
(California to Washington)

A large (to three inches across) most edible snail with a streaked yellowish brown shell, commonly considered a garden pest. This snail is particularly common in the gardens of southern California. Collecting a bucketful takes almost no time at all. There are also a number of native land snails, but little is known about their edibility.

DESCRIPTION

Marine and land snails are very easy to recognize by their whorled shells. Some marine snails have odd shells, such as abalones, limpets, and slipper shells. Snails have flattened feet and heads with prominent tentacles.

HABITAT

The majority of marine snails are found in the intertidal zone of rocky shores; most land snails are found in dense vegetation of woods, fields, and gardens.

METHODS OF CATCHING

Snails are very easy to collect. Gathering marine snails may involve climbing over slippery rocks (wear shoes with nonskid soles) and probing into crevices. Some marine snails can be trapped with bait like crabs or shrimps.

AVAILABILITY IN FISH MARKETS AND RESTAURANTS

Canned land snails called "escargot" are sold in just about every supermarket. Marine snails are harder to find, but I have discovered them at odd times and in varying quantities in Oriental seafood markets. If you cannot find any, ask your favorite fishmonger. He may be able to order them especially for you.

SEASONS

Year-round, except for filter-feeding slipper shells, which are subject to red tide restrictions. Land snails may hibernate in cold winter climates.

HOW TO CLEAN

Clean marine snails after cooking by rubbing off their intestines (the pointed part that goes up into the shell whorl). A few species, such as the Oregon triton, have a bitter, green gall or bile sac that must be removed, or it will spoil the meat (if you are in doubt, just remove the bile sac).

Land snails must be fed on greens for a couple of weeks after collecting to make sure they have not ingested any pesticides. Clean land snails by tossing them in coarse salt to draw out their sticky juices and kill them. Pull them from their shells, remove the operculum, gut them by cutting off the black tips of their tails, and rinse them well. Or cook them first and gut them after cooking.

HOW TO PREPARE

Cook only those snails that withdraw into their shell and close it with the trapdoor/operculum. Boil sea snails in salted water for about twenty minutes. Pull from the shell, remove operculum, and rub off intestines. Use them in any seafood recipe.

After cleaning, simmer land snails in water flavored with herbs (thyme, bay leaves, salt, and peppercorns) and wine. Or simmer them in a meat or chicken broth over very low heat for at least three hours. Cool in the liquid in which they were cooked.

Moon snails can be pulled from the shell by grabbing the

foot and twisting it off. Cut off remaining intestines, rinse the foot well, and prepare like abalone.

SERVES 6

Periwinkle Appetizers

This impromptu dish was cooked up after we came back from the beach with a mess of periwinkles and were surprised by unexpected guests. We enjoyed it with a good, chilled lager beer, but a semillon blanc works equally well.

48 *(or more) freshly gathered periwinkles or other small marine snails*
1 *gallon water*
1 *tablespoon salt*
½ *cup unsalted butter*
2 *teaspoons chopped parsley*
  Salt and freshly ground white pepper to taste
  Squeeze of lemon juice

1. Scrub periwinkles to remove any foreign matter.
2. Discard any snails not tightly closed (with the operculum/trapdoor plate in place).
3. Stir salt into water. Bring to a boil.
4. Drop snails into boiling water and remove as soon as operculum falls open (about 20 minutes).
5. Heat butter just to the point where it turns liquid, do not overheat. Stir in parsley, salt, pepper, and lemon juice. Serve as a dipping sauce for periwinkles. As an alternative, you may serve a simple soy dipping sauce.
6. Serve snails in small bowls; pick out meat with toothpicks and dip in parsley butter.

Forager's Sitka Periwinkle Salad with Watercress Dressing

SERVES 4

3 quarts periwinkles
½ bottle gewürztraminer (or other dry white wine)
2 cloves
2 sprigs lemon thyme
1 teaspoon green peppercorns
1 tablespoon chopped lovage stems or celery
6 cups loosely packed salad greens: chickweed, edible viola leaves and flowers, Swiss chard, sheep sorrel, lambs quarters, black Batavian lettuce, rocket lettuce (not more than 2 cups)*
½ cup walnut oil or peanut oil
2 tablespoons freshly squeezed lemon juice
1 tablespoon red wine vinegar
1 large bunch watercress, finely chopped
1 cup chopped rhubarb chard for garnish

This recipe comes from Sinclair Philip who says that periwinkles are very abundant on our beaches and are available in large quantities in the early spring. Although you can collect these little snails during the day, they are night creatures and your harvest will be more abundant at night. Periwinkles are easy to collect since they congregate in the medium to high tidal zones. In some areas of southern Vancouver Island they can be collected by the shovelful. Red turban and leafy hornmouth snails can be substituted but require a bit longer cooking time. The checkered periwinkle and the Sitka periwinkle are the snails the Sooke Harbour House staff prefers for this recipe.

1. Wash periwinkles thoroughly, and when the water is clean, put the snails in the pot. Cover them with water (clean salt water, preferably) and add wine, cloves, lemon thyme, peppercorns, and lovage. Bring to a boil with lid on and steam 4 to 7 minutes (depending upon size). Be careful not to overcook snails or much of the meat will break off inside snail when you attempt to remove it.
2. Remove meat with a pin and discard the disklike hard operculum. Keep snail meat lukewarm for salad.
3. Wash, break, and dry salad greens.
4. Make dressing by combining walnut oil, lemon juice, and vinegar with a whip. Stir in watercress slowly.
5. Place salad components and lukewarm periwinkle meat in a bowl; pour in dressing and toss. Sprinkle rhubarb chard over top as garnish and serve.

* Vary amount of each ingredient depending upon availability at different seasons. All of these wild and cultivated lettuces are interchangeable but should add up to the full 6 cups.

SERVES 8

40 hornmouth snails
4 cups water
2 tablespoons oil
½ cup vinegar
1 cup dry white wine
¼ cup sea urchin roe (rinse and
    discard black strands)
¾ cup unsalted butter, room
    temperature
1½ tablespoons finely chopped
    shallots
1½ tablespoons finely chopped
    parsley
1 tablespoon minced celery

Leafy Hornmouth Snails in Sea Urchin Butter

I first enjoyed this dish at the Sooke Harbour House on southern Vancouver Island. Other sea snails may be substituted for the leafy hornmouth. (Sinclair Philip notes that you must check Oregon tritons after cooking to make sure the bilious sac is not broken. If it is, a bitter flavor pervades the meat. The bilious sac must be removed before the triton can be eaten.)

1. Soak snails in fresh water for 1½ hours. Change water and resoak for 2 hours.
2. Boil sea snails for approximately 3 minutes from boiling point in a solution of water flavored with oil, vinegar, and wine. (The oil will facilitate removal of snail from shell.) Drain and cool.
3. When cool, remove snail meat from shells with a pin or crab pick and cut off horny operculum. Remove as much of animal as possible. If snail cannot be removed, cover shell with towel and break with a hammer. Remove meat from broken shell; pick over for shell fragments. All parts of the snail except the black bilious pouch are edible. The bile of the leafy hornmouth is quite mild; that of the Oregon triton is quite bitter. Cut the snail meat into small chunks, rinse briefly in diluted vinegar and save for stuffing. Scrub, clean, and boil the whole snail shells from which the meat has been successfully removed for 20 minutes. Reserve for stuffing.
4. In a mortar or bowl, pound together the sea urchin roe, butter, shallots, parsley, and celery until well mixed and of an even orange color. If light orange, add more roe until mixture is a clearly defined orange color.
5. Preheat oven to 400°. Mix sea snail butter with roe butter so that snail particles are well distributed. Stuff snail shells, place in oven-proof dish, and heat briefly, until butter begins to melt. Place any remaining stuffing in a small oven-proof porcelain dish and put into oven

at same time as snails.

6. Remove from oven when butter has melted. Serve hot and eat it all up. There is no sense in freezing the remaining mixture, since sea urchin roe becomes bitter and loses its fruitiness when frozen. But you need not fret about that. These snails are so delicious it is unlikely you will have any leftovers.

Turban Snails and Oyster Mushrooms in Herb Butter

SERVES 8

2 cups sliced oyster or fresh shiitake mushrooms
2 tablespoons chopped shallots
36 cooked and drained turban snails (cubed, if they are very large)
¼ cup unsalted butter
½ cup cream
1 teaspoon finely chopped thyme
1 small bay leaf
½ teaspoon nuoc mam
⅛ teaspoon freshly ground black pepper
½ cup Madeira wine

The red turban is a large (one or two inches across), cone-shaped marine snail common on rocks from the intertidal zone down to about sixteen fathoms. It is very good to eat and quite easy to collect. Make sure you gather only live snails, those that withdraw into their shells when disturbed and close the opening with their limy operculum/trapdoors. A bone-dry sauvignon blanc goes well with these snails.

1. In saucepan, cook mushrooms, shallots, and snails in butter until shallots are tender.
2. Stir in cream, thyme, bay leaf, nuoc mam, and pepper. Simmer very gently, uncovered, for 10 minutes. Remove bay leaf.
3. Add Madeira; heat through. Serve in preheated individual escargot dishes.

SERVES 6–8

48 cooked snails
½ cup dry white wine
1 tablespoon Cognac
1 teaspoon fresh thyme
2 bay leaves
1½ pounds unsalted butter
3 shallots, finely minced
2 cloves garlic, finely minced
½ cup finely chopped hazelnuts
½ cup finely chopped parsley

Escargots with Hazelnut Butter

Petit gris *snails, one of several land snails known as* escargots, *are gathered by Blaine Walker in the gardens of the Long Beach peninsula in Washington. They are cleansed, cooked, shucked, and served at the Shelburne Inn. These snails are amazingly superior to the canned snails commonly used (or rather abused) in our restaurants. I liked them so much I asked for the recipe, et voilà!*

1. Marinate snails in wine, Cognac, thyme, and bay leaves for at least 4 hours in refrigerator. Whip together all remaining ingredients until well blended; refrigerate.
2. Heat escargot serving dish. Sauté 6 snails per serving with 6 tablespoons hazelnut butter over medium heat until foaming. Serve immediately with plenty of fresh French bread.

MUSSELS

GIANT PACIFIC HORSE MUSSEL SAUCE

SWEET-COOKED MUSSELS

MUSSELS IN WHITE WINE SAUCE

HERBED MUSSELS

MUSSELS FARCI MARCELLE

BOTTOM FISH WRAPPED IN SWISS CHARD LEAVES
WITH SEA MUSSEL SAUCE

COZZE CON FINOCCHIO

SEAFOOD IN PHYLLO

MUSSELS WITH GREEN CHILE SAUCE

MUSSELS IN RED WINE BUTTER

COMMON NAME
Blue Mussel
(California to Arctic Ocean)

The blue mussel stays small, growing to a total length of only two inches. Its shell may have a brown, blue, or black periostracum; it is blue beneath. Its delicate, tan-colored flesh has the most refined taste of all the mussels. Blue mussels are naturally plentiful (though they have become rather scarce in the Bay Area), but the tender mollusks are also raised commercially in Washington, Oregon, and California.

Sea Mussel
(California Mussel)
(Baja California to Aleutian Islands, Alaska)

The large (to more than four inches across) sea mussel is brown or tan, but these colors are rarely visible: young shells are covered with a brittle, thin, black periostracum; old shells are heavily eroded and overgrown with all sorts of algae and other marine organisms. The sea mussel is ubiquitous on surf-washed rocks and the small bay (or blue mussel) occurs by the millions on rocks or pilings in protected waters. It grows in a wide, almost uninterrupted intertidal band all along our rocky shores. The orange meat is delicious.

Horse Mussels
(Baja California to Alaska)

Horse mussels (three to nine inches across) grow vertically in the sand, gravel, or mud of quiet bays. Only the upper end of the shell protrudes from the ground. The giant California horse mussel (up to nine inches across) is no longer common, but the smaller, ribbed horse mussel forms dense stands in southern San Francisco Bay. A thin-shelled Japanese horse mussel was accidentally introduced with oyster spat and is now found up and down the coast from Moss Landing, California, to Samish Bay, Washington. Up north, a giant horse mussel is still quite common, especially in deep water. The horse mussel has a lot of orange-colored meat high in vitamins and minerals (it has been suggested as a potential food concentrate or as a quick pick-me-up food pill for harried executives and astronauts) and is very tasty. Its slight toughness can be remedied by chopping or grinding.

Date Mussel
(California to British Columbia)

There are several species that burrow into rock. The largest, the falcate date mussel, reaches a length of four inches. It bores deep into hard rock. It is good to eat, if you can extract it from its lair.

*Freshwater Mussels
(streams and lakes from sea level
to timberline; California to
British Columbia)*

DESCRIPTION

Mussels (often referred to as freshwater clams) with medium- to large-sized oval shells (two to three and one-half inches across). The light-colored shells are covered with a dark brown to black periostracum. Freshwater mussels are edible.

Mussels are edible clamlike mollusks found throughout the world's oceans and are particularly plentiful on the West Coast of North America. Marine mussels attach their asymmetrical, elongated dark-hued shells to rocks or other supports by means of a cluster (beard) of slender byssus threads. Mussels are one of the most ubiquitous animals of our shores.

Freshwater mussels also have elongated shells, but these are rounder in outline than those of marine mussels. Freshwater mussels burrow in the sand of streams and lakes, with just the posterior of their shells exposed. They typically pass through a larval parasitic stage during which they infest fish.

Marine mussels are very good to eat and just about everyone who has tried these delectable blue- or brown-shelled mollusks likes them; freshwater mussels are edible, but only muskrats seem fond of them.

HABITAT

Mussels are most prolific in cool northern waters, but they are found in all seas, sometimes under strange conditions. Blue or sea mussels attach themselves to the tops of rocks. Horse mussels stand upright in sandy or muddy bottoms. Date mussels bore into rock (with the help of a rock-dissolving acid).

METHODS OF
CATCHING

Mussels are very easy to collect since they do not burrow but attach themselves to the substrate by slender byssus threads. Grab mussels firmly and cut the threads with a knife. Mussels can be torn or twisted off the rock, but this may damage the tender animal. They will stay alive longer if they are not traumatized during collection. Keep the mussels moist in a gunnysack or bucket. Horse mussels and freshwater mussels may be scooped up from the ground.

Collecting shellfish is quite easy on oyster beds, clam beaches and, particularly, mussel rocks; unless you are in an area where a strong and unpredictable surf protects the mollusks from hungry collectors. But none are as easy to gather as mussels. Mussels, our most visible bivalves, have little need to hide from their natural enemies (with the possible exception of the sun), whether man or beast, because they grow rapidly and disturbed clusters are quickly replenished.

AVAILABILITY IN FISH MARKETS AND RESTAURANTS

Cultured blue mussels (the only kind raised commercially) are far superior to wild mussels in taste and texture. Their meat is sweeter, they lack off-flavors, and their shells are thinner, allowing for quicker steaming.

The tastiest mussels are raised by a method called long-line culture: young mussels are strung onto lines suspended in nutrient-rich deep water, where the mollusks can grow fat quickly. Because these mussels are not exposed to the extremes of low tide, they need not grow thick protective shells. Because they are not subjected to stress, they grow to be sweet, buttery, and tender.

West Coast mussels are regularly sold in seafood markets and restaurants now, but demand is high. The supply is unfortunately spotty and is often augmented by inferior mussels imported from the East Coast. East Coast mussels can be told by their large coarse shells and often by their smell: they are rarely fresh by the time they reach the West Coast. I usually check to see how fresh the seaweed clinging to mussels is. If it is very fresh, the mussels are not long from the water.

SEASONS

The edibility of mussels is affected during warm weather by the presence of a toxic dinoflagellate called *Gonyaulax* (red tide) in the water (see Index). Mussels obtain their nutrients by straining food from the water. In the process they may ingest large quantities of this organism. *Gonyaulax* does not affect mussels, but it is toxic to man. Fortunately mussels rid themselves quickly of *Gonyaulax* once an outbreak has ended. Commercial mussels are always checked for their safe edibility. Check with a local health department before collecting wild mussels.

HOW TO CLEAN

Mussels have a tough cluster of byssus threads (the beard). This is the mussels' connection to the substrate to which they attach themselves. This beard should be trimmed off just before the mussels are cooked. The shells should be scrubbed clean with a stiff brush. Mussels may be shucked like oysters or steamed like clams.

HOW TO PREPARE

Shuck mussels like oysters and serve them raw on the half shell, or steam them open like clams and serve them on the half shell, or use them in salads, sauces, soups, and chowders. Mussels are excellent hot and steaming from the pan, and they are equally good served cold.

SERVES 2

Giant Pacific Horse Mussel Sauce

¼ cup very dry white wine or vermouth
1 shallot, finely minced
½ cup fish stock
½ cup whipping cream
½ cup finely chopped mussel meat
½ cup minced chervil or dill
Pasta or fish for 2

I really like using chopped horse mussels in a delectable sauce recipe given to me by Sinclair Philip of the Sooke Harbour House. Sinclair recommends using this sauce with such bland fish as the inexpensive Pacific cod. I like serving it over pasta for a quick and tasty luncheon dish.

1. In medium saucepan, bring wine and shallot to boil. Reduce heat and cook until wine/shallot mixture reaches a syrupy consistency. Add stock and cream and let mixture cook until it thickens (up to 10 minutes). Do not overheat, or cream may curdle. When sauce is ready, pour into blender with most of chopped mussels and chervil; blend well. Add remaining mussels for texture. Stir well to blend. (The sauce may be prepared earlier in the day up to this point.)
2. When pasta (or fish) is near serving point, reheat mussel sauce over low heat. Correct seasoning to taste. Pour sauce over strained pasta (or serve with fish).

SERVES 12 AS AN
HORS D'OEUVRE

½ cup sake
1 tablespoon honey
¼ cup soy sauce
1 teaspoon freshly grated
    gingerroot
3 dozen mussels, steamed and
    shucked
1 tablespoon cornstarch

Sweet-Cooked Mussels

This recipe is from Lila Gault's The Northwest Cookbook. *"This Japanese-style treatment sweetens the mussels nicely and makes a delicious hors d'oeuvre."*

1. Combine sake, honey, soy, and gingerroot in large frying pan and bring to a boil. Add mussels and cook over medium heat for 3 minutes.
2. Remove mussels from liquid and add cornstarch, mixing thoroughly. Bring to a boil and cook until thickened, stirring continually. Return mussels to sauce and coat evenly.

SERVES 4 AS AN APPETIZER

4 dozen mussels, well scrubbed
2 cups dry white wine or
    1¾ cups water and ¼ cup
    rice vinegar
1 medium onion, finely
    chopped
2 teaspoons dried basil
3 sprigs parsley or cilantro
1 tablespoon freshly squeezed
    lemon juice or ½ lemon
    and ½ lime
1 teaspoon coarse salt
1 teaspoon coarsely ground
    black pepper
4 tablespoons unsalted butter
4 tablespoons minced parsley
    or chervil

Mussels in White Wine Sauce
(MOULES À LA MARINIÈRE)

This is a traditional, very superb, way of preparing mussels. Accompany them with a very dry white wine; it will really bring out the flavor.

1. Place the mussels in a large kettle (exclude any that do not close when touched) with all ingredients except butter and parsley.
2. Bring to a boil and simmer shortly until mussels open (this should take just a few minutes). Remove the mussels with a slotted spoon; discard any that have not opened.
3. Add butter to liquid and raise heat; stir until the liquid is reduced by ½.
4. In the meantime, arrange the mussels in their shells in 4 individual serving bowls (if you do not mind the extra work, remove the top shell off each mussel and present the mussels on the half shell). Keep warm.
5. When liquid is reduced, pass it through a fine sieve into

a smaller pan; warm again. Pour some over each portion of mussels.

6. Sprinkle 1 teaspoon of chopped parsley over each serving.

Herbed Mussels

SERVES 4 AS AN APPETIZER

4 dozen mussels, well scrubbed
1 cup dry white wine or ¾ cup water and ⅓ cup rice vinegar
1 teaspoon salt
1 teaspoon freshly ground black pepper
4 tablespoons unsalted butter
6 shallots, finely chopped
4 tablespoons minced parsley or chervil
2 teaspoons finely chopped fresh thyme
1 tablespoon freshly squeezed limón juice or ½ lemon and ½ lime
½ cup (loosely packed) finely grated dry Sonoma Jack, Parmesan, or any other dry cheese

This recipe works equally well for blue mussels, sea mussels, and for some of the more exotic mussels found along our coast. If you use very large mussels, steam them open, chop them, and return them to the half shell before adding the butter.

1. Place mussels in large kettle (exclude any that do not close when touched) with wine, salt, and pepper.
2. Bring to a boil and steam shortly until mussels open (this should take just a few minutes). Remove mussels with slotted spoon; discard any that have not opened. Save pan juices for chowder.
3. Melt butter in sauté pan; add shallots, parsley, thyme, and limón juice. Cook until juice has reduced and sauce has thickened somewhat.
4. In the meantime, remove top shell of each mussel and arrange mussels in 4 individual oven-proof serving dishes, presenting the mussels on the half shell. Keep warm.
5. When sauce is reduced, spoon some over each portion of mussels.
6. Sprinkle about ¼ teaspoon cheese over each serving. Place dishes under broiler just until cheese melts. Serve hot.

SERVES 6

6 pounds fresh mussels
2 large cloves garlic
½ bunch parsley
1 cup fresh basil leaves
2 cups butter, softened
2 tablespoons Pernod
　Freshly ground black pepper
　to taste

Mussels Farci Marcelle

Jacques Boiroux of Le Tastevin restaurant in Seattle has fresh Penn Cove mussels delivered several times a week. Here is one of the inviting ways he prepares them. Accompany this dish with a crisp, very dry, white wine or sparkling wine.

1. In a large cooking pot, steam open the mussels; cool. Remove top shell from each mussel. Arrange mussels on the half shell in 6 oven-proof gratin dishes.
2. To make the butter, finely chop garlic, parsley, and basil, with a knife or in a food processor. Add butter, Pernod, and pepper. Fill each mussel in the half shell with ½ teaspoon of this butter. When all the mussels are filled, bake them in 400° oven, until butter starts sizzling. Serve at once.

SERVES 2

4 large Swiss chard leaves
2 quarts boiling water
¼ cup unsalted butter
1 cup angelwing, oyster, or
　shiitake mushrooms,
　sliced, then very finely
　chopped
1 tablespoon very finely
　chopped fresh parsley*
1 tablespoon very finely
　chopped fresh (French)
　tarragon*

Bottom Fish Wrapped in Swiss Chard Leaves with Sea Mussel Sauce

This recipe comes from Pia Carroll, head chef at the Sooke Harbour House. You may use any firm white-fleshed fish, such as lingcod, cabezon or other large sculpins, or rock fish. Accompany this dish with a dry sauvignon blanc.

1. Wash chard leaves and blanch for 10 seconds in boiling water (save water). Refresh in cold water. Drain leaves when cool, lay out on kitchen towels and pat dry.
2. Melt butter over low heat. Sauté mushrooms, herbs, and garlic; sprinkle with pepper. Set aside.
3. Prepare chard leaves. If stems are large and thick, remove

1 tablespoon very finely
   chopped fresh marjoram*
1 clove garlic, minced
   Freshly ground black
   pepper (to taste)
2 8-ounce fish fillets
24 sea (California) mussels
1 cup chard stock (the cooking
   water)
1⅔ cups fish stock
⅓ cup crème fraîche or
   whipping cream
1 teaspoon fresh (French)
   tarragon

and discard. With the outside of a leaf facing down, place a fillet in the middle, crosswise, and spread half of the mushroom mixture on top. Fold over the leaf into a small package. Place package on another chard leaf and repeat process. Then wrap second fillet with last 2 chard leaves. These may be prepared ahead of time, tightly covered, and refrigerated.

4. Steam open mussels in 1 cup chard water and 1 cup stock (throw out any that do not open); remove, shake meat from shells, debeard, and chop into small pieces.

5. Combine remaining stock and crème fraîche, bring to a boil and reduce until thickened. Add the tarragon. When ready to serve, stir in the mussel meat, heat through and pour onto plates.

6. On top of stove, in a metal-handled skillet, bring 3 cups of chard water to a boil. Add fillets (there should be enough water to go up halfway). Cover with foil and bake in preheated 450° oven approximately 4 minutes, or until fish is firm to the touch.

7. Remove from pan with slotted spoon and place in pool of sauce on plate.

* Any of these herbs can be varied according to the season and taste.

SERVES 4–6

2 tablespoons butter
½ cup chopped chives
1½ cups dry vermouth or
   spumante
1 teaspoon fennel seeds
1 bay leaf
2–3 pounds mussels, scrubbed,
   beards removed

Cozze con Finocchio
(MUSSELS WITH FENNEL)

This is an Italian dish from the kitchen of Vince Zizzo's superb Mona Lisa Deli. Accompany it with a zesty red country wine.

1. Melt butter in saucepan; add chives. Sauté until soft (5 minutes). Stir in vermouth, fennel seeds, and bay leaf. Add mussels. Cover, steam mussels open.

2. Remove mussels with slotted spoon to warmed deep bowl. Strain cooking broth. Pour over mussels.

SERVES 4–6

2 pounds small, cultured West
    Coast mussels
1 tablespoon chopped shallots
½ teaspoon thyme
2 bay leaves (California laurel
    or Oregon myrtle)
½ cup plus 1 tablespoon dry
    white wine
    Salt and freshly ground
    pepper to taste
1 cup bay scallops
1 cup water
1 cup tiny Alaskan shrimp
¾ cup sliced medium-sized
    mushrooms
2 tablespoons melted unsalted
    butter (or more as needed)
⅓ cup all-purpose flour
1 cup unsalted butter
¼–½ cup cream
    Pinch nutmeg
    Dash cayenne
4 sheets phyllo

Seafood in Phyllo

*A lot of the dishes served at the Rhododendron Cafe have a
distinctly Mediterranean flavor. This dish is a simple combination
of mussels, scallops, and shrimp in a light velouté sauce and
wrapped in phyllo dough. It is eminently delicious.*

1. Remove beards from mussels; combine mussels with
   shallots, ¼ teaspoon thyme, 1 bay leaf, ¼ cup wine,
   salt, and pepper. Reserve liquid for velouté.
2. Poach scallops in water, ¼ cup wine, 1 bay leaf,
   ¼ teaspoon thyme, salt, and pepper. Reserve liquid for
   velouté.
3. Sauté mushrooms in 2 tablespoons butter; season with
   salt and pepper.
4. Make a roux with 6 tablespoons butter and ⅓ cup
   flour. Cook over low heat for several minutes (do not
   brown). Slowly whisk in 1½ to 2 cups of the reserved
   scallop and mussel liquid and simmer over medium-low
   heat for 5 to 10 minutes, skimming foam off surface.
   Add ¼ to ½ cup cream (depending on the desired consistency). Season with nutmeg, a dash of wine, salt,
   pepper, and cayenne.
5. Set aside ⅓ of this velouté to top phyllo. Combine
   seafood and mushrooms with remaining velouté.
6. Layer 4 sheets of phyllo, brushing each with melted
   butter. Cut stack lengthwise into 3 pieces, and put
   spoonfuls (about ⅓ cup) of mixture into each strip,
   as you fold it into triangular packets.
7. Brush each packet with butter and bake in a 425° oven
   for 10 minutes. Top with reserved velouté. Serve hot.

SERVES 2–4

Mussels with Green Chile Sauce

3 tablespoons olive oil
1 medium onion, finely
   chopped
1 large clove garlic (or more,
   according to taste), minced
2 green chiles poblanos
   (anchos), roasted, seeded,
   peeled, and cut into small
   cubes (see p. 25)
½ cup (loosely packed) minced
   fresh cilantro
1 tablespoon freshly squeezed
   lime juice
1 tablespoon freshly squeezed
   lemon juice
1 cup dry sauvignon blanc
1 teaspoon coarse salt
1 teaspoon coarsely ground
   black pepper
8 dozen mussels, well scrubbed
8 lime wedges
   Tabasco or other hot sauce
   to taste (optional)

If you are in Mexico during the mussel season, and if you can find these mollusks fresh (or if you are at home in a dreary northern winter, dreaming of the warm shores of the Sea of Cortez), try this main course recipe.

1. In a large kettle heat olive oil; add onion and garlic and cook until translucent.
2. Add chiles, cilantro, citrus juice, wine, salt, and pepper; bring to a boil. Add mussels (exclude any that do not close when touched), cover, and simmer shortly until the mussels open (this should take just a few minutes). Remove the mussels with a slotted spoon; discard any that have not opened.
3. Raise heat, stirring until the cooking liquid is reduced by ½.
4. In the meantime, remove the top shell of each mussel and arrange the mussels in their shells in 4 individual serving bowls, presenting the mussels on the half shell. Keep warm.
5. When liquid is reduced, pour some over each portion of mussels.
6. Serve with lime wedges so guests may sprinkle their mussels with lime juice as desired. Make bottled hot sauce available for the same purpose.

SERVES 4

Mussels in Red Wine Butter

4 dozen mussels
1½ cups dry red country wine
   (do not use a heavy wine)
¼ cup finely minced shallots
¼ cup freshly squeezed lemon
   juice
½ pound unsalted butter, cut
   into small cubes
1 cup cooked fresh miner's
   lettuce, watercress,
   saltbush, or spinach
½ teaspoon freshly grated
   nutmeg

Use very fresh mussels for this dish—either blue or sea (California) mussels. If you cannot find fresh miner's lettuce or saltbush, you can use watercress or spinach with this recipe. The flavor will not be quite as fine, but the dish will still be delectable. Miner's lettuce grows all over shady woods and forest margins in the West during spring; saltbush is found at the coast and in inland alkaline areas.

1. Pick over mussels. Discard any that do not close when touched. Scrub mussel shells well. Debeard.
2. Heat 1 cup wine in large stainless steel or enameled pot. Add mussels. Cover, steam mussels open. Discard any shells that do not open.
3. In the meantime, cook remaining ½ cup of wine, shallots, and lemon juice in a heavy (nonaluminum) skillet. Reduce over low heat until liquid is almost gone. Stir in cooking juices from mussels. Reduce over medium to high heat until liquid thickens. (In the final stages, liquid may thicken very rapidly. Do not let it burn!)
4. Remove pan from heat and add 1 or 2 small cubes of butter. Stir steadily with wire whisk until blended. Butter should be consistency of mayonnaise (neither solid nor liquid). Quickly repeat step with remaining butter, 1 or 2 pieces at a time. (The skillet should retain sufficient heat to do this smoothly—if temperature drops, return skillet to low heat.) If butter separates, whisk rapidly to emulsify.
5. Steam greens. Drain. Chop.
6. Remove mussels from shell. Discard upper shells. Make small beds of chopped greens in lower shells. Place a mussel on each bed and cover with sauce. Serve warm.

OYSTERS

STUFFED OYSTERS

OYSTERS WITH LEEKS AND CHAMPAGNE
SOOKE HARBOUR HOUSE

WINED OYSTERS ON CUCUMBER SLICES

MANHATTAN OYSTER CHOWDER

NORTHWEST OYSTER STEW

OYSTER JINGLES AND SMOKED SALMON PANCAKES

OYSTERS ON THE HALF SHELL

BAKED OYSTERS

BAKED OYSTERS IN PHYLLO

OYSTER PIE WITH SPINACH AND PINE NUTS

OSTIONES CON CHILE VERDE

OYSTERS IN CHAMPAGNE CHESTNUT SAUCE

BRAISED PORK AND FRESH OYSTERS IN CLAY POT

CORTEZ (ISLAND) OYSTERS

PEPPER OYSTERS

OYSTERS MEUNIÈRE, "À MA FAÇON"

FRIED OYSTERS

HANGTOWN FRY

OYSTER FRITTERS

CHINESE FRIED OYSTERS

COMMON NAME
Native (Olympia)
West Coast Oyster
(Baja California to Alaska)

The tiny (to two inches long) native oyster is a much smaller and more delicate mollusk than the oysters introduced to the West Coast. Its superb taste — which accounts for its scarcity — more than makes up for its drab exterior. There is really only one way to eat this delicately flavored oyster: as fresh as possible and raw, on the half shell.

Pacific (Japanese) Oyster
(California to northern
British Columbia)

This oyster can grow to be very large (up to twelve inches long). But it is best eaten when it is between two and three inches long. Pacific oysters are much fatter than other shellfish. This gives them a very rich flavor. Young Pacific oysters are excellent raw, on the half shell; older (and much larger) oysters are good in stews and pies.

Kumamoto
(a farm oyster;
Oregon and Washington)

The Kumamoto, a small (two to three inches long) flavorful sport of the Pacific oyster, has a more deeply cupped shell than its close relative and a more complex and delicate flavor. But it grows very slowly, making it difficult for growers to make a profit. The Kumamoto adapts well to West Coast waters, but today it is grown by only a few oyster farmers. It is excellent eaten fresh on the half shell.

Hybrid Oyster
(a farm oyster; Westcott Bay,
San Juan Island, Washington)

Bill Webb of the Westcott Bay oyster farm on San Juan Island, Washington, has succeeded in crossing the Kumamoto with the common Pacific oyster to produce a hybrid with the growth rate of the Pacific, but the deep cup (to contain the precious liquid) of the Kumamoto. It has a fragile, deeply fluted, almost feathery shell, buffed with whitish and brownish marks, and can be told from other oysters by its beautiful shell alone. This hybrid oyster has a superb flavor when fresh. It should be eaten raw, on the half shell.

Atlantic Oyster
(occasionally from
San Francisco Bay, California,
to British Columbia)

The Atlantic oyster can reach a length of six inches, but it is best when less than three inches long. It is a favorite of American cooks from the East Coast and was once raised commercially in a number of Pacific estuaries, from San Francisco Bay north to Georgia Strait, British Columbia. But it did not adapt to West Coast commercial growing, and growers switched to the more prolific Pacific oyster. Yet the introduced eastern oysters spawned successfully in our waters, and small populations can be discovered here and there along our coast. Young Atlantic oysters are best eaten raw, on the half shell; older oysters are good in chowders or pies.

European Flat Oyster
(a farm oyster; California to
Puget Sound, Washington)

The latest newcomer to the West Coast oyster scene is the delectable European flat oyster (erroneously known in this country as the "belon" oyster). This oyster is a close — though larger — relative of our small native oyster. It has succeeded well in Washington State. It is adapting well to the different growing conditions that prevail in the inlets, and it is beginning to show a great and intriguing variation in flavor. The flat oyster should be shucked just before eating and must be eaten raw, on the half shell, with perhaps an accent of lemon. The taste is truly memorable and well worth the steep price this oyster commands.

Jingle (rock oyster)
(Mexico to southern Bering Sea)

The jingle is not a true oyster, though it more or less looks like one. This medium-sized (to five inches long) rock-dwelling mollusk has an uneven shell: the irregular top shell is cupped, the lower shell is almost flat and has a large hole through which the animal's byssus threads pass. We do not have another marine animal quite like this. The flesh is bright orange. The jingle's taste is even more unmistakable than its appearance. It is unique and mild, yet full of complex marine flavors. Many connoisseurs consider the jingle the finest flavored of our bivalves. The jingle is best eaten raw, on the half shell (in this case the upper, hollow one).

Peruvian Jingle
(Peru to southern California)

A small (to one inch long) jingle common in Baja California. Despite its small size it is worth collecting for its exquisite flavor.

Mangrove Oyster
(southern Baja California;
tropical oceans)

The (to three inches long) mangrove oyster is a tree oyster, only remotely related to true oysters. It attaches itself to the stilt roots and aerial roots of mangrove trees. Saltier than the oysters raised in the brackish waters of the Pacific Northwest, it is nevertheless thoroughly enjoyable. It is very good to eat on the half shell when fresh.

DESCRIPTION

True oysters are clamlike mollusks that spend their entire adult lives firmly attached to rocks, old shells, or other firm objects in shallow, brackish, or tidal waters. Because one shell is permanently attached to the substrate, oysters have only one adductor muscle, and they lack a foot. This makes them unusually tender.

Our native oyster is very tender and thrives only in beds that are never completely uncovered by the tide (it suffers from extremes of heat and cold). This is also true for the closely related (introduced) European flat oyster. The Pacific oyster and its sports and hybrids is tougher, as is the Atlantic oyster.

But the Pacific oyster has a finicky sex life and will not reproduce unless conditions are just right. In the past, West Coast oystermen had to import large quantities of oyster spawn from Japan. But now the Pacific oyster has begun to adapt to northwest waters after half a century of sojourn and produces copious quantities of spat.

The Pacific oyster shows fortuitous developments in flavor. As it adapts to West Coast growing conditions, and as an ever-increasing number of yearlings grow from local spat instead of imported seed, the flavor of our naturalized Pacific oyster improves and becomes more complex: different populations vary widely in flavor, depending on such growing conditions as water temperature, the type of substrate on which they are raised, the speed and direction of tidal currents flowing over the beds, available nutrients (both quantity and quality), and whether or not it has interbred with existing stocks of East Coast oysters. Oysters contain all sorts of necessary minerals — especially phosphorous — in an easily digested form. Contrary to a popular notion held several years ago, oysters are not high in cholesterol.

HABITAT

Unlike clams, oysters do not hide themselves by digging into the substrate. They grow in large numbers on tideflats, rocks, pilings, on hard ground, and on the roots of trees. At low tide they are exposed for all the world to see (and harvest). Their protection lies in their large numbers. Just like mussels, oysters multiply rapidly and grow quickly. Oysters are most plentiful in commercial oyster beds, partly because oyster growers have preempted the tidelands that oysters like best, partly because here oysters are protected from many predators.

The oyster's shape, size, and flavor are determined by the quality of the habitat. Oysters growing on rocks will have a cleaner taste than oysters growing half-submerged in the mud of tideflats. But there is no such thing as the "best" oyster. The taste of oysters varies from one season to the next, depending on the type of waterborne nutrients and the changes in salinity brought about by rainfall and runoff. It can also vary widely from one growing region to the next and even from one end of an inlet to the other.

Rather than looking for a "best" oyster, West Coast oyster lovers should try to taste the whole range of delectable oysters available locally and regionally. Just as there are differences in wines from central California, northern California, Oregon, and Washington, depending largely on climate and soil, there are differences in the taste of oysters from Morro Bay, Tomales Bay or Humboldt Bay in California. Oysters grown in Coos Bay, Oregon, are different from those raised in Tillamook, Oregon, or Willapa Bay, Washington, and these, in turn, differ from Puget Sound oysters. Perhaps the greatest variety of flavors comes from the Puget Sound region — oysters from no two bays taste alike.

Unlike true oysters, rock oysters or jingles are very good at mimicking the pitted surface of rough rock. Jingles, which vie with the rock scallop for the dubious honor of being considered our tastiest shellfish, are also very good at blending into the surfaces of tidal rocks. Jingles have been overharvested to such an extent that the survivors like to grow in strange holes and mysterious, hard-to-reach crevices beneath surf-tumbled rocks.

METHODS OF CATCHING

There is no skill in catching an oyster. They can be pried off the substrate by inserting a stout knife, screwdriver blade, or crowbar between the lower shell and the substrate. Large clusters may be broken off en masse. Always shuck oysters on the beach: oyster spawn will settle on the discarded shells.

This is one way to assure there will be a sufficient supply of oysters in years to come.

AVAILABILITY IN FISH MARKETS AND RESTAURANTS

Farm-raised fresh oysters are readily available in supermarkets, seafood markets, and restaurants almost anywhere in the West.

Today more than ninety percent of all West Coast oysters are grown in Washington State, and more than half of this state's production comes from Willapa Bay. Here a bevy of new growers has taken to growing oysters by the superior rack method: the oysterlings are placed in large bags of plastic netting and placed on racks that are a foot or more above the ground.

Rope culture is perhaps the best method of raising tasty oysters: the oyster *cultch* (the seedlings) is threaded onto long ropes suspended from platforms floating in deep water. Unlike oysters raised directly on tideflats, where the bivalves are exposed to the vicissitudes of tidal cycles, oysters suspended in deep water do not suffer much from climatic extremes and undergo little stress. They can feed for twenty-four hours a day, grow fat quickly, and often taste better than their earthbound brethren. They are also quite safe from predators. In rope culture nearly eighty percent of the oysterlings survive until harvest time; compared to only about twenty to thirty percent of the oysters grown on the bottom.

Excellent farm-raised oysters can be found in the seafood markets of San Francisco, Portland, and Seattle. Californians can buy Pacific oysters fresh from the farm at the Qualman Oyster Company in Morro Bay, at Johnson's Oyster Farm on Drake's Estero in the Point Reyes National Seashore, and at oyster farms on Tomales Bay. Oregonians can get excellent fresh Pacific oysters at the Hayes Oyster Company on Tillamook Bay. Washingtonians have the greatest numbers of farms to pick from. Oysters are raised commercially in Willapa Bay, lower Puget Sound, Hood Canal, Quilcene Bay, Samish Bay, Similk Bay, in a number of small inlets, and in the San Juan Islands. There is nothing like an oyster fresh from the farm.

SEASONS

Oysters spawn in summer. They can be eaten during the summer months, but they accumulate excess amounts of glycogen in their bodies and become flabby and translucent as they prepare to spawn. Their taste is much too sweet, their bodies are flabby, and they become quite milky as the warm weather induces spawn. Most growers will not sell them at this stage (which may not occur during cold summers). Oysters are also affected by *Gonyaulax* (red tide) outbreaks (see Index). They will not be sold at such times. Check with local health departments for closures of wild oyster beds.

HOW TO CLEAN

Grasp the oyster firmly in one hand, cupped shell down. (Protect hand with a glove if you have tender fingers.) Grasp oyster knife firmly in the other hand. Insert tip of oyster knife into shell either at the hinge or at the side of the shell. Cut adductor muscle. Remove the top shell. Cut oyster from lower shell. Do not rinse, or you will wash away a lot of flavor. Save or drink juices. Slurp!

HOW TO PREPARE

Oysters are best when they are slurped from the shell just after opening, accompanied by a squeeze of lemon juice. Large oysters (or oysters out of the shell for a few hours) are good in stews, chowders, or pies. Very large oysters may be cut into smaller pieces. Oysters may also be barbecued or broiled.

SERVES 2-4 AS
AN APPETIZER

1 chile poblano or chile verde,
    roasted, peeled, seeded,
    and finely diced
    (see p. 25)
1 ripe (red) Fresno chile or
    chile colorado
1 teaspoon dry mustard
    Salt and freshly ground
    white pepper to taste
1 egg
¼ cup homemade mayonnaise
½ cup cooked crab meat
1 dozen fresh medium oysters
6 teaspoons (approximately)
    thick crème fraîche for
    topping
    Dash California paprika

Stuffed Oysters

This is a dish for those who like their seafood hot. Make it as spicy as you like. Cool your palate with freshly squeezed fruit juices or with a red country wine.

1. Mix green and red chiles. Add mustard, salt, pepper, egg, and ¼ cup mayonnaise. Mix well. Add crab meat and mix in gently with fingers.
2. Shuck oysters and poach them lightly in their own liquor. Return to shell. Top with the crab mixture. Spread a little crème fraîche on top of each serving. Sprinkle with paprika.
3. Bake in a 350° oven until just golden brown. Serve hot.

SERVES 4 AS AN APPETIZER

6 small leeks (white part only),
    cut into julienne strips
    Boiling water as needed
12 fresh small oysters (the
    smaller, the better)
4 tablespoons unsalted butter
2 cups dry Champagne
    Dash cayenne (or to taste)
4 cups whipping cream
1 teaspoon freshly squeezed
    lemon juice

Oysters with Leeks and Champagne Sooke Harbour House

The Sooke Harbour House has an excellent kitchen garden and easy access to superbly fresh seafood from nearby waters. Little wonder Sinclair Philip and his kitchen staff have great fun experimenting with different foods. Here is one of their tasty dishes. Accompany it with, of course, Champagne.

1. Blanch leeks in boiling water. Set aside and keep warm.
2. Shuck oysters; reserve liquor.
3. Sauté leeks in butter in frying pan at medium heat for about 30 seconds (be careful not to burn). Remove from pan; set aside. Add Champagne to pan and reduce by ½ or more. Add oyster liquor and sprinkle on a

small amount of cayenne.

4. Poach oysters in reduced liquid for about 2 minutes. Remove from pan and keep warm. Stir cream into pan and reduce by ½ or until thick. Add lemon juice and stir for about 15 seconds.

5. Place oysters on hot serving plates, distribute sauce evenly, and decorate with leeks. Serve.

SERVES 4–6 AS AN APPETIZER

Wined Oysters on Cucumber Slices

This recipe comes from Karen E. Mack, special events manager at Chateau Ste. Michelle winery in western Washington. It is one of the recipes she prepares when Chateau Ste. Michelle entertains visitors. Accompany the oysters with a Chateau Ste. Michelle chardonnay.

1 tablespoon unsalted butter
¼ teaspoon freshly ground white pepper
½ teaspoon thyme
1 small onion, sliced
1 small carrot, chopped
1 stalk celery, chopped
1 cup water
1½ cups Chateau Ste. Michelle chardonnay
2 dozen fresh medium to small oysters, shucked and drained
24 slices English cucumber Topping

1. Combine first 7 ingredients in large frying pan over medium heat. Simmer for 20 minutes.

2. Add chardonnay.

3. Place oysters in liquid. Cook until oysters are plump and edges begin to curl, approximately 2 to 3 minutes. Turn once to assure even poaching. Remove and drain, let cool.

4. Place each oyster on an English cucumber slice, garnish with topping.

2 tablespoons chardonnay
1 cup Robiola (a soft, fresh Italian cheese)
1 tablespoon minced fresh thyme
1 tablespoon minced fresh parsley
1 tablespoon minced fresh sweet red pepper
1 tablespoon minced fresh lemon zest

TOPPING

1. Blend ingredients; spoon into pastry bag; pipe over oysters.

SERVES 4

½ cup diced bacon fat
2 medium onions, chopped
3 cloves garlic, pressed
1 quart chopped fresh oysters
3 pounds fresh tomatoes,
    chopped
3 large potatoes, diced
3 ribs celery, chopped
½ green pepper, finely chopped
1 teaspoon fresh thyme
    Salt and freshly ground
        black pepper to taste
½ cup tomato paste
1 quart water
½ cup dry white wine

Manhattan Oyster Chowder

This is a very tasty dish from the Rhododendron Cafe in northwestern Washington. I like it even better than Manhattan clam chowder. Accompany it with a microbrewery ale.

1. In large stock pot, sauté bacon fat, onion, and garlic for 5 minutes.
2. Add remaining ingredients. Simmer 1 to 2 hours; adjust seasonings. Serve hot.

SERVES 4

1 pint (or 18) fresh oysters
1 cup heavy cream
3 cups milk
1 teaspoon salt
1 tablespoon Worcestershire
    sauce
    Cayenne to taste
2 tablespoons butter
    Chopped parsley

Northwest Oyster Stew

This recipe is from Lila Gault's The Northwest Cookbook.

1. Shuck oysters if necessary, reserving liquor.
2. In large Dutch oven, simmer oysters in liquor over low heat for about 3 minutes or until edges begin to curl.
3. Add cream and milk, and heat until bubbles form around edge of pot, but not until boiling.
4. Add salt, Worcestershire sauce, and cayenne in pinches to taste. Remove from heat and add butter. Garnish with parsley.

MAKES ABOUT
16 PANCAKES

Oyster Jingles and Smoked Salmon Pancakes

Sinclair Philip of the Sooke Harbour House is a great collector of fresh seafood from the shores of Juan de Fuca Strait. Oyster jingles are not true oysters, though they are closely related. They are delicious.

24 fresh oyster jingles
3 eggs, separated
¾ cup milk
¼ cup unsalted butter, melted
1 cup all-purpose flour
1 teaspoon baking powder
¼ pound smoked salmon,
 chopped into small pieces
2 tablespoons finely chopped
 chives
¼ cup unsalted butter, melted
¾ cup crème fraîche
5 tablespoons salmon caviar,
 drained

1. Pry off backplate of jingles with fingers or knife. Discard roe (it is too bitter for the pancakes). Coarsely chop meat.
2. Preheat grill to 325°, or have a heavy skillet ready over moderate heat.
3. Mix together the egg yolks, milk, and butter. Set aside.
4. In another bowl, mix the flour, baking powder, jingles, smoked salmon, and chives.
5. Beat egg whites to soft peaks.
6. Combine egg yolk mixture with the jingles/salmon mixture; carefully fold in beaten egg whites.
7. Brush grill or skillet with melted butter and ladle out batter in approximately ¼ cup portions. Continue until all the batter has been turned into pancakes. Keep warm until ready to serve. Garnish with crème fraîche and salmon caviar.

SERVES 2–4

2 dozen freshly shucked
    oysters on the half shell
    Dipping Sauce

Oysters on the Half Shell

The Japanese, who love fresh oysters almost as much as the French do, have their own fashion of presenting oysters on the half shell: this version requires a special dipping sauce. It must be noted that the Japanese take their dipping sauces very seriously: K. Watanabe, a Japanese seafood fancier who regularly travels to Alaska, Baja California, and Europe, to indulge in the best of locally available fish and shellfish, carries his special dipping sauce all the way from Tokyo so that he can enjoy a civilized meal wherever he may be, in a small cafe, on a fishing dock, or on the beach. Accompany these oysters with well-chilled lager beer, room temperature porter, or sake (either warmed or "on the rocks").

1. Pick up each oyster with chopsticks (or cocktail fork) and dip it into sauce before eating it.

MAKES ABOUT ¼ CUP

¼ cup soy sauce
4 teaspoons apple cider or
    2 teaspoons white vinegar
2 teaspoons Japanese hot red
    pepper (do not use chile
    powder)
1–2 teaspoons lightly toasted
    white sesame seeds
2–3 teaspoons sugar (optional)
1 green onion, finely chopped
    (optional)

DIPPING SAUCE

1. Blend soy sauce, cider, hot pepper, sesame seeds, and sugar just before serving. Sprinkle with green onions.

SERVES 8-10

1 quart freshly shucked Pacific
      oysters
½ cup butter, melted
1 pound mushrooms, sliced
1 cup chopped green onions
2 cups chopped white onions
4 cloves garlic, minced
1 cup sliced celery or ¾ cup
      chopped lovage
1 bay leaf (California laurel
      or Oregon myrtle)
¼ teaspoon thyme
¼ teaspoon salt (or to taste)
1 teaspoon nuoc mam or
      Worcestershire sauce
½ cup dry French bread
      crumbs or cracker crumbs

Baked Oysters

*This is a recipe designed for the height of the oystering season,
when you have had your share of freshly shucked oysters on the
half shell and want to use the delectable critters in a more
substantial dish. Accompany it with a good lager beer.*

1. Drain oysters; reserve liquor.
2. Combine all ingredients except bread crumbs.
3. Place mixture in a well-buttered, oven-proof baking
   dish. Top with bread crumbs. Bake 40 to 45 minutes in
   preheated 350° oven. Remove bay leaf before serving.

Note: This dish may be made up to a day in advance and
may be stored, tightly covered, in the refrigerator until
baking time.

SERVES 1

4 extra small oysters
4 large leaves spinach, washed
2 slices bacon, cooked but still
      limp
4 sheets phyllo, brushed with
      melted butter and stacked
   Melted unsalted butter as
      needed
   Hollandaise Sauce as
      needed (see p. 19)

Baked Oysters in Phyllo

*This is an exceptionally delectable dish from the Rhododendron
Cafe in Skagit County in northwestern Washington. It makes
great appetizers served with well-chilled bone-dry sparkling
wine.*

1. Wrap each oyster in a spinach leaf and then in ½ strip
   of bacon. Cut the stacked phyllo into 2 strips lengthwise, then fold them over in triangular pockets. Wrap
   2 oysters in packets per strip. Brush with melted
   butter.
2. Bake in a well-oiled pan in a 425° oven for 10 minutes
   or until lightly browned and puffed. Serve laced with
   Hollandaise Sauce.

Oyster Pie with Spinach and Pine Nuts

SERVES 4–6

2 bunches fresh spinach
1 small yellow or white onion, finely chopped
2 cloves garlic, pressed
1 tablespoon unsalted butter
2 tablespoons olive oil
20 fresh small oysters, whole or large pieces
2 eggs
¼ cup half-and-half
¼ cup pine nuts
　Salt and freshly ground pepper to taste
　Short crust dough for double crust pie

This is another uniquely savory dish from the Rhododendron Cafe. Be sure both your oysters and your pine nuts are very fresh, it gives the dish a flavor edge. Serve a chilled sauvignon blanc or pinot blanc with this pie.

1. Wash and chop spinach; steam until soft. Cool and squeeze almost dry.
2. Sauté onion and garlic in butter and olive oil until they soften; add oysters. Beat together eggs and half-and-half; add to onions and oysters. Add spinach, pine nuts, salt, and pepper; blend well.
3. Roll out pie crust; press into pie dish and fill with oyster mixture. Cover with top crust.
4. Bake for 10 minutes in 425° oven, then reduce heat to 375° for 30 minutes, or until pie is golden brown. Cool slightly before serving.

Ostiones con Chile Verde
(OYSTERS IN GREEN CHILE SAUCE)

SERVES 2

2 tablespoons olive oil
1 shallot, finely chopped
12 freshly shucked oysters, with the liquor
　Olive oil as needed
　Sea salt and freshly ground pepper to taste
2 green chiles poblanos (or chiles anchos or chiles verdes), roasted, peeled, seeded, and cut into strips (see p. 25)

Not all of the fine oysters growing in the Sea of Cortez are eaten raw. Local cooks prepare them in many different ways. We asked a cantinero in southern Baja for a recipe. This is the one he gave us. On returning home, we discovered that it works equally well with the cultivated Pacific oysters of the California, Oregon, and Washington shores. Serve hot with freshly toasted croutons of French bread and well-chilled Mexican lager beer.

1. Heat oil in frying pan. Add shallot; sauté until transparent. Transfer to oven-proof *cazuela* (pottery or porcelain dish). Add oysters and oyster liquor. Sprinkle

1–3 *teaspoons finely chopped*
    fresh cilantro

with olive oil, salt, and pepper. Lay chile strips on top.
2. Bake in hot (400° to 425°) oven until the oysters
   plump up and edges begin to curl (about 10 minutes).
   Sprinkle with cilantro.

SERVES 2

2 *dozen oysters*
2 *pounds fresh chestnuts*
1 *medium white onion,*
    chopped
7 *tablespoons unsalted butter*
⅓ *cup heavy cream*
⅓ *cup unsalted chicken stock*
⅓ *cup Champagne*
¼ *teaspoon freshly ground*
    white pepper (or to taste)
⅛ *teaspoon cayenne*
¼ *teaspoon freshly grated*
    nutmeg
¼ *cup grated Parmesan cheese*
    (or to taste)

Oysters in Champagne Chestnut Sauce

*While walking along the beach New Year's Eve 1984, Betty
Swift and Virginia Felton came upon some excellent oysters.
A huge snowfall that day made it impossible for them to keep
a dinner engagement. Instead, they returned to Betty's island
retreat with these fresh and frosty oysters and put together their
own special feast. This is an exceptional dish for bringing in the
new year.*

1. Shuck oysters, saving the juices.
2. Gently steam chestnuts to open. Remove skins with
   sharp paring knife.
3. In heavy skillet, sauté onion in butter until soft. Stir
   in oyster liquor, cream, stock, and Champagne. Season
   with pepper, cayenne, and nutmeg. Reduce by ½.
4. Lay chestnuts and oysters into sauce to warm them
   through. Sprinkle with just enough Parmesan for
   saltiness and texture. Serve hot.

SERVES 4

Braised Pork and Fresh Oysters in Clay Pot

Marinade

½ pound boneless pork butt,
  cut into 1½-inch cubes
½ cup almond or apricot oil
1½ cups warm water
1 tablespoon brown bean
  sauce*
1 tablespoon dark soy sauce
1 tablespoon fresh
  gingerroot, minced
1 piece dried orange peel
2 tablespoons dry sherry or
  Shaoxing wine
4 green onions, trimmed
  and cut diagonally into
  2-inch pieces
8 fresh medium Pacific oysters
  Cornstarch paste as
  needed (see p. 37)
  Chinese or Italian parsley
  for garnish

Chinese sandy pots have such good heat distribution that they cook food very evenly. But there is also some magic going on during the slow-cooking; a delicate balancing and harmonizing of flavors take place, difficult to define, but highly delectable. Strange as the marriage of pork and oysters may seem, here it is a happy one.

1. Combine marinade ingredients in bowl large enough to hold pork; mix well. Add pork; cover and marinate at room temperature for 1 hour.
2. Drain pork, taking care to remove any pieces of garlic clinging to the meat. Heat oil in wok until it begins to smoke. Fry pork cubes, a few at a time, until brown and crusty. Sear meat without cooking it through. Drain on clean kitchen towels. Strain and save cooking oil.
3. In sandy pot, combine water, bean sauce, soy sauce, gingerroot, orange peel, and sherry. Bring to boil. Add braised pork cubes. Reduce heat, cover pot, and simmer for 30 minutes.
4. Drain oysters.
5. When pork has simmered 30 minutes, add onions and oysters. Turn up to boil, slowly pour in cornstarch paste to thicken. As soon as broth has sufficiently thickened (to taste) dish is ready to serve. Garnish with parsley.

* Available in Oriental markets.

¼ cup medium sherry
2 teaspoons light soy sauce
2 cloves garlic, minced
1 teaspoon Chinese 5-spice
    powder*
1 teaspoon freshly squeezed
    lemon juice

MARINADE

1. Blend ingredients well.

* Available in Oriental markets and some supermarkets.

SERVES 4

2 tablespoons butter
2 tablespoons flour
1 cup light cream
¼ teaspoon salt
⅛ teaspoon white pepper
½ teaspoon dill
    Dash nutmeg
18 oysters in shell
4 strips bacon, cooked and
    crumbled
1½ cups grated Cheddar or
    Monterey Jack cheese

Cortez (Island) Oysters

This recipe is from Lila Gault's The Northwest Cookbook. *"Cortez natives could fill several cookbooks with tasty oyster recipes. These deviled oysters top the list."*

1. Melt butter in small saucepan and add flour, cooking for several minutes over low heat and stirring constantly.
2. Remove from heat and add cream, salt, and pepper, and stir until smooth. Return to medium heat and stir until thick. Add dill and nutmeg and set aside.
3. Shuck oysters, reserving lower shells. Cut oysters into small pieces or put through a food mill. Put 2 tablespoons sauce into each shell and fill with ground oysters. Top with bacon bits and grated cheese. Place under hot broiler for 4 minutes or until cheese melts.

SERVES 6

6 tablespoons butter
3 teaspoons minced garlic
3 tablespoons cracked black
    pepper
36 freshly shucked small
    Pacific oysters (preferably
    Willapa Bay)
¾ cup freshly squeezed lime
    juice
¾ cup fish fumet
3 tablespoons butter

Pepper Oysters

Sometimes a restaurant will really surprise me with a dish. That is what Shelburne Inn owners Tony and Ann Kishner did when they gave me this recipe. It is the kind of dish I would not have dared try a few years ago (oysters and all that pepper!), but it is delicious. Try for yourself.

1. Melt butter in sauté pan over medium heat; add garlic and black pepper. Sauté 1 minute. Add oysters, lime juice, and fish fumet; cook, turning oysters once, until liquid is reduced by ½. Add the remaining 3 teaspoons butter; stir and cook just until butter has melted into the sauce. Serve immediately.

SERVES 6

36 medium-sized oysters
½ cup flour
3 eggs, lightly beaten
¼ cup corn oil
¼ pound butter
½ cup capers
    Juice of 1 lemon
    Sprigs of parsley
    Lemon wedges

Oysters Meunière, "À Ma Façon"

This recipe comes from Jacques Boiroux of Le Tastevin Restaurant in Seattle. These are not simple fried oysters. There is a refinement in the taste not found in the standard fried oyster dish. I have enjoyed them at light luncheons and found them to be superb. Once we had these oysters at a wine writers' luncheon where a great variety of different white and red wines were served. The oysters held up surprisingly well.

1. Shuck and drain oysters. Flour each oyster and dip in eggs. Pan fry in a large hot skillet with a little oil. When oysters turn golden brown on one side, turn them over and drain the excess oil by tilting the skillet.
2. Add butter in small amounts, then capers, and lemon juice. When butter starts foaming, serve at once. Garnish with parsley and lemon wedges.

SERVES 2–4

2 dozen freshly shucked oysters
½ teaspoon salt
½ cup all-purpose flour
3 eggs, lightly beaten
    Almond or apricot oil for
        frying (do not use animal
        fat or shortening)
    Dipping Sauce

Fried Oysters

This recipe, from Korean chef Young Kim, is crisp, nongreasy, and just heated through. Needless to say, it calls for very fresh oysters. To make sure this dish is as good as it can be, shuck your own oysters and avoid the positively horrid things that come in jars. If you use more than two dozen oysters, keep the quantity of eggs and flour the same. Dip each fried oyster into dipping sauce before eating it. Accompany with hot sake or well-chilled lager beer.

1. Quickly wash oysters in very cold water (just enough to clean).
2. Place oysters in a basket (at this point Young Kim ran into the kitchen and returned with a small 8-inch open-textured bamboo basket) to drain out the water. Salt the oysters and let them sit and drain until you feel no moisture (about 10 minutes).
3. Roll oysters in flour, coating them very lightly, then drop into eggs and coat.
4. Heat oil in frying pan; fry oysters. Fry them, Young Kim says, as though you were cooking a steak and wanted it to come out medium rare. (They should not be well-done.)

2 teaspoons white (rice)
    vinegar
¼ cup soy sauce
½ chopped green onion (green
    and white parts)

DIPPING SAUCE

1. Mix ingredients together. Sauce is ready to use.

SERVES 2-3

6 small to medium oysters
4 tablespoons butter
Flour as needed
6 eggs, well beaten
3 tablespoons cream
½ teaspoon salt
¼ cup chopped parsley

Hangtown Fry

This recipe is from Lila Gault's The Northwest Cookbook. *"The Hangtown Fry was supposedly invented during the California Gold Rush days and is said to have been the village specialty of a place known as Hangtown, which was later renamed Placerville by its image-conscious citizens. This oyster-and-egg combination is a standard on many Northwest restaurant menus and makes a fine luncheon and supper dish. The oysters should be dusted in flour and browned in butter before adding the beaten eggs to the pan. Try sprinkling freshly grated Parmesan cheese over the finished product."*

1. Dust oysters in flour and fry until golden in melted butter in medium frying pan.
2. Blend together eggs, cream, salt and parsley, and pour over oysters. Reduce heat to low and cover. Serve when eggs are set.

SERVES 6

1 cup flour
1 teaspoon baking powder
½ teaspoon salt
1 egg, lightly beaten
⅔ cup milk
1 cup cooked corn, fresh if possible
½ cup parsley, chopped
½ cup onions, finely chopped
2 cups oysters, drained and chopped
Cooking oil for deep frying

Oyster Fritters

This recipe is from Lila Gault's The Northwest Cookbook. *"Oyster fritters should be eaten with the fingers and can be dipped into small bowls of applesauce, soy sauce, sour cream, or yogurt."*

1. Mix flour, baking powder, and salt together. Add egg and milk and stir until smooth.
2. Add vegetables and oysters and blend until thoroughly mixed.
3. Drop by tablespoon into hot fat in deep pot and let cook for 3 minutes or until golden.

SERVES 4

5–6 cups water
2 dozen shucked oysters
1 teaspoon ginger wine (made by steeping crushed gingerroot in sake or dry sherry for 4 to 6 hours)
1 teaspoon light soy sauce
1 teaspoon baking powder
1 cup all-purpose flour
3 tablespoons cornstarch
½ teaspoon coarse salt
1 large egg (preferably a fresh duck egg), well beaten
½ cup plus 2 tablespoons cold water
5 tablespoons almond or apricot oil
4 cups almond or apricot oil
Cornstarch for dusting oysters as needed
Lemon wedges

Chinese Fried Oysters

Fried oysters call for a good lager beer to wash them down, particularly a Mexican beer, which is much better than Chinese beer for washing down fried seafood. There is a trick to drinking Mexican beer straight from the can. We learned it in La Paz: after you open the can, you rub the rim thoroughly with limón, the unique small green citrus fruit of Mexico (which appears to be akin to the Key lime of Florida), then you sprinkle it liberally with salt.

1. Bring water to boil. Drop in the oysters and cook for about 10 seconds until they begin to curl at the edges. Remove and immediately rinse under cold water; drain well.
2. Place oysters in ceramic bowl; add ginger wine and soy sauce. Marinate for 10 minutes.
3. Combine baking powder, flour, cornstarch, and salt in a bowl. Mix well, then gradually add first the beaten egg, then the water. Beat to a smooth batter, then beat in 5 tablespoons oil. Beat until smooth.
4. Heat 4 cups oil in wok to 350°.
5. Sprinkle oysters with cornstarch; then dip in batter. Deep fry 8 to 10 at a time until they turn golden brown. Remove to a platter when done. Serve with lemon wedges.

SCALLOPS

SCALLOP SUNOMONO

SEVICHE

SCALLOP MOUSSE WITH SAUVIGNON BLANC/SAFFRON SAUCE

ROCK SCALLOPS WITH ORANGE BELL PEPPER SAUCE

ENGLISH CUCUMBER WITH SCALLOPS IN WINE SAUCE

CLEAR SCALLOP SOUP

WEATHERVANE SCALLOP SOUP

MARINATED SQUID AND SCALLOP SALAD

BLANCHED CURLY KALE, APPLE, AND FRESH ROCK SCALLOP
SALAD WITH A BLUEBERRY VINAIGRETTE

FRESH SCALLOPS IN THE SHELL RHODODENDRON CAFE

BAKED ROSEMARY SCALLOPS

SCALLOPS BAKED WITH OYSTER MUSHROOMS

WINED SCALLOPS IN BROTH

SCALLOPS IN CHINESE SPICY SAUCE

SCALLOPS IN BEAN SAUCE

SCALLOPS WITH VEAL STOCK AND CREAM

FRESH SCALLOPS NIÇOISE

SCALLOPS VICTORIA

SCALLOPS CAROL ANNE

RIESLING SCALLOPS

BROILED SCALLOPS

SCALLOPS IN PUFF PASTRY

BARBECUED SCALLOPS

CALIFORNIA SUNSHINE SCALLOPS

STIR-FRIED VEGETABLES WITH SCALLOPS

DEEP-FRIED SCALLOPS

COMMON NAME	
Weathervane Scallop *(Giant Pacific Scallop)* *(California to Alaska)*	This is our largest (to nine inches across) swimming scallop (larger even than the Atlantic sea scallop). It is harvested commercially in deep water offshore. The color of its strongly ribbed shell is variable and may be brown, yellow, orange, rose, lavender, or white. Only the large adductor muscle of this large scallop is harvested.
Iceland Scallop *(Washington to Arctic seas)*	This small (two and one-half inches across) scallop is harvested commercially in deep water offshore. The grayish white shell has fifty or more thin ribs. Only the muscle is harvested.
Pink (Swimming) Scallop *(California to Alaska)*	A small (two inches across) scallop with a colorful, ribbed shell. This scallop is very common in the inland waters of the Pacific Northwest. It is now harvested commercially. It is exceptionally good to eat whole, lightly steamed.
Kelpweed Scallop *(Baja California to* *central California)*	A small (one inch across) scallop with a mottled, brownish white shell. It is common in kelp beds. The kelpweed scallop is very good to eat whole.
San Diego Scallop *(California)*	A large (four inches across) very pretty scallop with twenty-two or twenty-three flattened ribs on its upper (convex) shell. Despite its size, it is good to eat whole.
Pacific Lion's Paw *(Ecuador to southern California)*	A large (six inches across) reddish scallop. Good to eat whole, despite its size.
Hind's Scallop *(California to Alaska)*	A small (two inches across) scallop with a colorful shell. May be steamed open and eaten whole.
Giant Rock Scallop *(Purple-Hinged Rock Scallop)* *(Gulf of California to Alaska)*	A large (to ten inches across) scallop that swims free like other scallops in its youth, but then settles down on a rock for life, grows a heavy shell, and waxes fat. After the rock scallop gives up its power of flight, its pretty shell becomes coarse and thick (the animal opts for armor instead of speed) and quite lumpy. It can still be recognized as a scallop, however, because the original, finely fluted juvenile shell remains embedded near the hinge of the adult shell.

The rock scallop is the most sweetly flavored of our

shellfish—its flesh has the highest glycogen content of any bivalve—and many connoisseurs claim it is also the tastiest. Young rock scallops should be eaten raw, like oysters; older ones may be prepared like other scallops or like mussels and oysters.

DESCRIPTION

Scallops are beautiful to look at and to eat. They have delicate meat with good flavor, large adductor muscles, and thin, winglike shells, which allow them to swim through the water. Their brightly colored red, pink, orange, or purple shells blend surprisingly well with stands of eelgrass or kelp. Scallops make a very attractive meal when served in the shell.

Most bivalves have two small adductor muscles for opening or closing their shells; the scallop has one large, tender, juicy, and very savory adductor muscle. The rest of the scallop's body is a bit of an enigma. It is more or less nothing but a large gut wrapped around the muscle. The whole animal is exceptionally tasty.

HABITAT

Scallops live in eelgrass meadows and kelp forests. They are found in fairly deep estuaries, bays, and coastal areas to offshore waters. Since they can swim, scallops may migrate for short distances.

The sessile rock scallop is not as common in Canadian and United States waters as it once was, but it is still very common in Mexico. It is so common that you may get rock scallop in a restaurant when you order oysters or abalone. The name *abulón*, in fact, may be applied indiscriminately to both the abalone and the rock scallop. The rock scallop may be found attached to beach rocks in the lower tidal zones, but it is encountered more commonly in deep water.

METHODS OF CATCHING

Scallops may be caught by divers using hand-held nets, or they can be dredged up from deeper waters. Commercial scallopers use huge dredges to scrape scallops off the ocean floor.

AVAILABILITY IN FISH MARKETS AND RESTAURANTS

Scallops are harvested only intermittently on the West Coast. Their presence cannot be predicted accurately, which makes dredging a risky proposition. The West Coast scallop industry also suffers from a lack of motivated shuckers. But they are well worth searching out. Keep on good terms with your fishmonger to assure yourself of a mess of tasty West Coast scallops whenever they become available.

Fortunately for scallop lovers, things are changing. A couple of years ago the small delightful pink scallops were not available commercially, and gourmets who wished to savor these tender and flavorful mollusks needed to dive for them or make the acquaintance of a diver willing to share his catch. Then the delectable mollusks started showing up regularly in Chinatown fish markets in Vancouver, British Columbia, then in other fish markets; now they are available in special United States seafood markets as well.

Rock scallops are not currently sold by our fishmongers (their scarcity has led to protective legislation) but Bill Webb, at Westcott Bay on San Juan Island, Washington, is experimenting with their commercial production.

SEASONS

Year-round.

HOW TO CLEAN

Scallops can be shucked like oysters or steamed open like clams. The whole animal (not just the white adductor muscle) should be eaten.

HOW TO PREPARE

For who knows what reason, the large adductor muscle is the only part of the scallop commonly sold in our fish markets. This is a shame, for the rest of the scallop is just as delicious and very tender. Scallops are excellent raw, on the half shell, or steamed. The less they are cooked, the better. But they may be added to salads, sauces, soups, and chowders.

SERVES 2–4 AS AN APPETIZER

1 cucumber (preferably
    Japanese kyuri), thinly
    sliced
½ teaspoon salt
½ teaspoon gingerroot, crushed
    and very finely chopped

Scallop Sunomono

Scallops can be served in a vinegared dish of Japanese origin called sunomono. *This is a very delicate dish, perfect as an appetizer for a light meal. Make sure the scallops are absolutely fresh! Accompany it with sake, a light sauvignon blanc, or a good lager beer.*

1½ cups rice vinegar
1 cup tiny shucked scallops or
large scallops cut into
8 pieces each

1. Place cucumber in ceramic or stainless steel bowl; salt. Let stand for 15 minutes. Press liquid from cucumbers and drain (cucumber slices should be limp).
2. Combine remaining ingredients; add to cucumber and toss.
3. Refrigerate for a minimum of 1 hour; preferably overnight.

SERVES 4–6 AS
AN APPETIZER

2 pounds shucked scallops
4 limes, juiced
3 ripe tomatoes, peeled and chopped
2 green chiles poblanos, cut crosswise in thin strips
1 red onion, sliced paper-thin
2 cloves garlic, minced
Sprigs parsley, chopped
Sprigs cilantro, chopped
Salt and freshly ground black pepper to taste
1 teaspoon oregano
⅛ teaspoon sugar
3 tablespoons olive oil
Fresh red chiles (optional)
Green pepper (optional)
Ripe-green olives (optional)
Avocado slices for garnish
Raw red onion slices for garnish

Seviche

Raw fish or shellfish marinated in lime juice and spices is a popular dish in tropical Latin American countries. "Cooking" seafood in lime juice is a quick method of preserving it and keeping it from spoiling. I got this recipe from Sue Schellenberger, who now lives in Skagit County in northwestern Washington. Sue has spent quite a bit of time in Latin America and brought this recipe home with her. Accompany it with good Mexican lager beer or Margaritas.

1. If scallops are large, cut them into quarters; leave small scallops whole. Marinate overnight in lime juice.
2. Drain scallops and add remaining ingredients. Serve.

SERVES 6 AS AN APPETIZER

1 *pound fresh scallops, cold*
2 *cups whipping cream, cold*
1 *egg, cold*
  Salt and freshly ground
    white pepper to taste
6 *timbales (appetizer portions)*
  Sauvignon Blanc/Saffron
    Sauce
  Whole prawns cooked in
    butter for garnish
  Caviar for garnish
    (optional)
  Fresh dill sprigs for garnish
  Fennel sprigs for garnish
    (optional)

Scallop Mousse with Sauvignon Blanc/Saffron Sauce

I enjoyed this lovely dish at a luncheon prepared by Jon Kasky, who is the executive chef for Almadén Vineyards. The setting was lovely too; we ate at the Cienega mansion in San Benito County, which is a restored manorial farmhouse surrounded by vineyards and oak woods. This is a truly sumptuous dish. Enjoy it with an Almadén or Charles Lefranc sauvignon blanc.

1. Trim side muscles from scallops and save for use in sauce. Puree scallops fine in a food processor blender.
2. With machine running, add cream in a steady stream, then egg.
3. Add ½ teaspoon salt and a pinch of white pepper.
4. Poach a teaspoon of the mousse until done and adjust seasoning.
5. Divide mousse into 6 buttered timbales (scallop shape if available).
6. Poach in water bath in a 400° oven until firm, about 20 to 25 minutes. Do not overcook, or they can be rubbery.
7. To present, make a pool of the sauce on a warm plate. Unmold the warm mousse, drain any water, and place on sauce. Garnish with cooked whole prawns or caviar and fresh dill or fennel sprigs. Serve warm.

Note: This recipe makes an elegant appetizer course when served with the same wine used in the sauce. Use only fresh scallops. For an interesting variation, put ½ the finished mousse into the timbales, and puree the remaining half with fresh dill or tarragon; then fill the molds with the green mousse. You could even place a small, whole scallop between these 2 layers for garnish.

SAUVIGNON BLANC/SAFFRON SAUCE

Pinch saffron threads or
  ½ teaspoon powdered
2 *shallots, very finely diced*

1. Place saffron threads in 1 tablespoon sauvignon blanc

½ cup mushroom stems and
  trimmings
½ cup unsalted butter, cut into
  8 pieces
  Trimmed muscles from
  1 pound fresh scallops
¾ cup Almadén sauvignon
  blanc
¼ cup water
1 cup whipping cream
  Sea salt and freshly ground
  white pepper to taste

to extract flavor and color.

2. In saucepan, sauté shallots and mushrooms in 1 piece
   of butter. Do not brown.
3. Add scallop trimmings, remaining wine, and water.
   Bring to a boil, skim, lower heat, and simmer to reduce
   to about ¼ cup.
4. Add cream, boil, and reduce by ½.
5. Whisk in remaining butter, 1 piece at a time, until
   incorporated. Add saffron and wine.
6. Add salt and pepper. Taste and adjust seasoning. Serve
   warm under scallop mousse.

SERVES 4 AS
AN APPETIZER

Cooking oil as needed
2 large yellow bell peppers,
  seeded and chopped into
  small pieces
1 large red bell pepper, seeded
  and chopped into small
  pieces
2 tablespoons minced shallots
1 tablespoon minced garlic
4 tablespoons blackberry or
  blueberry vinegar
1 teaspoon good brandy
½ cup dry white wine
3 tablespoons freshly squeezed
  lemon juice
½ pound rock scallops (about
  6 average scallops)
½ cup unsalted butter
  Petals of 4 calendula flowers
  for garnish (optional)

Rock Scallops with Orange Bell Pepper Sauce

This is another exceptionally delicious recipe from the Sooke Harbour House, a restaurant that may well be the most adventurous seafood house on the coast.

1. Warm oil in saucepan over low heat for 1 minute. Add
   peppers, shallots, and garlic, and cook for 10 minutes,
   stirring constantly. Add vinegar, and continue reducing
   sauce at low heat for about 5 minutes. Add brandy, wine,
   and lemon juice. Reduce sauce by ½ (approximately
   10 minutes).
2. Pour sauce into blender or food processor and puree
   until smooth. Press through sieve.
3. Steam scallops open; remove each scallop as it opens and
   place in oven to keep warm.
4. To finish sauce, slowly incorporate butter at low heat
   until completely absorbed.
5. Remove scallops from oven and arrange on serving
   platter. Pour sauce around scallops. Decorate scallops
   with orange calendula petals.

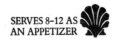

SERVES 8–12 AS
AN APPETIZER

1 English cucumber or more
   as needed
4 tablespoons unsalted butter
⅛ teaspoon freshly ground
   white pepper
¼ teaspoon dried basil or
   1 to 2 leaves fresh, minced
1 pound sea scallops, shucked
   and cut in half
   horizontally
½ cup Chateau Ste. Michelle
   fumé blanc
½ cup heavy cream
   Minced hazelnuts as needed

English Cucumber with Scallops in Wine Sauce

English cucumbers do very well in western Washington. They develop a firm texture and crisp taste. This crispness makes them a good foil for fresh seafood. This recipe, from Chateau Ste. Michelle winery, brings out the best in cucumber and scallop. Accompany the dish with a Ste. Michelle fumé blanc.

1. Wash and score cucumber; cut into ½-inch thick slices. Using a medium melon baller create a bowl in the center of each slice. Turn bowl upside down on paper towels to drain.
2. Combine butter, pepper, and basil in medium saucepan over medium heat. Add scallops; lightly sauté scallops over medium heat 2 to 3 minutes, do not overcook; remove scallop slices and keep warm.
3. Add fumé blanc and cream and reduce to ½, return scallops and toss. Scallops should be lightly coated with sauce.
4. Place one slice of scallop in cup of each cucumber slice. Dust with minced hazelnuts.

SERVES 4

4 cups unsalted chicken stock
1 bunch very fresh spinach
8 slices winter bamboo shoots
½ pound very fresh, shucked
   scallops
1 teaspoon salt (or to taste)
1 tablespoon sherry
1 tablespoon almond or
   apricot oil

Clear Scallop Soup

Like many good soups, this one makes a good luncheon dish as well as a perfect soup course for a multicourse dinner. Accompany it with a well-chilled very dry wine or sparkling wine.

1. Heat stock.
2. Cut off root ends of spinach and thoroughly wash. Slice bamboo shoots into paper-thin strips; add to stock as it is heating.
3. Using a wire strainer, blanch scallops in boiling water for 15 seconds; set aside. Add salt to water. Blanch spinach for 10 seconds; drain and set aside.
4. When stock reaches rapid simmer (do not let boil), add scallops, spinach, and sherry. Cook for 3 minutes. Heat oil in ladle over flame. Mix oil into soup. Transfer soup to serving bowl.

SERVES 4

¾ pound fresh weathervane
   scallop meat
5 cups light fish stock
3 thin slices young gingerroot
¼ cup dry sherry
10 small beach crabs, scrubbed,
   watch those pincers
   (optional)
1 medium carrot, peeled and
   cut into very fine
   julienne strips
1 small leek with 1- or 2-inch
   green leaf, cut into very
   fine julienne strips
16 wild onion flowers (optional)

Weathervane Scallop Soup

This is another one of those most exquisite dishes from the Sooke Harbour House. Accompany it with a chilled fino sherry or good, light ale.

1. Cut scallops into fine julienne strips and briefly put into freezer while preparing the other ingredients.
2. In a saucepan, bring stock, gingerroot, sherry, and small crabs to a boil. Strain out gingerroot and crabs. (You may save crabs for garnish or other dishes.)
3. Add carrot. Add scallops and leek. Simmer for about 30 seconds.
4. Pour soup into warmed soup bowls, garnish with wild onion flowers and serve.

Marinated Squid and Scallop Salad

SERVES 6

The Shelburne Inn is without a doubt one of the most delightful country restaurants on the entire coast. Yet despite its country setting, it has an admirable sophistication about food, which expresses itself in dishes like this.

4 green peppers, cut into
 ¼-inch strips
½ cup olive oil
6 squids, cleaned and cut into
 ¼-inch rings
1 pound very fresh, shucked
 scallops
½ cup marinara sauce
8 cloves garlic, minced
4 red onions, sliced
⅓ cup olive oil
⅓ cup red wine vinegar
2 bay leaves
 Salt and freshly ground
 black pepper to taste

1. Sauté green peppers in ½ cup olive oil until softened. Add squid and scallops and sauté 2 to 3 minutes.
2. Pour off cooking oil; add marinara sauce and garlic to peppers, squid, and scallops; pour into bowl.
3. Add onions, ⅓ cup olive oil, vinegar, bay leaves, salt, and pepper. Toss well.
4. Marinate for 48 hours, tossing occasionally.

Blanched Curly Kale, Apple, and Fresh Rock Scallop Salad with a Blueberry Vinaigrette

SERVES 4

This recipe comes from Pia Carroll and Kelly Bullock; chefs at the Sooke Harbour House. It is very popular in winter, when kale is one of the few greens that will do well in the cool Vancouver Island climate.

 Leaves from 4 to 8 curly
 kale stems
2 apples, cored and cut into
 wedges
 Unsalted butter as needed
4 large rock scallops
1½ cups olive oil
½ cup blueberry vinegar
 (substitute other fruit
 vinegars according to
 availability — bright colors
 are more attractive)

1. Remove kale leaves and discard stems. Tear into bite-sized pieces and wash.
2. Bring a quart of water to boil; blanch kale leaves for 15 seconds. Place in a colander and rinse immediately under cold water to stop the cooking. Spin dry.
3. Sauté apple wedges in butter. (They should be just

2 tablespoons Dijon or
  Meaux mustard
¼ cup whipping cream

cooked and warm when served.)

4. If the scallops have been caught within the tide (4 to 8 hours), shuck them and cut them into crescent slices. Set raw scallop crescents aside. If the rock scallops are more than a day from the water, sauté them lightly with the apple and butter.

5. To make blueberry vinaigrette, pour oil and vinegar into mixing bowl. Whisk in mustard until mixture is well blended. Blend in the cream. The dressing should be of an appealing blue-red color.

6. Place dressing in bottom of (preferably) white serving plate. Arrange other ingredients decoratively around rim of plate. Serve.

SERVES 2-4

Fresh Scallops in the Shell Rhododendron Cafe

2 tablespoons unsalted butter
2 tablespoons dry white wine
1 bay leaf
  Pinch thyme
  Dash cayenne
  Salt and freshly ground
    white pepper to taste
2 dozen fresh scallops in shells
  (buy only scallops whose
  shells are firmly closed)

While just about all of the dishes served at the Rhododendron Cafe in northwestern Washington can make for a most rewarding repast, the fresh scallops cooked in the shell are a special treat. They are amazingly simple to prepare. Just make sure to use only the freshest of scallops (if you cannot get scallops in the shell, use fresh tiny bay scallops). I have had best results with this dish using fresh thyme and a crisp nonweedy sauvignon blanc or semillon.

1. Melt butter in deep saucepan. Add wine, bay leaf, thyme, cayenne, salt, and pepper. Bring mixture to rolling boil. Add scallops and cover. Cook about 1 minute. Scallops have very thin shells (otherwise they would never get off the ground as they try to swim) and take almost no time to cook.

2. Serve hot, in the shell in small bowls; pour pan juices over scallops. Accompany with freshly baked bread (preferably hot from the oven).

SERVES 6-8

Baked Rosemary Scallops

Serve this flavorful herbed dish with garlic French bread and an amusing little country wine such as a pinot blanc or green hungarian.

2 pounds shucked scallops
   (white muscle only)
½ cup half-and-half
¼ cup dry sauvignon blanc
2 teaspoons freshly squeezed
   lemon juice
1 white onion, chopped
½ teaspoon finely chopped fresh
   rosemary or ⅛ teaspoon
   dried
   Salt and freshly ground
   white pepper (to taste)
¾ cup soft bread crumbs
   Unsalted butter as needed

1. Spread scallops in shallow baking dish. Mix together half-and-half, wine, lemon juice, onion, rosemary, salt, and pepper. Pour over scallops. The dish may be prepared ahead of time to this point and cooked later. Be sure to cover it tightly and refrigerate.
2. Top mixture with bread crumbs and dab with butter.
3. Bake in preheated 450° oven for 15 minutes. Quickly broil to brown the top.

SERVES 4

Scallops Baked with Oyster Mushrooms

I will use any excuse to cook oyster mushrooms, especially when I can match them to seafood. The delicate flavor of oyster mushrooms goes particularly well with scallops. Enjoy this dish with a dry riesling or chenin blanc.

4 tablespoons unsalted butter
1 cup sliced oyster mushrooms
1 stalk celery or lovage,
   chopped
3 shallots, chopped
1 small chile verde, roasted,
   peeled, and chopped
   (see p. 25)
   Pinch dried basil
1 pound shucked scallops
2 cups Béchamel Sauce
   (see p. 18)
½ cup cracker crumbs
½ cup grated dry Sonoma Jack
   cheese

1. Melt butter in heavy saucepan; add mushrooms, celery, shallots, chile, and basil. Sauté gently for 5 minutes.
2. Add scallops and cook 5 minutes longer.
3. Add Béchamel Sauce; mix well.
4. Pour mixture into an oven-proof glass or ceramic dish. Sprinkle cracker crumbs, then cheese over scallops.
5. Bake in preheated 325° oven until cheese melts and crust turns golden, about 30 minutes.

SERVES 4

Wined Scallops in Broth

2 pounds large shucked scallops
2 teaspoons salt
½ cup good-quality sake
4 Napa cabbage leaves
2 cubes hard (Chinese-style)
   tofu
2 green onions
1 teaspoon almond or apricot
   oil
3 cups unsalted chicken stock
½ teaspoon fresh gingerroot,
   minced
   Salt and freshly ground
   white pepper to taste

The unique character of this dish derives from the marriage of firm-textured scallops with a good rice wine. Use a first-rate sake only. Do not stint on the quality of the wine; its flavor is important here. This dish is an entrée, not a soup course; the amount of broth is less than you would expect for a soup.

1. Wash scallops. Mix 2 teaspoons salt and sake in bowl; add scallops and toss. Cover bowl and refrigerate for 6 hours. After 2 hours, turn scallops to mix with marinade.
2. When scallops have finished marinating, rinse and drain.
3. Wash cabbage; slice leaves down middle, then into 2-inch sections. Rinse tofu; cut into 1-inch cubes. Wash, trim, and shred green onions, greens and all. Heat almond or apricot oil to point of smoking. Remove from heat; reserve.
4. Heat stock, tofu, gingerroot, salt, and pepper in saucepan. Reduce heat; cover pan and simmer for 10 minutes.
5. When you are ready to add scallops and cabbage, bring stock to boil; add scallops and cabbage; cover pan. Cook about 3 to 5 minutes. Cabbage leaves will be bright lime green.
6. Ladle scallops, cabbage, and tofu into warm shallow serving bowl; add broth. Sprinkle with cooked oil, minced green onion and pepper. Serve.

SERVES 4

¼ pound snow peas, strings
and ends removed
1 pound small Oregon scallops
2 tablespoons light soy sauce
2 tablespoons dry sherry or
Shaoxing wine
1 teaspoon sugar
Cornstarch as needed
½ cup almond or apricot oil
6 pieces dried chile (do not use
Oriental peppers for this,
they are too hot)
5–6 pieces dried orange peel
(1½- by 1½-inch pieces)
2 whole star anise
5 whole cloves
6 pieces peeled gingerroot, cut
into ¼-inch slices
3 green onions (white part
only, cut on the bias into
2-inch pieces)
4 cloves garlic, peeled
Chinese Spicy Sauce

Scallops in Chinese Spicy Sauce

The contrasting flavors are what make this dish unique. The spicy sauce does not penetrate the mild-flavored scallops. Accompany it with a fino sherry or amontillado.

1. Bring 1 quart of water to boil; add snow peas. Blanch for 10 seconds or until color turns deep green. Remove and plunge into cold running water (to stop further cooking). Pat dry with clean kitchen towels and set aside.
2. Place scallops in a bowl and add soy sauce, wine, and sugar. Mix gently. Add cornstarch and stir gently until scallops are thoroughly coated.
3. Heat wok until it smokes. Add oil; heat for 15 seconds. Add dried chile. When these have turned almost black, add orange peel and anise; cook until peel is charred. Reduce heat; add cloves, gingerroot, green onion, and garlic. Stir over low heat to extract the flavors. Do not burn garlic. After a few minutes, remove all solid ingredients from oil.
4. Make Chinese Spicy Sauce.
5. Mix water and cornstarch in separate bowl.
6. Bring oil back to high temperature. Stir fry ½ the scallops until they begin to brown lightly around the edges. Remove with strainer; stir fry remaining scallops.
7. Reduce heat to low. Remove all but 1 tablespoon oil from wok. Increase heat to high. Add snow peas and stir briskly for 10 seconds. Return scallops to pan; toss.
8. Stir spicy sauce and slowly pour into wok with one hand while stirring contents of wok with the other. Mix well. At this point you may reduce and thicken sauce to desired consistency, or you may thicken it with the cornstarch mixture. (Using the cornstarch mixture is easier, you do not risk burning the contents of the wok as the sauce cooks down, but the flavor will not be as fine.)

2 tablespoons light soy sauce
1 tablespoon sugar
2 tablespoons water
2 tablespoons oyster sauce*
1 teaspoon Chinese sesame
oil (do not use other
sesame oil, the flavor
will be different)
1 teaspoon Chinese chili
oil* (or to taste)
1 teaspoon cornstarch
1 tablespoon water

CHINESE SPICY SAUCE

1. Combine all ingredients except cornstarch and water in ceramic bowl. Set aside until needed. Combine cornstarch and water separately in small bowl or cup. Use cornstarch mixture to thicken sauce as needed.

* Available in Oriental markets and in some supermarkets.

SERVES 4

½ pound small shucked scallops
½ cup dry sherry or Shaoxing
wine
1 teaspoon sugar
½ teaspoon light soy sauce
⅔ cup unsalted chicken stock
½ teaspoon Sichuan soybean
paste*
½ teaspoon fresh gingerroot,
minced
1 tablespoon thinly sliced fresh
water chestnuts (peeled)*
1 teaspoon cornstarch paste
(see p. 37)
½ teaspoon Chinese sesame oil
(do not use other sesame
oil — it will change the
flavor of the dish)
Thinly sliced green onion
for garnish

Scallops in Bean Sauce

Cook this dish quickly so scallops stay flavorful and tender. Accompany it with a fino sherry.

1. Marinate scallops in sherry, sugar, and soy sauce for 15 minutes. Mix stock and soybean paste; stir in ½ the marinade after scallops are removed.
2. Heat wok to high. Add stock mixture; when it begins to simmer, add gingerroot and water chestnuts; cook for about 1 minute. Dribble in cornstarch paste stirring constantly. Sauce should reach a medium-thick consistency. Allow sauce to cook for another minute. Reduce heat to medium, then add scallops. Poach for about 1 or 2 minutes, just until scallops begin to turn opaque. Avoid overcooking. Stir in sesame oil. Garnish with green onion. Serve.

* Available in Oriental markets and in some supermarkets.

SERVES 6

Scallops with Veal Stock and Cream

The Shelburne Inn, at the corner of Columbia River and Long Beach peninsula, has access to superbly fresh seafood. Chefs Cheryl and Eric Jenkins obtain their fresh Oregon scallops from the nearby fishing port of Astoria.

1 cup all-purpose flour
  Salt and freshly ground
    pepper to taste
2½ pounds small shucked
    scallops (preferably small
    Oregon scallops)
¾ cup butter
¾ cup dry white wine
1 cup fish stock
1½ cups chopped ripe tomatoes,
    peeled and seeded (about
    2 to 3 medium tomatoes)
1½ cups veal stock
¾ cup heavy cream
¼ cup chopped fresh basil
  Salt and freshly ground
    white pepper to taste
  Chopped parsley for garnish

1. Mix flour, salt, and pepper in bowl. Lightly dredge scallops in flour mixture.
2. Melt butter over moderate heat in sauté pan. Add scallops and sauté on each side until golden brown (be careful not to burn the butter during this step).
3. Remove scallops from pan and drain off butter. Deglaze pan with wine. Turn up heat; add stock and tomatoes. Reduce over high heat until it reaches a syrupy consistency. Add veal stock; reduce by ⅓. Add cream, basil, salt, and pepper; continue reducing until sauce thickens and coats the back of a spoon.
4. Return scallops briefly to sauce to reheat. Serve with a sprinkling of parsley.

SERVES 6

Fresh Scallops Niçoise

This recipe comes from Jacques Boiroux of Le Tastevin in Seattle, the most respected "French" restaurant in the Northwest. Accompany this dish with a dry chardonnay.

30 medium-sized shucked
    scallops
½ cup all-purpose flour
3 tablespoons olive oil
8 cloves garlic, chopped
½ pound unsalted butter
1 cup veal stock
3 ripe tomatoes, diced
  Freshly ground black pepper
    to taste
½ cup chopped fresh basil
    leaves

1. Lightly dredge scallops in flour; shake off excess.
2. Heat olive oil in skillet; sauté the scallops quickly.
3. When scallops are golden brown, add garlic, butter, and veal stock. Stir until butter and stock are well blended. Add tomatoes and pepper. Sprinkle with basil just before serving.

SERVES 2-4

2 cloves garlic, pressed or
   finely minced
1 tablespoon unsalted butter
1 tablespoon olive oil
   All-purpose flour as needed
¾ pound shucked scallops
2 tablespoons diced ripe
   tomatoes
2 tablespoons tomato sauce
¼ cup slivered almonds, toasted
½ cup freshly squeezed orange
   juice
   Salt and freshly ground
   black pepper to taste
   Dash cayenne (or to taste)
2 tablespoons chopped green
   onions

Scallops Victoria

This dish comes from the Rhododendron Cafe, a delightful small country restaurant in the northern Puget Sound region. The scallops are excellent served over fresh pasta or with rice.

1. Briefly sauté garlic in butter and oil.
2. Flour scallops and add to pan. Cook 1 to 2 minutes. Add tomatoes, tomato sauce, almonds, orange juice, salt, pepper, and cayenne. Simmer for 2 minutes more (be careful not to overcook scallops). Add green onions just before serving.

SERVES 4

1 tart apple, diced
12 medium mushrooms, sliced
1 tablespoon minced shallots
¼ cup unsalted butter
1 pound fresh, shucked bay
   scallops
   All-purpose flour as needed
1 teaspoon mustard
   Pinch basil
1 teaspoon chopped parsley
   Salt and freshly ground
   black pepper to taste
1 teaspoon freshly squeezed
   lemon juice
1 cup dry white wine

Scallops Carol Anne

This light sauté features small bay scallops simmered with apples, mustard, and basil in white wine. It is one of the many delectable seafood dishes served at the Rhododendron Cafe.

1. Sauté apple, mushrooms, and shallots in butter.
2. Lightly dredge scallops in flour. Briefly sauté with apple/mushroom mixture.
3. Stir in mustard, basil, parsley, salt, pepper, lemon juice, and wine.
4. Simmer until scallops are not quite opaque (leave slightly undercooked). Serve hot.

SERVES 4

Riesling Scallops

This is a delightful dish. Just make sure the scallops you use are very fresh. Accompany it with, of course, a dry riesling.

2 pounds shucked scallops
  Salt and freshly ground
    white pepper to taste
½ teaspoon California paprika
2 tablespoons unsalted butter
2 tablespoons olive oil
1 cup dry riesling
¼ cup chopped fresh dill

1. Season scallops with salt, pepper, and paprika.
2. Heat butter and oil in a heavy skillet almost to the smoking point.
3. Drop scallops into skillet; sauté for 5 minutes over high heat, turning constantly to brown evenly.
4. Remove scallops to heated platter.
5. Add wine to pan juices; stir to blend. Cook over high heat, stirring and shaking pan, until sauce is reduced by ½. Pour sauce over scallops. Serve garnished with dill.

SERVES 4

Broiled Scallops

This is one of those recipes that seems to have been around forever and will probably remain forever popular, because it is easy to prepare and tasty. It goes well with just about any of the lighter white wines or with a first-rate (microbrewery) lager beer.

1 clove garlic, cut lengthwise
    down the middle
6 tablespoons unsalted butter,
    melted
1 pound shucked scallops
  Salt and freshly ground
    white pepper to taste
  Dash cayenne
  All-purpose flour as needed
1 teaspoon California paprika
8 lemon slices

1. Rub bottom and sides of medium-sized, shallow glass or ceramic baking dish with garlic; add half the melted butter and swish around in the dish.
2. Lay scallops in dish (flat side down); season with salt, pepper, and cayenne; lightly dust with flour and paprika. Pour remaining butter over scallops.
3. Place under hot broiler. Cook 8 minutes, or until golden. Serve hot with lemon slices.

SERVES 8

Scallops in Puff Pastry

This delightful dish comes from western Washington's Chateau Ste. Michelle winery. Despite its elegant appearance, it is surprisingly simple to prepare. Serve it on festive occasions, accompanied by a Chateau Ste. Michelle fumé blanc.

4 shallots, minced
2 cloves garlic, minced
1 tablespoon minced fresh parsley
1 cup Chateau Ste. Michelle fumé blanc
¼ teaspoon freshly ground white pepper
Pinch lemon zest
1¼ pound bay scallops, shucked
8 pastry cups

1. Combine all ingredients except scallops and pastry cups; simmer for 20 minutes.
2. Add bay scallops. Simmer 3 to 4 minutes; do not overcook.
3. Spoon mixture into pastry cups. Serve immediately.

PASTRY CUPS

1. Use a standard puff pastry recipe, or take your favorite pie crust recipe, roll it to a thickness of ⅛ inch, spread it with butter, fold, and reroll. Repeat 3 to 4 times and you will have a "mock" puff pastry dough. On the final roll, roll to a thickness of ¼ inch.
2. Cut dough into circles and rings of the same diameter. Place a ring on top of each circle. As this is baked, it will rise and create a cup.
3. Prebake cups in a 375° oven. Time varies according to size. If entrée size is 5 or 6 inches, bake approximately 20 to 25 minutes. Prick any bubbles in the dough after 10 minutes.

SERVES 2-4

1 pound shucked scallops
8 slices bacon, quartered
1 clove garlic, crushed
1 green onion, minced
1 tablespoon chopped chervil
    or parsley
2 tablespoons olive oil
2 tablespoons unsalted butter
    Garlic toast

Barbecued Scallops

Here is a simple way of barbecuing scallops. Bacon keeps the scallops moist, acting as a sort of self-basting sauce while the scallops are cooking. By the way, do not, as a friend once did, pour the sauce over the scallops while they are still on the grill. Olive oil and butter burn quite readily. Accompany this dish with a light dry white wine: a chenin blanc or a dry riesling.

1. Thread scallops and bacon slices alternately onto 4 skewers (fold quartered pieces in half before skewering, if they seem too unwieldy). Barbecue over hot coals until lightly browned on all sides.
2. Meanwhile, in a small saucepan, gently sauté garlic, green onion, and chervil in oil and butter until garlic softens. Do not brown.
3. Remove skewers from grill. Pour sauce over skewered scallops. Serve hot with garlic toast.

SERVES 4

8 bay leaves, cut in half
¼ cup lemon juice
¼ cup white wine vinegar
¼ cup olive oil
2 tablespoons finely chopped
    shallots or white onion
2 tablespoons finely chopped
    chervil or parsley
    Salt and freshly ground
    black pepper to taste
1 pound shucked scallops
2 ripe nectarines, cut into
    wedges

California Sunshine Scallops

What could be more California-like than the combination of luscious fruit and scallops? Accompany this dish with an off-dry muscat.

1. Combine first 8 ingredients in a jar. Shake well. Pour marinade over scallops and nectarines and let marinate 1 hour.
2. Thread scallops, bay leaves, and nectarines onto skewers.
3. Barbecue over mesquite charcoal 2 to 4 minutes on each side, or until just tender. Baste with marinade while cooking. Serve immediately.

SERVES 4

Stir-Fried Vegetables with Scallops

This dish can be prepared ahead and served at room temperature, or it may be served right from the wok.

2 stalks celery
1 large carrot
½ cup giant bamboo shoots, cut into sticks
½ medium white onion
½ cup unsalted chicken stock
¼ teaspoon salt (or to taste)
Pinch sugar
½ teaspoon fresh gingerroot, minced
2 teaspoons sherry or Shaoxing wine
½ teaspoon Chinese sesame oil
6 cups boiling water
1 teaspoon almond or apricot oil
2 cups tiny shucked scallops
Cornstarch paste as thickener (see p. 37)

1. Wash and trim celery and carrots; trim strings from back of celery; cut into sticks then cubes the size of the scallops. Peel carrot, treat like celery. Wash and cube giant bamboo shoots across grain the size of the scallops. Peel onion, take apart layers; cut into cubes.
2. Combine stock, salt, sugar, gingerroot, sherry, and sesame oil in bowl. Reserve.
3. Put carrots in rapidly boiling water; in 15 seconds, add celery; in another 15 seconds, drain and plunge vegetables into running cold water to stop cooking. Drain and reserve.
4. Heat wok until it smokes; add almond oil. Let oil heat for a few seconds, then add onions; toss for 10 seconds. Add celery, carrots, and bamboo shoots; toss for 1 minute. Slowly pour in stock mixture around sides of pan so it will heat quickly. When liquid boils, add scallops. Thicken liquid slightly with 1 to 2 dribbles of cornstarch paste. Keep stirring gently to reduce liquid. Remove to serving platter.

SERVES 4

2 pounds small shucked
    scallops or large scallops
    cut in half across the grain
Salt and freshly ground
    white pepper to taste
2 whole eggs
Pinch cayenne
Pinch freshly grated nutmeg
Cracker crumbs as needed
Oil as needed
Homemade Tartar Sauce
    (see p. 28)

Deep-Fried Scallops

Deep-fried scallops will always remind me of the Clampeddler restaurant on the Redondo Beach fishermen's wharf, where, as an undergraduate, I whiled away long hours with friends. Wine and deep-fried foods do not enhance each other. Try this dish with a well-chilled Mexican or Japanese lager beer.

1. Season scallops with salt and pepper.
2. Beat eggs with cayenne and nutmeg.
3. Dip scallops first into egg, then into cracker crumbs.
4. Deep fry scallops in hot oil (at least 350°). Remove as soon as they turn golden. Drain on clean kitchen towels. Serve hot with Homemade Tartar Sauce.

COCKLES

SPICY BAKED COCKLES
BAKED COCKLES
STEAMED STUFFED COCKLES
FRIED COCKLES ON THE HALF SHELL
COCKLE CHOWDER
SCATTERED SUSHI
LINGUINE WITH COCKLES
BASKET COCKLE AND SORREL OMELET
CURRIED COCKLES
COCKLE BARBECUE

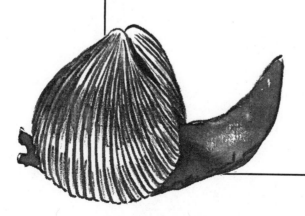

COMMON NAME	
Giant Pacific Cockle *(Baja California to* *southern California)*	This tan-colored cockle (to five inches across) has pronounced, squarish ribs with spiny protuberances. Moderately common, it is found in soft ground from shallow waters to a depth of about two hundred feet.
Giant Pacific Egg Cockle *(Panama to southern California)*	This is a yellowish cockle with closely spaced weak ribs, which may be blurred in the older mollusk. It is common and likes relatively shallow water from six to thirty feet. Its size (to six inches across), and that of the giant cockle, make them ideal for sushi and sashimi. Only the large foot is used.
Common Pacific Egg Cockle *(Baja California to* *southern California)*	This tan-colored cockle (to four inches across) is quite common and easy to collect on sandy beaches from the lower tidal zones to two hundred feet. A very flavorful cockle, the small specimens may be eaten raw, on the half shell.
Pacific Basket Cockle *(Nuttall's Cockle or Heart Cockle)* *(California to Alaska)*	The shell of this whitish gray cockle is usually higher than long (to four inches across; larger in the northern part of its range). Strong crescent-shaped riblets cut across the radial ribs. Old shells may be worn smooth. It can be found from the low tidal zones down to eighty feet in sandy or muddy/sandy areas close to the mouth of bays. An excellent stewing cockle.
Iceland Cockle *(Washington to Alaska)*	This small (to two inches across), thin-shelled, yellowish brown cockle is quite common in depths of twenty to six hundred feet. Very good to eat on the half shell, especially if you like the assertive flavor.
Fucan Cockle *(Puget Sound, Washington, and* *Juan de Fuca Strait, Washington)*	This small (two inches across), common cockle is often mistaken for a steamer clam. It is found on sandy bottoms from twelve to one hundred feet. Very good to eat, especially raw, on the half shell.
DESCRIPTION	Cockles, also known as "heart clams," are bivalves with thick shells, commonly marked by strong, radiating ridges. Seen from the side, the shells are heart shaped. Cockles have very short or nonexistent siphons, and they have evolved a large, sickle-shaped foot. This foot is rather huge in relation to the cockle's size. One wonders how all of it fits into the shell. But it does, and it can suddenly spring forth and propel

the cockle off the ground—quite an achievement for such a heavy-shelled mollusk.

But taste, even more than appearance, sets cockles apart from clams: cockles have a more pronounced (and rather unique) flavor, which makes them a perfect ingredient for sushi or seafood chowders.

HABITAT

Cockles prefer soft sandy or sandy/muddy ground in fairly protected waters. In general they do not tolerate dense mud as well as clams do.

METHODS OF CATCHING

It is quite easy to pursue tasty cockles in their lair. Cockles must stay close to the surface of the ground, because their siphons are short or nonexistent. They might choke to death if they stayed below the surface too long.

Cockles can often be spotted by the furrows they make in the sand as they plow along in search of food. Their powerful foot allows them to spring forward to escape slow-moving predators like starfish.

A bucket (or gunnysack) for holding the cockles is necessary during the hunt; a shovel is optional. Cockles are easy to dig out with the hands. But watch it! They are surprisingly active bivalves. They may jump from the hand and quickly dig back into the sand, or jump a few inches off the ground when touched.

AVAILABILITY IN FISH MARKETS AND RESTAURANTS

Cockles may be found in Italian or Oriental seafood markets in metropolitan areas. They are difficult to find in small town seafood markets, but they are very easy to gather. Cockles are served in some sushi parlors, but they are otherwise quite rare in restaurants (unless they inadvertently went into the chowder pot as "clams").

SEASONS

Cockles are good to eat all year round, except when beaches are closed during outbreaks of red tide (see Index).

HOW TO CLEAN

Cockles may be shucked like clams or oysters, with the oyster or clam knife inserted carefully at the front of the shell.

HOW TO PREPARE

In Europe, cockles are more highly esteemed than clams, because they make excellent food. Cockles may be a bit tough, but they have a delicious marine flavor. Many people, particularly those who do not really care for seafood, find them too strong tasting and do not like to eat them steamed or sautéed, but they add a superb taste to clam chowders. There is nothing quite like a "clam" chowder made with cockles alone. It is a seafood aficionado's dream.

I like to eat small cockles on the half shell, served with a little lemon, a Chinese vinegar and ginger sauce, or with a fresh salsa. Cockles are one shellfish that stands up very well to the spiciness of hot sauces.

Large cockles are best eaten in the Japanese fashion — on sushi. However, cockles are not commonly served in sushi parlors on the West Coast. For an obscure reason, the Japanese, who are very fond of other delectable West Coast shellfish, such as geoduck and abalone, have not yet taken full advantage of our native cockles. (I find the flavor of our native West Coast cockles in no way inferior to their Japanese cousins.)

Only the cockle's large foot is used for sushi, and this should be absolutely fresh. (Cockles are quite tender when fresh and raw. They toughen during freezing.) It should be sliced very thin. To the Japanese, the dark end of the Japanese cockle's foot looks like a chicken's beak and the flavor (by a creative act of the imagination) is supposed to resemble that of (raw) chicken. Thus the name *torigai*, from *tori*, chicken, and *gai*, shellfish.

SERVES 4–6 AS
AN APPETIZER

2 tablespoons minced red onion
2 tablespoons chopped chile
   jalapeño
2 tablespoons chopped red
   chile Fresno
2 tablespoons unsalted butter
   Juice from ½ lemon
   Salt and freshly ground
   black pepper to taste

Spicy Baked Cockles

Some people find the taste of cockles to be strong. Make it even stronger by spicing this dish as hot as you want, or as hot as you and your guests are willing to tolerate. Accompany it with a red country wine.

1. Cook onion and chile in butter over low heat until tender. Stir in lemon juice, salt, and pepper.
2. Shuck cockles; coarsely chop, add to pan. Cook for

24 cockles
4 slices chopped and fried lean
   bacon, crumbled
½ cup dry bread crumbs
  Rock salt as needed
3 tablespoons finely chopped
   cilantro

2 minutes.

3. Spoon mixture into cleaned half shells. Cover with chopped bacon and bread crumbs. Place half shells with meat on a bed of rock salt in a shallow baking dish. Bake in 450° oven for 5 to 7 minutes, or until bread crumbs are nicely browned. Sprinkle with cilantro. Serve hot.

MAKES 12 APPETIZERS

¼ cup sliced fresh morels
2 tablespoons chopped green
   onions
  Dash cayenne
3 tablespoons unsalted butter
3 tablespoons all-purpose flour
  Salt and freshly ground
     black pepper to taste
¾ cup milk
1 beaten egg yolk (at room
   temperature)
2 tablespoons dry sherry
12 cockles in the shell
  Rock salt as needed
4 teaspoons olive oil
   (or more, as needed)
3–4 teaspoons salmon caviar,
   drained

Baked Cockles

You may use other wild or even cultivated mushrooms for this dish. Among cultivated mushrooms I am particularly fond of shiitake and oyster mushrooms. A good, not overly demanding, white wine really brings out the flavors of this dish.

1. In heavy skillet, cook mushrooms, onions, and cayenne in butter until vegetables are just tender. Slowly blend in flour (be sure no lumps form), salt, and pepper. Cook for 2 minutes, stirring constantly. Stir in milk; cook until thickened and bubbly. Gradually stir the sauce into the egg yolk. Do not rush this step or yolk may curdle. Return to pan. Cook 1 minute more; stir in sherry.

2. Shuck cockles. Coarsely chop meat. Return to shells. Place half shells with meat on a bed of rock salt in a shallow baking dish. Dab with olive oil. Bake in 350° oven for 5 minutes. Spoon about 1 tablespoon sauce over each cockle. Bake 5 minutes longer.

3. Remove to a bed of rock salt on serving platter. Make sure cockle half shells are level. Place a few salmon eggs atop each serving.

12 cockles (about 2 inches
  across)
1 cup water
½ cup fresh shrimp, finely
  chopped into a paste
¼ pound ground lean pork
3 tablespoons finely chopped
  fresh water chestnuts
  Salt and freshly ground
  white pepper to taste
1 tablespoon Shaoxing wine,
  dry sherry, or sake
½ tablespoon light soy sauce
½ tablespoon cornstarch
1 teaspoon minced gingerroot
2 tablespoons chopped green
  onions
1 teaspoon Chinese sesame oil

Steamed Stuffed Cockles

This is a great little appetizer dish, designed to turn even those few holdouts who claim not to like shellfish into avid aficionados. Accompany the cockles with a bone-dry fino sherry or sparkling wine. Use Shaoxing wine or sherry for your cooking wine if you plan to serve sherry; use sake if you plan to serve Champagne.

1. Scrub and rinse cockles thoroughly. In saucepan, bring cockles and 1 cup water to a boil; cover and steam over high heat until they just open. Drain off liquor; remove meat from shells and dice. Set aside 18 half shells.
2. In a bowl, combine diced cockles, shrimp, pork, and the remaining ingredients. With a flexible spatula, stuff the reserved half shells with the mixture. Set onto steamer rack.
3. Heat water in steamer. When it is at a full, rolling boil, add rack with cockles. Cover and steam for 10 minutes. (Do not lift lid during steaming.) Serve hot.

48 cockles (about 2 inches
  across)
2 medium eggs, lightly beaten
  All-purpose flour, seasoned
  to taste with salt and
  pepper
½ cup olive oil
½ teaspoon hot paprika
  (or more, to taste)
2 tablespoons finely chopped
  cilantro or parsley
2-4 tablespoons salmon caviar,
  drained or fresh sea
  urchin roe

Fried Cockles on the Half Shell

I commonly make this quick and easy appetizer with clams. It is a standby I serve when friends drop in unexpectedly. One day I had no fresh clams handy, but I had a goodly mess of cockles. They worked beautifully. The cockles I used had a more pronounced flavor than the clams, just right for a good microbrewery porter (I served Blackhook from Seattle). But they also go well with a big fumé blanc.

1. Open cockles with clam knife. Cut from top shell, but leave attached to bottom shell. Discard top shell. Throughly clean cockle by rinsing. Drain on clean kitchen towels.
2. Dip cockles, shell up, first in egg, then in seasoned flour.

3. Heat oil in heavy iron skillet. Place cockles in oil, shell on top; fry until golden brown. (Depending on the size of your skillet, you may have to do this in batches.) Sprinkle with paprika and cilantro, and top with a dollop of salmon caviar. Serve hot.

Cockle Chowder

SERVES 4

¼ pound salt pork, diced
1 medium red onion, coarsely chopped
2 cloves garlic, minced (or more, to taste)
1 cup cubed potatoes
2 cups tomatoes (preferably the meaty kind—either red or yellow or both), peeled and chopped
2 chiles poblanos or chiles verdes, roasted, peeled and diced (see p. 25)
2 cups uncooked cockle meat, chopped
½ teaspoon fresh thyme or ¼ teaspoon dried
Salt and freshly ground pepper to taste or use ½ teaspoon nuoc mam instead of salt

When using cockles in chowders, add them raw, coarsely chopped, a few minutes before the chowder is done. This keeps their flavor at its peak and avoids toughening the meat further by overcooking.

1. Place salt pork in deep, heavy saucepan and cook slowly until fat melts.
2. Add onion, garlic, and potatoes; simmer for 15 minutes and then add tomatoes and chiles.
3. Add cockle meat, season with thyme, salt, and pepper; simmer for 3 minutes.

SERVES 4

Scattered Sushi

12 dried morels
1 medium carrot, cut into
    ¼-inch slices and shaped
    into florets
    Sauce for simmering
    vegetables
5 cups prepared sushi rice
16 snow peas
4 large shrimp
4 cockle feet, trimmed
½ pound fresh raw tuna
    (otoro), sliced crosswise
    against the grain into
    ¼-inch slices
1 omelet
4 scallops in the shell, steamed
    open
    Sprigs of cilantro for garnish
    Soy sauce as needed
1 tablespoon prepared Japanese
    horseradish (wasabi)★
    Sliced pickled gingerroot★

½ cup dashi (Japanese soup
    stock)★
¼ cup dark soy sauce
¼ cup mirin★
1½ teaspoons sake

Cockles are a traditional ingredient in the popular Japanese dish chirashi-zushi, known in English as scattered sushi. This dish gives you a chance to use your imagination: almost anything goes, as long as it is fresh. Accompany it with a well-chilled Japanese beer.

1. Cover morels with cold water; soak until they are soft, about 30 minutes.
2. Simmer softened morels and carrots in simmering sauce until carrots are just beginning to turn soft. Let rest in liquid about 15 minutes. Drain; save liquid. Set aside carrots. Cut the best looking 8 morels in half lengthwise. Coarsely chop the remaining 8 mushrooms and mix with the sushi rice.
3. Parboil snow peas. Refresh under cold running water.
4. Shell shrimp, remove sand vein, and drop shrimp into boiling water; cook just until shrimp turn opaque. Coarsely chop. Cut cockle and tuna into strips.
5. Make omelet; cut into strips.
6. Toss cooled sushi rice with chopped mushrooms, shrimp, and cockle and lightly pack into decorative shallow bowl. Top with a layer of omelet strips. Season with a little of the vegetable cooking liquid (to taste). Arrange (or simply scatter) carrot florets, halved morels, and scallops on top of omelet strips and garnish with cilantro sprigs.
7. Serve soy sauce in a small bowl on the side for dipping. Serve *wasabi* on the side (may be mixed with soy sauce to give it a tangy edge). Serve gingerroot slices on the side as a palate refresher.

SAUCE FOR SIMMERING VEGETABLES

1. Blend ingredients together; add vegetables. Simmer.

1 whole egg
3 egg yolks
   Dash soy sauce
   Pinch sugar (optional)

OMELET

1. Beat whole egg with yolks, soy sauce, and sugar. Make a thin omelet in a large, buttered skillet. When omelet has cooled, fold over several times; cut into thin strips.

* Available in Oriental markets and in the gourmet sections of some supermarkets.

SERVES 4-6

6 pounds fresh small cockles
2 cups cold water
½ cup dry white wine
1 small onion, diced
1 bay leaf
1½ teaspoons finely chopped garlic
6 tablespoons butter
3 tablespoons finely chopped parsley
   Salt and freshly ground black pepper to taste
1 pound linguine, cooked al dente

Linguine with Cockles

This is a variation on a classic dish more commonly made with clams. I feel the cockles add more flavor (of the right kind). Enjoy your pasta and cockles with a simple pinot blanc or semillon.

1. Wash cockles under cold running water, then put into large stainless steel or enamel pot.
2. Add water, ¼ cup wine, onion, and bay leaf to pot. Cover, bring to a boil over high heat and steam until cockles open (very small cockles will open almost immediately). Discard any that do not open. Drain pot. Reserve ½ cup of liquor.
3. Remove cockles from shells.
4. Sauté garlic in butter in a large skillet over medium heat, being careful not to burn either butter or garlic.
5. Add cockle meat, liquor, and parsley to butter and garlic. Stir until well blended. Reduce lightly by simmering over medium heat for 4 minutes. Add remaining wine. Reduce by simmering on medium heat for 2 minutes. Season with salt and pepper. Add linguine. Toss to coat well. Keep in pan just long enough to reheat linguine (this should be timed so linguine is just fresh from the kettle and still hot).
4. Transfer to warm serving bowl or warmed plates. Serve.

SERVES 4

1 quart cockles in the shell
7 tablespoons unsalted or
   clarified butter
1 cup dry white wine
1 6-inch branch lovage with
   leaves or celery
1 shallot, finely chopped
1 egg yolk
½ cup cream
6 young sorrel leaves, washed
   and julienned
1 tablespoon chopped chervil
⅓ cup crème fraîche
6 eggs

Basket Cockles and Sorrel Omelet

Basket or heart cockles are very common on the coast, and they are easy to collect because they have no syphons and do not dig deeply into the substrate. You may substitute other cockles, like the Fucan cockle, for basket cockles. Just use whichever cockle you find, they are all good to eat. This recipe comes from the Sooke Harbour House; Sinclair Philip recommends a Uniacke gewürztraminer from Uniacke in British Columbia or a Mont Elise gewürztraminer from Washington State.

1. Wash and scrub the cockles in fresh water until they are quite clean. Twist cockle shells sideways to make sure they are alive and not full of sand.
2. Place cleaned cockles in pot with 4 tablespoons butter, wine, lovage, and chopped shallot. Cook over high heat, shaking pan. Remove cockles from pot 1 by 1, as they open. Remove cockles from shell. Save liquor. Strain liquor through muslin cloth placed over a strainer. Discard shells.
3. In saucepan over low heat, mix egg yolk and cream, stirring constantly. Stir in 2 tablespoons of cockle liquor. Add cockle meat, and keep warm over very low heat.
4. In a large skillet, melt 2 tablespoons butter over low heat and incorporate sorrel as butter melts. Meanwhile, mix chervil, eggs, and crème fraîche, and beat lightly until the whites are mixed with the yolks.
5. Add remaining tablespoon butter to skillet. As soon as it has melted, pour in egg mixture. Cook omelet until almost at desired doneness; fold in cockle mixture. Place a dollop of butter under omelet (to brown omelet) and cook for another 30 seconds. Serve.

SERVES 2–4

2 dozen cockles (about
  2 inches across)
2 tablespoons almond or
  apricot oil
¼ cup chopped green onion
1 teaspoon minced gingerroot
½ tablespoon chopped fresh
  chile serrano
1 tablespoon curry powder
  (see p. 233)
1 cup diced ripe tomato
2 tablespoons Shaoxing wine
  or dry sherry
1 tablespoon soy sauce

Curried Cockles

Freshly baked, crusty French bread and a bottle of dry fumé blanc are perfect accompaniments for this spicy dish. You may use any cockle for this dish, from very small ones to the huge egg and basket cockles. If your cockles are smaller than about two inches across, double the number used for this recipe. If they are much larger, use only half the number. Coarsely chop very large cockles after they are shucked.

1. Scrub cockles well.
2. Heat oil in wok over medium heat. Add green onion and stir until slightly brown. Add gingerroot, chile, curry powder, and cockles. Toss for 1 minute. Add tomato, wine, and soy sauce. Mix thoroughly with cockles.
3. Cover and cook for 4 to 5 minutes until all cockles open. Discard any that did not open. Transfer to a large bowl and serve immediately. (Very large cockles should be shucked and chopped before being added to the wok.)

SERVES 4

2–3 dozen cockles in the shell
  Dry white wine as needed
1 cup unsalted butter
  Salt and freshly ground
  pepper to taste
½ cup finely chopped cilantro
  or parsley

Cockle Barbecue

This is one of the easiest ways to prepare cockles. But the simplicity is deceptive: the result is exceptionally tasty. Barbecues like this call for beer or jug wine. Use a good lager beer or inexpensive Parducci white or red generic wine.

1. Place cockles on hot barbecue grill. Cook until shells open. Remove upper shell; discard. Return lower shell with cockle to grill.
2. Place approximately 1 teaspoon wine and butter into each shell. Sprinkle with salt, pepper, and cilantro. Allow butter to melt. Serve hot.

CLAMS,
HORSE CLAMS,
and
GEODUCKS

PALOURDES FARCIES
BAKED CLAMS
SMOKED CLAMS
CLAMS VERACRUZ
CALIFORNIA CLAM CHOWDER
YOUNG KIM'S CLAM SOUP
HORSE CLAM CHOWDER
GEODUCK SOUP
DUCK SOUP
RAW GEODUCK SALAD
BAKED CLAMS ON THE HALF SHELL AU GRATIN
CLAMS TARRAGON O'REILLY
ASPARAGUS AND GEODUCK IN BLACK BEAN SAUCE
WATER SASHIMI
MARINATED GEODUCK
SAKE STEAMED CLAMS
STEAMED CLAMS
TENDER BROCCOLI STEMS WITH CLAMS
FRIED CLAMS
CLAM FRITTERS
HORSE CLAM AND CORN GRIDDLE CAKES
CLAM PATTIES
GEODUCK STEAK
QUICK-FRIED GEODUCK

COMMON NAME
Butter Clam
(Washington Clam)
(Baja California to Alaska)

Two species (to three and one-half inches across) occur on the West Coast. Curiously this clam is called the Washington clam in California. There is little (if any) difference between the species, especially in taste. Found on sandy/gravelly beaches down to five fathoms. Much of the commercial product is canned.

Native Littleneck Clam
(Rock Cockle)
(Steamer Clam)
(Baja California to
Aleutian Islands, Alaska)

A medium-sized (to two and one-half inches across) oval to round clam. The striated shell is mostly white. It occurs just below the surface on tideflats and sandy/muddy/gravelly beaches from midtide level down. This is the native "steamer" clam of the West Coast. It is delicious, but has been replaced in the fancy of gourmets by the even tastier Japanese littleneck.

Thin-Shelled Littleneck Clam
(Baja California to Vancouver
Island, British Columbia)

A larger (to four inches across) steamer clam with a dull gray-white shell. It is found on intertidal sandy/gravelly beaches to deep water. Not common. It is very good to eat.

Japanese Littleneck Clam
(Manila)
(central California to
British Columbia)

This medium-sized (to two and one-half inches across) clam occupies muddy/gravelly/sandy beaches above the half tide level. It does not compete for space with the native littleneck clam. This introduced clam has increased rapidly and is now more abundant than the native littleneck clam. The commercial clam industry harvests the Japanese littleneck almost exclusively. Delicious on the half shell, steamed, in soups, and sauces.

Horse Clam
(Gaper)
(Baja California to Alaska)

The gaper's foot-long siphon is thick, black, and wrinkled and protrudes from an off-white shell that is blotched with loose, mangy-looking pieces of brown periostracum. This neck is topped by two leatherlike flaps at the tip (often colonized by tiny algae, barnacles, sea anemones, and hydroids). The inner edge of the siphon opening is lined with small tentacles. This large clam (shell to eight inches across) is common buried deep in intertidal mud (or gravelly mud). This chowder clam is used by the Japanese for sushi. The Japanese, however, prefer the geoduck to the horse clam and use it as a substitute whenever possible. The same species of horse clam is native to both sides of the Pacific Ocean.

Geoduck
(Baja California to Alaska;
most common in Puget Sound)

Our largest clam (shell to nine inches across; syphon to three feet long) is common in mud below the high tide line, about three or four feet below the surface. A most delicious clam, excellent for sashimi, sushi, soups, chowders, and stir frying.

California Mactra
(Panama to Washington)

This small (to one and one-half inches across) whitish clam is common in the intertidal areas of local bays and lagoons. It is a soup or chowder clam.

Soft-Shell Clam
(central California to
British Columbia)

This medium to large (three to six inches across) clam is the "steamer" clam of the East Coast. Once thought to be an introduced clam, scientists now declare it to be a native of the West Coast. The soft-shell clam prefers a more gooey, muddy habitat than other clams. It occurs quite high in the intertidal zone. Good steamed, though the flavor is not as fine as that of the Japanese littleneck.

Blunt Soft-Shell Clam
(California to British Columbia)

A medium-sized (to three inches across) clam found in hard sand and mud. Prepare like the soft-shell clam.

Chubby Soft-Shell Clam
(California to British Columbia)

A medium-sized (to three inches across) clam that burrows in hard clay or soft rock. Prepare like the soft-shell clam.

Pacific White Venus
(Mexico to southern California)

A medium-sized (to three and one-half inches across) clam with a glossy ivory shell marked by numerous neat, concentric ridges. Common on sandy bottoms in the subtidal zone down to five fathoms. Delicious; excellent on the half shell, steamed, in sauces, and chowders.

Common California Venus
(Baja California to California)

This medium (to two inches across) clam is closely related to the East Coast quahog. The ridged and ribbed off-white shell is tinged with purple. The California Venus is common in muddy bottoms from the intertidal zone down to thirty-five fathoms. It is excellent on the half shell, steamed, in sauces, and chowders.

Smooth Pacific Venus
(Baja California to California)

A medium-sized (to two inches across) clam with a ribbed, off-white (tan to brown) shell. It is fairly common in sandy/muddy bottoms in the intertidal zone. The Smooth

Venus is excellent on the half shell, steamed, in sauces, and chowders.

Frilled California Venus
(Peru to southern California)

This medium-sized (to two inches across) venus has a fatter shell than its relatives (and thus usually more meat). The shell is patterned with numerous concentric ribs and striations. The Frilled Venus is common in sand from the intertidal zone to a depth of five fathoms. It is excellent on the half shell, steamed, in sauces, and chowders.

Pismo Clam
(Baja California to Monterey Bay, California)

This large (four to seven inches across) clam has a thick, heavy, roughly triangular shell, which is covered by a brown periostracum that looks like a coat of varnish. The shells of young clams are marked with brown to purplish rays. The Pismo clam burrows in the sand of surf-swept beaches just below the surface in the intertidal zone. The flesh is easy to recognize: it is pink with hemoglobin. This tasty clam has been overharvested and is now quite uncommon. Back when these clams were still plentiful on the beaches of southern California, they were turned up in huge quantities by horse-drawn plows and carted away by the wagonload. Today they are almost extinct.

Stout Cardita
(California to Washington)

A small (to three-fourths inch across) soup clam that looks somewhat like an immature cockle (which it is not). It is closely related to marsh clams, of which the most prized is the Japanese *shijimi*. Found in sandy ground from the subtidal zone down to a depth of one hundred fathoms.

Shijimi
(Marsh Clam or Corbicula Clam)
(aquaculture; California)

A small grayish black freshwater clam (about one inch across) raised commercially in California's Central Valley. Shijimi is one of the best soup clams I have tasted. Like the Manila clam, it was introduced from Japan. I first encountered *shijimi* in bowls of *miso shiru* at a sushi parlor in Santa Barbara and discovered them later at a Japanese seafood market in Los Angeles. These delicious clams will become more widely available in the next couple of years.

Ark Shell
(Bittersweet)
(Baja California to Aleutian Islands, Alaska)

A small (to one inch across) whitish clam with a heavy brown flaky periostracum. Found in gravel from the intertidal zone down to a depth of twenty-five fathoms.

Bodega Clam
(Gulf of California to Queen Charlotte Islands, British Columbia)

A medium-sized (to two inches across) flat white clam that prefers beaches exposed to the open ocean. Like other tellins, it has two long, slender siphons. A good soup clam.

Butter Tellin
(California to Alaska)

This small (three-fourths inch across) clam, and the closely related salmon and carpenter tellins, is found on sandy shores to a depth of thirty-five fathoms. It is too small for anything but soup.

Inconspicuous Macoma
(southern California to Arctic Ocean)

A small (to one inch across) white clam with a yellow periostracum. It is very common in sandy bottoms in sheltered waters from the intertidal zone down to ten fathoms. Soup clam.

Sand Clam
(Gulf of California to Vancouver Island, British Columbia)

A white, medium-sized (to four and one-half inches across) clam found in sheltered waters from the intertidal zone down to twenty-five fathoms. It may burrow to a depth of eighteen inches. Steamer clam.

Bent-Nose Clam
(Baja California to Alaska)

This small (to two inches across) steamer clam lives in the mud and sand of protected waters from the intertidal down to twenty-five fathoms. It is very common in San Francisco Bay, where it was widely dug in the past (before pollution closed the Bay to shellfish harvesting).

Rose Petal Semele
(Mexico to Alaska)

A small (to two inches across) steamer clam found in gravel or sand. In California it prefers deep water (from twenty-five to fifty fathoms). In British Columbia it is found in the intertidal zone. Like all semeles, this is a delicious clam. Good on the half shell, steamed, or in soups.

Rock-Dwelling Semele
(Baja California to California)

A common, small (to one and one-half inches across) yellowish clam of rocky subtidal shores. Delicious on the half shell, steamed, or in soups.

California Cumingia
(Baja California to California)

A common, small (one inch across) semele clam found in rock crevices and on pilings from the tidal edge to deep water. Delicious on the half shell, steamed, or in soups.

Bean Clam
(Mexico to southern California)

This small (to three-fourths inch across) purplish brown clam was once so common, it was canned commercially. It is delicious. Commercial production has ceased, but the clam is still common in the intertidal zone of sandy beaches. It is often possible to find a sufficient number of bean clams for a good-sized pot of chowder by combing the sand at low tide just beneath the surface. The bean clam is a tasty addition to soups, salads, and sauces.

California Donax
(Baja California to California)

This yellowish white small (to one inch across) clam is slightly larger than the bean clam. The shell is covered with a tan to brown periostracum. This donax is common in the intertidal zone of bays and estuaries. It is delicious in salads, soups, and sauces.

Mahogany Clam
(Baja California to
southern California)

This medium-sized (to three inches across) clam has a whitish shell with purplish rays and is covered with a strong mahogany-brown periostracum. A chowder clam common in bays and estuaries.

Razor Clam
(northern California to
Arctic Ocean)

A large (to six inches across) thin-shelled clam with a thin and brittle sharp-edged shell. The shell is covered with a smooth, glossy olive-brown or yellowish brown periostracum. A very tasty (and very popular) clam for cooking and frying.

Blunt Jackknife Clam
(Baja California to
Queen Charlotte Islands,
British Columbia)

This clam (to six inches across) looks like a narrow, square version of the razor clam. It is common in sand or mud from intertidal flats down to twenty-five fathoms. Prepare like razor clams.

California Jackknife Clam
(southern California)

This uncommon, small (to two inches across) clam closely resembles the Atlantic Jackknife clam. It is found on sandy shores below the low tide line. Prepare like razor clam.

West Coast Jackknife Clam
(Panama to California)

A common, medium-sized (to three and one-half inches across) mud flat jackknife clam (not closely related to the sand-dwelling jackknife clam) occurs from intertidal areas down to twenty fathoms. Prepare like razor clam.

Sunset Clam
(southern California to Japan)

This medium-sized (to three inches across) clam has a thin, whitish shell with purplish and reddish rays and tints.

Rare and in deep water in California; intertidal in British Columbia. A chowder clam.

Surf Clam
(California to British Columbia)

We have four species of surf clams, which look more or less alike and grow to a length of three to six inches. Surf clams are more common in California, and they grow larger than their northern relatives. Found just below the surface of sandy beaches from the intertidal zone down to twenty fathoms. Surf clams are a nice addition to chowders.

Pacific Mud Piddock
(Chile to Oregon)

The fragile shell gapes at both ends (to two inches across). As in all burrowing clams, the body is much larger than the shell. Common in intertidal clay. Tasty.

Common Piddock
(Baja California to
Arctic Ocean)

A medium-sized burrowing clam (to three inches across) with a whitish shell covered by a hard gray or brown periostracum. This rock clam is common. It bores into hard clay, sandstone, and even concrete. It is very good in chowders.

Wart-Necked Piddock
(Gulf of California to
Bering Sea)

A medium-sized (to three inches across) boring clam. The whitish shell is covered with a gray-brown periostracum. The siphons are white and irregularly covered with pustules. The wart-necked piddock bores into hard clay and fairly solid rock. It is very good to eat; a good chowder clam.

Rough Piddock
(California to Bering Sea)

This is the largest of our boring clams (shell to six inches across). This clam's body is very much larger than the shell. The rough piddock bores into stiff clay, hard mud, and even rocky reefs. The rough piddock yields a lot of tasty chowder meat per clam.

DESCRIPTION

Clams are mollusks, whose soft body is protected by two hinged shells. The shells may be thin and brittle or thick and dense; they may measure only a fraction of an inch in diameter, or they may reach a length of seven inches. A few shells are very colorful.

Unlike mussels or oysters, clams live in burrows they dig in sand, gravel, mud, clay, and soft rock. They feed by means of siphons extended up into the water. A few clams with weak shells, or with shells too small to hold the entire animal, are fast or deep diggers.

All West Coast clams are edible, but some taste better than others. A clam's body consists of siphon(s), the body proper, an anterior and a posterior adductor muscle (attached to the shell, and used for opening and closing it), and the foot (the organ used by the clam for digging). The entire clam is edible, though large ones are commonly gutted. Small clams are eaten whole. Small, tender clams collected in unpolluted waters may be eaten raw, on the half shell. Some large clams are very tough and must be pounded to tenderize or ground for chowder.

HABITAT

Clams are found in every type of marine habitat on the West Coast. Many species are found along the entire coast, though they may be abundant in only one or two locations.

Both the native littleneck and the introduced Manila clam, for example, can be harvested on tideflats from California to British Columbia. There are centers of regional abundance, like Tomales Bay or southern Puget Sound, but these tasty bivalves are encountered in most bays and inlets with a suitable habitat.

METHODS OF CATCHING

One way or another, all clams are dug up. The only tool the clam digger needs is a shovel, accompanied by a bucket or a gunnysack for storing the catch. Short-siphoned forms are quite easy to find just below the surface. Several of the small steamer or sand-dwelling clams can be scooped from the ground with the hands. A few clams, such as the razor clam, require expertise on the part of the clam digger because they can dig themselves down (and out of the collector's reach) in a matter of seconds. The geoduck and horse clam dig themselves several feet below the surface. Their position is given away by the tip of the siphon. Piddocks and other burrowing clams may be difficult to dislodge from hard rock (do not use a sledge hammer; the tasty tidbits are not worth the environmental damage).

Clams gathered from muddy or sandy ground should be allowed to clean themselves of ingested grit before they are eaten. The best method is to hang them off a dock or boat in a clean bay for a few days.

AVAILABILITY IN
FISH MARKETS AND
RESTAURANTS

The Japanese littleneck steamer clam is currently the most widely available West Coast clam. Geoduck has become more widely available in recent years in the shell and in a processed fresh or frozen form. It is harvested commercially in the Pacific Northwest, but for some reason it is eaten more in California. Perhaps this has a lot to do with the way this huge clam is marketed: in Pacific Northwest seafood markets, it is usually sold whole and alive (and a gross sight this can be, scaring off inexperienced cooks); in California it is sold primarily in a processed form. If you live in California and want to see what a geoduck really looks like you should go to a Chinatown fishmonger. With the geoduck, the assumption that the larger the mollusk, the coarser and more inferior the taste, does not hold true. Butter clams are available mostly canned. Fresh *shijimi* are delightful. They are becoming increasingly available in California seafood markets. Many of the other clams we have listed are available from time to time in Oriental seafood markets. If you like them very much and would like a regular supply, you must be prepared to dig your own.

There is only one way to buy clams; when they are still alive. (Do not buy clams whose shells do not close when touched or clams whose shells do not open during cooking.) Fortunately, modern methods of cooling plus speedy jet freight make it possible to have fresh clams shipped to all parts of the coast within hours after capture. This sort of thing is essential if you want to serve up clams for sashimi or sushi or on the half shell. Look for truly fresh clams in Japanese or Chinese fish markets.

SEASONS

Sexual cycles have a different effect on the palatability of clams than they have on the taste of oysters during the spawning season. Unlike oysters, which turn soft and milky during the spawn, clams stay firm. The stimulated gonads of littleneck and butter clams affect the flavor of these bivalves very positively. These clams are thus most savory during the early summer months when they prepare to spawn. Immediately after spawning, they are tough, dark in color, and tasteless.

However, by fall and winter they have fully recovered and are once again very tasty.

Razor clams should be safe to eat throughout the year (whenever it is legal to harvest these increasingly scarce mollusks). They must, however, be carefully trimmed: the parts that absorb *Gonyaulax* (red tide) toxin (see Index) — the liver and the viscera — must be cut out and thrown away. Once that is done, there seems to be little danger from eating these exceptionally tasty clams.

Butter clams really soak up the *Gonyaulax* organism and can store it for several years. Proper trimming takes expertise: this is one reason butter clams are mostly sold in canned form.

The edibility of clams is also affected by the presence of raw sewage or industrial pollutants in the water. Always check with a health department to make sure the clams in a given locality are free of toxins.

HOW TO CLEAN

Nothing cleanses clams as well as a few days spent in clean salt water. Once they have rid themselves of grit, they may be steamed or shucked. To shuck a clam, insert a clam or oyster knife in the front, between the two halves of the shell. Probe with the tip of the blade to find and cut the adductor muscles. Remove clam from the shell. Save the juices.

Geoducks and horse clams have tough outer skins and must be skinned before they can be prepared. I have run into all sorts of instructions on how to do that — most of them call for throwing away all but the siphon — the best and most tender part of the clam, the belly. Skinning is a very simple process if done properly.

Bring a pot of water large enough to hold your geoduck to a vigorous boil. When the water spouts, gurgles, and forms big bubbles and throws dense steam into the air, quickly immerse the clam, shell and all. Pull the clam out after a few seconds (with tongs, of course) and chill it immediately under cold running water. The skin and shell should have loosened sufficiently to come right off. You can now cut off the siphon and remove the guts in one piece by running a sharp paring (or boning) knife along the long, crescent-shaped chunk of belly meat.

HOW TO PREPARE

Proper methods for preparing clams differ depending on type, size, and age. For example, young butter clams make good steamers, old butter clams are tough and best cooked in chowders.

Eating small clams raw, on the half shell, has long been part of the East Coast culinary tradition. But, surprisingly, though our West Coast clams have a greater flavor and are in high demand as steamers, few West Coasters eat them raw. Only in the fishing ports of Baja California have I been offered local clams raw, on the half shell, accompanied by a spicy dipping sauce. They are quite delightful. Just make sure that any clams you eat raw come from clean, unpolluted beaches.

Some clams should never be eaten raw, of course. Particularly clams living in very muddy habitats where all sorts of organisms live. These clams should be neutralized by thorough cooking. This is especially true of the soft-shell clam, which should always be steamed before it is eaten.

Geoducks, like turkeys, have two kinds of meat: the somewhat tough meat of the "neck" or siphon (which is the portion most people eat), and the much more tender belly meat. The siphon meat can be beaten to tenderize (like the abalone muscle it resembles), and it may be fried as a "steak" or ground for chowder. The tender belly meat (which includes the mantle and the foot muscles) can be served raw as sashimi, or cubed and sautéed lightly in butter or olive oil. It can also be added to stir-fried vegetables. Eating geoduck as sashimi or sushi may be an acquired taste.

Razor clams should always be cooked as quickly as possible after digging (and they should still be alive — since razor clams spoil very quickly once they have died), and they must be treated delicately in the kitchen. In my opinion, the worst thing you can do to a razor clam is to overpower the flavor by breading and deep frying it.

If you find yourself in a spot where Pismo clams are still plentiful — on a remote beach in Baja California — and if you can get them fresh, you might just want to steam them open and serve them with a simple lemon butter as a dipping sauce. Or dip them into a well-balanced mignonette sauce or serve a salsa verde if you like your food *picante.*

Instead of using razor or Pismo clams in gratin dishes, you can use the diminutive clams so common on sandy beaches up and down the California coast, especially the small (one inch) wedge-shaped bean clam. Bean clams also may be used in any chowder recipe (they are so small you do not need to chop). If you want to fully savor their unique flavor, try them in a more delicate clam soup.

SERVES 3–4 AS AN APPETIZER

48 bean clams (more or less, depending on the size)
12 well-scrubbed scallop shells or porcelain baking shells
1 shallot, chopped
1 teaspoon chopped fresh parsley
1 tablespoon unsalted butter
½ cup extraheavy cream*
1 heaping teaspoon of finely grated dry Monterey Jack cheese or other hard cheese
2–3 teaspoons toasted bread crumbs
Salt and freshly ground pepper to taste

Palourdes Farcies

The French do not, as a rule, like clams, for who knows what reason (perhaps for the same reason that they do not like crab), but they do eat the tiny palourdes of the coast of Brittany raw, and they sometimes bake them in a gratin dish. Our bean clams work just as beautifully in this breton dish.

1. Place clams in baking shell, 3 to 4 per shell, depending on size, and set shells into a flat oven-proof baking dish.
2. Finely mince shallot and parsley together. Cook them in butter until shallot begins to turn golden.
3. Slowly stir in cream and let bubble for about a minute (do not overheat, or cream may curdle). Add cheese, then a teaspoon of bread crumbs. Keep stirring. Sauce will thicken very rapidly. Season with salt and pepper.
4. Pour some of the sauce over each of the shells. Sprinkle lightly with more bread crumbs. Place under broiler for about 2 minutes. Serve immediately. This dish cannot be kept waiting.

* Let whipping cream sit in refrigerator for 1 or 2 days; skim off the thick part that has risen to the top.

SERVES 6 AS AN APPETIZER

½ cup cold-pressed olive oil
  Salt and freshly ground
    white pepper to taste
1 tablespoon chopped shallots
1 pint freshly steamed clams
½ cup finely grated dry
  Sonoma Jack cheese
1 cup dry bread crumbs

Baked Clams

Baked clams make a nice party appetizer. They go very well with the uncomplicated white wine we serve at the beginning of a party, and they have just enough substance to counteract the alcohol. Serve them with a well-chilled dry pinot blanc, aligoté, or other unpretentious wine.

1. Mix oil, salt, pepper, and shallots.
2. Place clams in mixture for 1 minute. Remove and drain; roll in cheese, then in bread crumbs. Place on a well-greased baking sheet; bake in a 450° oven for about 10 minutes, or until golden brown.

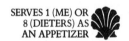

SERVES 1 (ME) OR
8 (DIETERS) AS
AN APPETIZER

4 dozen clams, steamed open
  Brine as needed (depending
    on the size of your clams)
  Apple wood chips as needed

Smoked Clams

These are just great when presented on an appetizer platter with such delicacies as smoked salmon, smoked sea snails, smoked oysters, smoked shad or sturgeon, and smoked mussels. Accompany them with a stout beer.

1. Shake meat from clam shells; rinse clams in cold water to remove any remaining particles of grit. Place in brine for 30 minutes.
2. Rinse clams lightly in warm water and allow to air dry for 30 minutes to 1 hour, depending on the relative humidity. (I open the back door and front window of my apartment and let them dry in the draft, there always seems to be a wind blowing either up or down the lake.)
3. Place clams on an oiled screen in your smoker. (I use a most admirable contraption called a "Little Chief," an efficient little machine about which even Craig Claiborne waxed lyrical.)
4. Smoke for about 2 hours, using 2 pans of apple wood chips.

SERVES 4

Clams Veracruz

This is a spicy, hearty clam stew served at the Rhododendron Cafe in northern Washington. Don Shank, one of the chefs at the cafe, says that the Marinara Sauce is best when made with fresh tomatoes, onions, garlic, fresh Italian herbs, and a hint of red wine.

2 tablespoons olive oil
1 pound hot Italian sausage
    cut into bite-sized chunks
4 cloves garlic
4 tablespoons chopped onion
12 medium mushrooms, sliced
6–8 dozen fresh Pacific
    littleneck clams
1½ cups Marinara Sauce
    Parmesan cheese as needed
    Parsley and/or fresh basil
    for garnish

1. Heat olive oil in heavy saucepan. Cook sausage until just underdone. Add garlic, onions, and mushrooms and sauté lightly. Add clams and Marinara Sauce and cover.
2. Cook over medium heat until clams steam open (steam will escape from pot when they are ready).
3. Ladle clams into serving dish. Pour sauce and sausages over clams, grate Parmesan on top. Garnish with chopped parsley or basil. Serve hot.

MAKES ABOUT 6 CUPS

MARINARA SAUCE

3 tablespoons olive oil
1 large onion, finely chopped
7 cups stewed meaty tomatoes
    in their liquid
2 tablespoons tomato paste
4 cloves garlic, minced
1 bay leaf
1 teaspoon fresh oregano
½ teaspoon fresh basil
½ cup dry red wine
    Salt and freshly ground
    black pepper to taste

1. Heat 2 tablespoons olive oil in heavy saucepan. Sauté onion over medium heat until transparent. Add tomatoes and their liquid, tomato paste, garlic, bay leaf, oregano, basil, and wine. Bring to a boil over high heat, stirring frequently. Simmer, uncovered, over low heat for 1 hour.
2. Season to taste with salt and pepper.
3. Strain sauce through a fine sieve. Sauce should be rich and thick. If it seems too thin after straining, continue to simmer over low heat; if it is too thick, stir in a little water.
4. When sauce has reached the desired consistency, remove from heat. Pour 1 tablespoon olive oil on top; do not mix in (this will keep the sauce from oxidizing). Allow sauce to cool, uncovered and unrefrigerated, in a cool spot for at least 4 hours. It may be refrigerated for up to 2 weeks.

SERVES 6

¼ cup chopped salt pork
¼ cup chopped shallots
2 chiles poblanos or chiles
    verdes, roasted, peeled,
    seeded, and diced
    (see p. 25)
1 cup clam liquor
1 cup diced potatoes
    Salt and freshly ground
    white pepper
1 pint freshly shucked clams,
    chopped
1 cup whole milk
1 cup cream
    Chopped cilantro for garnish

California Clam Chowder

*It seems that almost everywhere you eat in California these days,
you will find chiles in your soup. I even found them in several
clam chowders. When taken in small doses, chiles can add
a pleasant tang to the chowder.*

1. Fry salt pork over low heat until lightly browned.
   Do not pour off grease. Add shallots and cook until
   translucent.
2. Add chiles, clam liquor, potatoes, salt, and pepper; cook
   until potatoes are tender, about 15 minutes.
3. Add clams. Cook for 5 minutes.
4. Add milk; heat, stirring constantly. Do not boil.
5. Add cream; reheat carefully. Do not bring to a boil,
   or cream will curdle.
6. Pour into individual serving bowls; garnish with
   cilantro.

MAKES ABOUT 4 CUPS

3 cups cold water
1 teaspoon whole black
    peppercorns
1½ teaspoons salt
½ pound small clams in shell
1 teaspoon sake

Young Kim's Clam Soup

*A Korean friend of mine swears by the restorative power of his
clam soup. He gave me the recipe when I had suffered from a bad
cold for several days. It must have worked, since my cold went
away. This soup is also good when made with tiny nut clams,
bittersweets, or salmon tellins. I like it best made with highly
flavored small clams.*

1. Pour water into saucepan, bring to boil; add peppercorns and salt, then clams. Boil for 30 minutes until the
   color of the soup changes to white.
2. Stir in sake. Serve hot.

SERVES 6–8

2 pounds chopped horse clams
3½ cups cold water
¼ pound salt pork, diced
2 cups onion, diced
4–6 garlic cloves (or more,
    according to taste),
    chopped
1 cup celery or lovage, finely
    diced
2 chiles verdes, roasted, peeled,
    and diced (see p. 25)
1 teaspoon freshly ground
    pepper
    Salt to taste (optional)
1½ cups hot milk
1½ cups hot cream
    Borage flowers for garnish

Horse Clam Chowder

The horse clam is a good clam to eat if you cannot get geoduck. Just remember that its flavor will not be as fine as that of the geoduck. That makes little difference if you use the horse clam in the dish it is most suited for: chowder. Be brave and try it.

1. Place clams in saucepan. Cover with cold water, slowly bring to a boil. Simmer for about 5 minutes. Strain, reserve liquid.
2. Combine salt pork, onions, garlic, and celery in saucepan. Gently sauté for about 3 minutes; do not brown. Add reserved broth, clams, chiles, and season with pepper (and salt, if you must).
3. Remove from heat; slowly stir in heated milk and cream. Garnish with borage flowers.

SERVES 4

1 medium cucumber (Japanese
    kyuri or English)
1 bunch cilantro leaves
    as needed
½ pound fresh geoduck belly
    meat
4 cups unsalted chicken stock
1 slice fresh gingerroot
1 cup bean thread noodles,
    soaked
2 tablespoons cornstarch paste
    (see p. 37)

Geoduck Soup

This soup is refreshing to the palate, very tasty and filling. In other words, it is a perfect luncheon course. Drink a glass of cold lager beer with it.

1. Slice cucumber in half lengthwise (peel if using an American waxed cucumber). Thinly slice crosswise. Or, use fancy vegetable cutter to make animal figures.
2. Wash cilantro; remove stems.
3. Cut geoduck meat into dollar-sized pieces.
4. Combine stock and gingerroot in saucepan; bring to just under boil. Remove gingerroot slice. Add noodles and cornstarch paste; stir. Add geoduck and cucumber. Cook at high simmer until geoduck is done, about 3 to 5 minutes. Do not allow broth to boil; you want it to remain clear. Remove to covered serving bowl. Garnish with cilantro leaves. Serve hot.

SERVES 4

2–3 geoduck stomachs
  4 tablespoons butter
  2 garlic cloves, minced
  1 cup thinly sliced celery
  3 green onions, chopped
  2 cups whole milk
    Salt and freshly ground
      black pepper to taste

Duck Soup

This recipe is from Lila Gault's The Northwest Cookbook. *"Geoduck stomachs have the same qualities as good sweetbreads. They have different summer and winter characteristics, as a result of the absence or presence of plankton in their diet. The digested algae is replete with nutrients, and it tastes good too."*

1. Carefully slice stomachs into bite-sized chunks and sauté gently in medium saucepan in butter and garlic.
2. Add celery and green onions and stir to blend.
3. Add milk, salt, and pepper, and simmer gently over medium heat for 20 minutes.

SERVES 4

Raw Geoduck Salad

2 cups plus 2 tablespoons
    almond or apricot oil
3 tablespoons cool water
2 teaspoons light soy sauce
3 slices fresh gingerroot (the
    size of a half-dollar)
½ teaspoon ground cinnamon
¼ teaspoon freshly ground
    white pepper
½ pound fresh geoduck belly
    meat, sliced into ½-inch
    by 2-inch strips
2 ounces thin transparent rice
    noodles
1 tablespoon white sesame
    seeds
½ head lettuce (inner leaves
    only, shredded)
¼ cup pickled red gingerroot,
    shredded or minced
½ cup coarsely chopped
    watercress
1 fresh lemon, cut into wedges

*For a starter course on a warm fall evening, this dish is just right.
Especially if you accompany it with well-chilled off-dry riesling.*

1. Combine 2 tablespoons almond oil, water, soy sauce,
   gingerroot slices, cinnamon, and pepper. Pour into
   bowl with geoduck meat; toss well. Cover and marinate
   in refrigerator 3 to 8 hours.
2. Heat remaining oil in wok to medium high. Toss
   2 strands of noodles into oil to make sure it is hot
   enough. (Noodles should puff up instantly without
   browning.) Deep fry noodles until they expand; drain
   on clean kitchen towels; set aside. (Watch this step.
   The noodles puff up almost immediately and burn very
   quickly.) Remove from the wok as soon as they turn
   opaque white.
3. Toast sesame seeds in a dry wok at low to medium heat
   until they are a light tan; set aside.
4. Drain marinated geoduck and remove gingerroot slices.
   Put geoduck, noodles, lettuce, pickled gingerroot, and
   watercress onto large serving platter.
5. Sprinkle salad with sesame seeds; toss. Squeeze lemon
   over salad and toss again.

SERVES 6

Baked Clams on the Half Shell Au Gratin

1 *pint clam meat, raw*
¾ *cup cold water*
¼ *cup dry white wine*
¼ *teaspoon salt*
  Sprinkle cayenne
1 *small onion, chopped*
2 *tablespoons butter*
2 *tablespoons all-purpose flour*
½ *clove garlic, minced*
1 *teaspoon minced parsley*
1 *egg yolk, beaten*
6 *large Pismo clam shells, well scrubbed and buttered*
¾ *cup buttered bread crumbs*
2 *tablespoons grated Parmesan cheese (optional)*

The clams in a dish of Baked Clams on the Half Shell Au Gratin we had at Plessas Tavern in Pismo Beach were finely chopped and so well disguised, they were unrecognizable, though savory. This dish has been served at Plessas Tavern since 1921. This is not a bad little dish, and it may be made with other clams as well. Geoducks and horse clams and even chopped butter clams work equally well. I could not get the original recipe, but here is my reconstruction.

1. Simmer clam meat for 5 minutes in water, wine, salt, and cayenne mixture. Drain. Reserve liquid.
2. Sauté onion in butter until tender; blend in flour. Slowly stir in cooking liquid drained from clams and cook until thickened, stirring constantly. Add garlic and parsley and cook 5 minutes longer.
3. Gradually add mixture to egg yolk, mixing well.
4. Chop clams and add to mixture.
5. Divide mixture among clam shells, top with buttered crumbs and cheese. Brown in 400° oven. Serve hot.

SERVES 4–6

2–3 pounds fresh clams
¼ cup water
¼ cup white wine
    Pinch fresh thyme
    Pinch fresh dill
    Herb Butter
    Bread crumbs as needed

MAKES ¾ CUP

½ cup unsalted butter
¼ cup chopped shallots
1 tablespoon fresh tarragon or
    tarragon preserved in
    vinegar
    Salt and freshly ground
    pepper to taste
1 tablespoon fresh parsley,
    chopped

Clams Tarragon O'Reilly

This dish was created by Rick O'Reilly of Olympia. Everyone who has tried it just loves it. Accompany it with a good sauvignon blanc or very dry riesling.

1. Lightly steam clams in water, wine, and herbs, until they just pop open.
2. Snap off upper half shell of clam, place other half shell with clam in it in oven-proof dish.
3. Place a dab of herb butter on each clam. Sprinkle with bread crumbs.
4. Bake for 5 to 7 minutes in 375° oven until bubbling. Serve immediately.

HERB BUTTER

1. Mix ingredients until well blended.

SERVES 6

1 tablespoon dry sherry or
   Shaoxing wine
2 teaspoons light soy sauce
1 teaspoon cornstarch
1 cup diced geoduck meat
12 medium asparagus spears
2 teaspoons fermented black
   beans
3 cloves garlic, minced
½ teaspoon brown sugar
2 teaspoons dark soy sauce
¾ cup unsalted chicken stock
3 tablespoons almond or
   apricot oil
   Cornstarch paste as needed
   (see p. 37)

Asparagus and Geoduck in Black Bean Sauce

I sometimes think that the Chinese must—at one time or another—have matched every and any seafood to black beans. Of course, it works. Accompany this dish with a rich ale or hearty country wine.

1. Combine sherry, soy sauce, and cornstarch in bowl. Add geoduck. Massage liquid into meat with your fingers. Marinate for 15 to 30 minutes.
2. Wash asparagus; break off tough ends; slice on diagonal into 2½-inch pieces.
3. Rinse black beans.
4. In bowl, combine and mash black beans with garlic, sugar, soy sauce, and chicken stock; stir; set aside for 15 minutes.
5. Pour 2 tablespoons of oil into hot wok; when oil is very hot, add geoduck. Stir fry for about 3 minutes on high heat, or until geoduck begins to shrink and firm up. Remove geoduck and set aside in another bowl.
6. Reheat wok to high, add remaining oil. When oil is hot, add bean sauce. Stir fry for 1 minute. Add asparagus; mix with sauce. When sauce boils, add cooked geoduck; toss to combine.
7. Pour in a little cornstarch paste if needed to thicken sauce.
8. Toss ingredients until very little liquid remains and is reduced to glaze. Dish is ready when asparagus is done. If you have too much liquid, remove ingredients, continue to reduce sauce, then return ingredients to wok to coat them with sauce. Serve in individual bowls.

SERVES 4

2 cups very cold water (not
  iced water)
1 peeled garlic clove
1 teaspoon salt
3 teaspoons soy sauce
4 teaspoons Korean or
  Japanese hot red pepper
  powder (do not use
  Mexican chili powder as
  a substitute)
5 teaspoons honey or sugar
  (If honey is used, bring to
  a boil, or it will not melt
  into the cold water.)
1 teaspoon sesame seeds,
  untoasted
2 teaspoons white (rice)
  vinegar
1 teaspoon sesame oil
2 pieces Japanese kyuri
  cucumber (about 1½ inches
  long), cut lengthwise into
  thin shreds
1 pound assorted shellfish (or
  fish) (preferably 3 to 4
  kinds, such as abalone,
  geoduck, clams, or
  scallops), cut into thin
  shreds and mixed together

Water Sashimi

*Young Kim, whose father was the famous Korean chef Doo C.
Kim, and whose mother ran a successful sushi shop in Osaka
before her marriage, loves West Coast shellfish. Here is one of
his favorite recipes, which he claims has restorative powers. This
is a very traditional Korean dish for which any kind of shellfish
or fish (with the exception of salmon or tuna) may be used.
The ingredients must be perfectly fresh, however, or the flavor
will be poor.*

1. Pour water into bowl; add all other ingredients except
   shellfish; mix well for 20 to 30 seconds. Let rest for
   5 minutes.
2. Drop in shellfish. Let mixture rest for another 5 minutes.
   Eat from bowl with chopsticks. Sauce may be sipped like
   miso shiru. (But be careful—it will be hot!)

SERVES 6

2 geoduck breast pieces,
    unpounded
½ cup soy sauce
¼ cup lemon juice
1 teaspoon freshly grated
    gingerroot
2 garlic cloves, minced

Marinated Geoduck

This recipe is from Lila Gault's The Northwest Cookbook. *"Marinated geoduck is elegant, flavorful, and very healthful. Try different combinations; I like this soy and gingerroot marinade."*

1. Cut breast pieces into ⅛-inch strips.
2. Combine soy, lemon juice, gingerroot, and garlic, and pour over clam strips. Add more juice if strips are not entirely covered. Marinate 30 minutes.

SERVES 4–6

4–6 dozen littleneck clams
  1 cup sake (or more, as needed)
  2 slices fresh gingerroot, peeled
  2 tablespoons fresh lemon juice
  ¼ cup soy sauce
    Wedges of lemon

Sake Steamed Clams

This dish was first served to me by Takahashi-san of the Maneki restaurant in Vancouver, British Columbia. I could not get the recipe, so I made up my own. As far as I can tell, it comes very close to Takahashi-san's version.

1. Rinse shells well. Scrub off any remaining sand or mud.
2. Pour sake into bottom of stainless steel or enamel pot large enough to accommodate clams in 1 or 2 layers. There should be about ½ inch of sake in bottom of pot. Add gingerroot. Bring to boil over high heat. Add clams. Cover tightly with close-fitting lid. Remove clams from steamer as soon as they have steamed open.
3. Make a dipping sauce by combining the lemon juice and soy sauce. Strain sake/clam juice; serve on the side.

SERVES 2

2 dozen clams
   Salt and freshly ground
     pepper to taste
   Unsalted butter as needed
   Fresh or dried herbs, finely
     chopped

Steamed Clams

Be sure to use only the freshest clams for this dish. Clams that have been out of water too long develop an off-flavor. Accompany this dish with a dry sauvignon blanc or semillon.

1. Scrub clams with stiff brush; rinse thoroughly. Place the washed clams in a large kettle with ½ inch water at the bottom (or use a dry white wine or sake). Season with salt and pepper. Cover. Steam over medium heat until all clams have opened (about 5 minutes). Do not overcook. Overcooking makes the clams tough. Discard any clams that do not open; they were dead before they went into the pot and should not be eaten. Reserve broth.
2. While clams cook, melt butter. Season with chives, tarragon, chervil, parsley, dill, basil, or other herbs of your choice.
3. Serve clams immediately with melted and seasoned butter for dipping. Serve cups of hot broth on the side.

SERVES 4

2 pounds broccoli
1 tablespoon fermented
    soybeans
4 large cloves garlic
¼ cup shucked baby clams
½ cup clam broth
3 tablespoons almond or
    apricot oil
    Cornstarch paste (see p. 37)

Tender Broccoli Stems with Clams

This is a standard Chinese dish popular along the West Coast wherever Chinese cooks and fresh clams meet up. I tried it with a microbrewery porter, and it worked.

1. Wash broccoli and cut off florets (save for another dish). With small paring knife, carefully peel outer skin off broccoli stems, beginning at the base. Leave inner stems whole. Cut stems on the bias into ¼-inch slices.
2. Rinse fermented soybeans. Peel garlic. Blend soybeans and garlic together in blender or food processor; set aside.
3. Drop clams into stock.
4. Heat wok until it smokes, then add 2 tablespoons oil. When oil begins to smoke, add broccoli and toss quickly to avoid burning. Stir fry about 1 minute. Turn heat down to moderate. Push broccoli up on sides of wok; add remaining oil; add soybean mixture. Press and stir until a strong odor of beans and garlic rises from the wok.
5. Return to high heat and immediately push down broccoli. Stir for about 30 seconds. Beans and garlic will burn easily, so keep mixture moving. Quickly add clams and stock; stir fry for another 30 seconds. Cover for 30 seconds to finish cooking broccoli. Remove cover; thicken with cornstarch paste to a light saucy consistency.

SERVES 6

1 quart fresh clams, shucked
2 eggs, beaten
2 tablespoons milk
½ teaspoon fresh tarragon,
    finely chopped or
    ¼ teaspoon dried
    Salt and freshly ground
    black pepper to taste
3 cups dry bread crumbs
    Oil for frying
    Homemade Tartar Sauce
    (see. p. 28)

Fried Clams

Fried clams call for beer. If you cannot get a good lager beer from a microbrewery, accompany this dish with a Japanese or Mexican lager.

1. Drain clams (save nectar for chowder).
2. Combine egg, milk, tarragon, salt, and pepper. Dip clams in egg mixture and roll in crumbs. Set aside and let dry in a cool place for about 10 minutes.
3. Fry in a wok or deep fryer at 350° until golden brown (about 1 or 2 minutes).
4. Drain on absorbent paper. Serve hot with Homemade Tartar Sauce.

SERVES 6-8

2 cups all-purpose flour
2 teaspoons baking powder
    Salt and freshly ground
    black pepper to taste
1 cup milk
½ cup clam liquor
2 eggs, lightly beaten
24 chopped clams

Clam Fritters

Here is a dish that is quick to make and quite good if the clams are fresh. It is the kind of dish that has been around seemingly forever and has not lost an iota of its popularity. Accompany with a well-chilled lager beer.

1. Sift dry ingredients. Slowly stir in milk, clam liquor, and eggs. Stir carefully and steadily to be sure no lumps form (or use a food processor). Mix well.
2. Add clams.
3. Drop mixture spoonful by spoonful onto a well-greased griddle. Fry until golden brown.

MAKES ABOUT 18 CAKES

2 cups fresh minced horse
   clams
1½ cups all-purpose flour, sifted
1 cup yellow cornmeal
5 tablespoons baking powder
   Salt and freshly ground
      pepper to taste
¾ cup clam liquor
¾ cup milk
2 eggs, beaten
⅓ cup olive oil
2–4 tablespoons butter, melted
   Peach Relish

MAKES ABOUT 5 PINTS

7 medium-sized meaty
   vine-ripened tomatoes
2 cups celery, sliced or
   1½ cups lovage
2 cups coarsely chopped red
   onion
2 chiles verdes or chiles
   poblanos, roasted, peeled,
   seeded, and chopped
   (see p. 25)
3 ripe peaches, cut into
   ½-inch-thick slices
1 cup rice vinegar
½ teaspoon salt (or to taste)
1½ teaspoons mixed pickling
   spices, tied in a cheesecloth
   bag
1 cup sugar (or less, to taste)

Horse Clam and Corn Griddle Cakes

This is one simple country dish that will even make those who claim not to like clams clamor for more. Accompany the griddle cakes with a hearty ale.

1. Drain clams; reserve liquor.
2. Sift dry ingredients together. Slowly stir in clam liquor, milk, eggs, and olive oil, making sure no lumps form.
3. Drop batter onto hot, well-greased griddle ¼ cup at a time. Fry until brown, about 1 to 2 minutes; carefully turn with spatula, and fry on other side for 1 or 2 minutes, until golden brown. Serve with melted butter and cranberry sauce or Peach Relish.

PEACH RELISH

1. Peel and coarsely chop tomatoes. (This should yield 1½ cups tomato pulp.) Put into large, heavy pan (preferably 8-quart capacity) with remaining ingredients. Simmer carefully, stirring regularly, until thickened (about 2 hours).
2. Remove bag of pickling spices and discard.
3. Pour relish into hot (sterilized) pint-sized canning jars; leave ¼-inch headspace. Adjust caps. Process for 10 minutes in boiling water bath. Or use relish immediately.

SERVES 6

Clam Patties

Clam patties are just great for a quick lunch if you have a lot of fresh clam meat on hand. Enjoy them with a well-chilled lager beer or a good, room temperature porter.

1¼ cups minced fresh clams
2 cups mashed potatoes
2 tablespoons unsalted butter, softened
¼ teaspoon fresh thyme or a pinch dried
Salt and freshly ground pepper to taste
½ tablespoon freshly squeezed lemon juice
½ tablespoon freshly squeezed lime juice
2 eggs, lightly beaten

1. Drain minced clams and mix with potatoes, butter, thyme, salt, pepper, and citrus juice. Slowly add beaten eggs; mix well (be sure no lumps form).
2. Shape mixture into 12 patties of equal size and fry in hot fat until lightly browned on both sides.

SERVES 6

Geoduck Steak

This recipe is from Lila Gault's The Northwest Cookbook. *"Geoduck steak should be cooked quickly in very hot oil. One good cook I know says the oil must be smoking; others use thermometers to measure 400 degrees."*

Oil for frying
1 live geoduck, cut into 4-inch steaks
½ cup whole wheat flour
½ teaspoon thyme
Salt and freshly ground black pepper to taste

1. In large frying pan heat oil to 400°.
2. Combine flour, thyme, salt, and pepper. Dredge steaks from neck and breast in flour mixture and fry until golden, usually about 4 to 5 minutes.

Variation: Instead of flour mixture, combine 2 lightly beaten eggs with 1 cup cracker crumbs and salt and pepper to taste.

MAKES 2–4 SERVINGS

4 small or 2 large geoduck
   necks, skinned (horse
   clam may be substituted
   for the geoduck)
2–4 tablespoons freshly made
   unsalted butter
4 tablespoons shallot, minced
½ cup dry sauvignon blanc
   Juice from 1 lime or ½ lime
   and ½ lemon
½ cup California champagne
   mustard

Quick-Fried Geoduck

Unlike oysters, geoducks do not suffer a loss in flavor as they grow large. They are good to eat no matter how they are prepared: as steaks, in chowders, or — the most delicious way of all — sliced very thin as sashimi. (When cut across the muscle fiber, the flesh is slightly crunchy, but not tough.) You can slice, pound, and sauté the large siphon as a substitute for the less common — and much more expensive — abalone. Be assured that most of your gourmet friends will not be able to tell the difference. Here is a simple dish, which has frequently made dinner guests think they are eating abalone instead of geoduck. Serve hot with steamed vegetables and fresh pasta or hot flour tortillas. Accompany with a well-chilled sauvignon blanc.

1. Skin geoduck (see Index). Cut siphons off geoduck and slice tips off siphons. Open siphons by inserting sharp knife at wide ends and carefully cutting upward; flatten and pound with wooden mallet for a couple of minutes to tenderize. Cut large siphon steaks into 2 pieces crosswise.

2. Melt butter in pan, heat until foamy. Add minced shallots and cook until transparent. Add geoduck steaks; sauté for about 30 seconds on each side. If pan is too small to cook steaks at once, add extra butter after each set of steaks is done; add new steaks when butter foams. Remove shallots from pan if they start to brown. Keep cooked geoduck warm.

3. Pour wine into pan; add lime juice. Heat until wine foams, scraping off browned bits of geoduck and butter from bottom of pan. Add mustard, blend in well. Reduce liquid until it has thickened slightly. Pour over individual steaks.

OCTOPI
and
SQUIDS

MARINATED OCTOPUS

OCTOPUS SALAD

CHINESE OCTOPUS SALAD

CURRIED OCTOPUS SALAD

FLYING SQUID IN ROSEMARY SAUCE
ON A BED OF SQUID INK PASTA

OCTOPUS IN TOMATO SAUCE

SQUID IN INK

MARINATED SQUID RINGS

SEPPIE CON PISELLI

KALAMARAKIA TIGHANITE

OCTOPUS FRITTERS

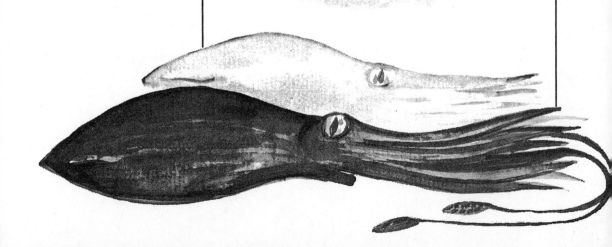

COMMON NAME
Octopus
(along entire West Coast;
in tide pools from
Santa Barbara, California,
south to Baja California)

Squid
(Calamari)
(common offshore,
inshore particularly in
Monterey Bay, California,
and Puget Sound, Washington)

DESCRIPTION

There are several species of octopus on the West Coast, all of which are good to eat. They seem to differ primarily in size, habitat, and minor morphological features. Even experts have trouble telling them apart. But that should not concern you: any octopus you get into your kitchen is good to eat — as long as it is fresh.

We have several species of squid on the West Coast; all look more or less alike to the layman. There is little difference in taste between the different kinds. Here, too, freshness is more important than variety. You do not have to worry about which species you encounter on the beach or at your fish-monger's. Like octopi, all are good to eat.

The order to which octopi and squids belong is aptly named Decapoda, "head-feet," for that is exactly how these animals look: they have large heads with many feet protruding from the base.

Octopi, with their big heads and bulging eyes and long tentacles crowded with suction cups, are mistakenly called "devilfish." But, while they may not look pretty, they are highly intelligent animals. They use their intelligence to devise ways of catching delectable crabs and mollusks. Octopi are very finicky eaters and, one might say, since they eat only the very best food, they themselves have an excellent taste. Octopi have always been a highly prized food by people of Mediterranean or Oriental descent. Only quite recently have they come to be appreciated by Americans with northern European roots.

Squids look more or less like octopi, but their heads are more elongated and streamlined with a pair of stabilizing fins at the apex, and their legs are shorter and less motile. They have ten legs, while octopi have eight. Squids are very fast swimmers. They propel themselves through the water (and at times into the air) by squirting water from a flexible jet nozzle. Squids eat what they can catch, mostly fish or other squids. Squids are now one of the most popular sea-foods on the West Coast.

HABITAT

Octopi are nocturnal. During the day they like to hide under rocks, in crevices, and in small marine caves. They are very agile and fast on their feet. They have been observed running across tideflats and beaches in pursuit of crabs. They can fit themselves into incredibly small places. Occasionally small octopi may be observed floating in the water at night.

Squids travel through the open water in large schools. When they do come inshore, they can be caught from small boats or docks. The schools of squid range up and down the coast. One year they may be common off Monterey, California, the next off San Pedro, California, or Oregon, then off the Olympic Peninsula. Small squids are quite common in the waters of Puget Sound, the Strait of Georgia, and Juan de Fuca Strait. Giant pelagic squids occasionally come close to shore, but these are not good to eat because of their iodine taste.

METHODS OF
CATCHING

The key to catching octopi lies in the fact that they like darkness, and the trick in catching squid lies in the fact that they are attracted to light.

Octopi like to hide in dark places and may be discovered in gloomy marine recesses. They can also be caught in ceramic jars lowered to the ocean floor. This fishing method, which has remained more or less unchanged since Homeric times, has recently been introduced to the commercial fisheries of the West Coast, because it is so very effective. Care needs to be taken in handling live octopi: the animals have very sharp parrotlike beaks (the only solid parts in their bodies), and the bite of some species may be mildly poisonous. Octopi can regenerate lost limbs. Some fishermen or divers slice off an arm at a time and return the animal to the water to grow a new limb.

Squids are attracted to lights at night. They may be caught from docks or boats with jigs or dip nets. They should be kept moist until they reach the kitchen.

AVAILABILITY IN
FISH MARKETS AND
RESTAURANTS

Octopi and squids are widely available in supermarkets and fish markets. You will find the best and freshest in Oriental or Italian seafood markets. Octopi usually come precooked —

which makes them very easy to handle: you just slice it and warm it in your favorite octopus dish (or pasta sauce).

SEASONS

Octopi and squids are good to eat year-round. Check local fishing regulations for seasons and catch limits.

HOW TO CLEAN

Cooked octopus is already cleaned. To clean an uncooked octopus, first remove the skin by rubbing it with coarse salt. Rinse in cold water, and rub on more salt until all the skin has been removed. Gutting an octopus is easy: there is almost nothing inside the animal. Cut off the eyes, remove the beak, pull out the ink sac, and the intestines.

To clean squid, pull the head and tentacles from the mantle cavity. Save the ink sac for sauce. Cut off the tentacles just below the beak. Discard the rest of the head (most of the innards come off with the head). Remove the plasticlike, transparent quill from the mantle, rinse out the inside, and rub off the skin under cold water.

HOW TO PREPARE

Select an octopus weighing about one and a half pounds (just right for tenderness). The Italians tenderize octopus by pounding it like abalone. The Japanese tenderize octopus by kneading it in a bath of finely grated daikon (use one large daikon — about four to six cups per one-and-one-half-pound octopus). Clean octopus and turn it inside out. Knead. The radish will turn gray. Continue the kneading process for five minutes. The octopus should have a fresh, clean ocean smell.

Cook the octopus in a large pot filled with lightly salted boiling water and one tablespoon dark soy sauce. Slowly dunk the octopus into the water, tentacles first, holding it by the orifice in the head with kitchen tongs. This will allow the tentacles to curl up. Repeat two or three times, then cook, uncovered, over medium heat for five to six minutes. Do not overcook, or the octopus will toughen. The skin side should change color from steely gray to a reddish pink. Hang the octopus from a hook inserted into the orifice and let it cool. Slow cooling will make it tender. The cooled octopus should be firm and slightly chewy, but not tough.

Once octopus has been cooked very little need be done to it. It is best served cold or heated very briefly (excessive heating may overcook and toughen it). Sliced cold octopus is perfect for sandwiches, sashimi or sushi. Cubed or julienned octopus may be used in any seafood salad recipe calling for firm white fish or shellfish.

Be careful when reheating octopus. Always add it to a dish at the very last moment so it will reheat but not cook. Extra cooking will toughen it, often beyond redemption.

Squid may be boiled, pan fried, deep fried and, best of all, stir fried. It should never be cooked for more than a minute or two. Squid may also be eaten in the Japanese fashion: raw.

Marinated Octopus

SERVES 4 AS AN APPETIZER

This simple dish makes a great appetizer. It stimulates the taste buds and prepares the stomach for the coming feast. If you cannot find freshly cooked octopus, substitute raw squid. Accompany it with a fino sherry or a cool sauvignon blanc.

2 cups cooked octopus meat, cut on the bias into ¼-inch-thick slices, then cut into ¼-inch-wide strips
1 cup virgin olive oil
¾ cup red wine vinegar
2 cloves garlic, minced
½ cup chopped fresh parsley
Juice of 1 lemon
1 teaspoon oregano
Salt and freshly ground black pepper to taste
Green nori flakes (ao-nori) as needed

1. Place octopus in shallow bowl; add remaining ingredients except nori flakes. Toss to mix well. Make sure all of the octopus pieces are covered by marinade.
2. Cover and refrigerate 1 hour. Drain; sprinkle with nori flakes. Serve cold.

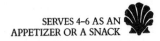

SERVES 4–6 AS AN
APPETIZER OR A SNACK

2¼ cups diced, cooked octopus
¼ cup chopped sweet pickle
¼ cup diced celery
¾ cup prepared mustard (use
    Dijon or Düsseldorf)★
    or prepared wasabi
¾ cup homemade mayonnaise
Salt and freshly ground
    black pepper to taste

Octopus Salad

This is a very simple salad. It is quickly made and just perfect for a warm summer afternoon. Accompany it with a cool white country wine or with a chilled microbrewery lager beer.

1. Combine octopus, sweet pickle, and celery in a large bowl.
2. Blend mustard with mayonnaise and stir into octopus mixture. Toss and stir until well coated. Season with salt and pepper.

★ If you can get it, use the excellent mustard by the sisters of Our Lady of The Rock Convent on Shaw Island, Washington.

SERVES 8

4 cups coarsely diced octopus
    arm
1 cup diagonally sliced green
    onion (½-inch pieces)
1 cup peeled and sliced fresh
    water chestnuts
1 cup lightly toasted white
    sesame seeds
1 pound sugar snap pea pods,
    trimmed and cut on the
    bias into ½-inch pieces
    or snow peas
Sherry Mustard Dressing
Salt and freshly ground
    black pepper to taste

Chinese Octopus Salad

The firm, almost crunchy, texture of the octopus, and the crisp consistency of the sugar snap pea pods combine to make this salad a special treat. Accompany this dish with a cool fino sherry.

1. Mix octopus, onion, water chestnuts, sesame seeds, and pea pods in large bowl. Toss with Sherry Mustard Dressing to taste. Season with salt and pepper. Serve chilled.

MAKES 2 CUPS

1 ½-inch piece of gingerroot,
    peeled
¼ cup fino or amontillado
    sherry
2 egg yolks
2 tablespoons mustard
    (Düsseldorf or Dijon)
2 teaspoons sugar
    Juice of 1 lemon
1 cup olive oil
    Dash Chinese sesame oil
2 tablespoons light soy sauce
    Salt and freshly ground
    black pepper to taste

SHERRY MUSTARD DRESSING

1. Marinate gingerroot in sherry overnight.
2. Beat egg yolks with mustard. Add sugar and lemon juice; stir until dissolved.
3. Beat oils together.
4. Pour oils in thin stream into yolk mixture, whisking constantly until thickened and smooth.
5. Remove gingerroot from sherry; beat sherry and soy sauce into yolk/oil mixture. Season with salt and pepper.

SERVES 8

3½ cups cooked octopus arm,
    cut into ¼-inch cubes
½ cup chopped chiles anchos,
    roasted, peeled, and seeded
    (see p. 25)
½ cup chopped red onion
½ cup chopped celery
½ cup coarsely cut prunes
½ cup golden raisins
½ cup seedless grapes
½ cup diced honeydew melon
    Curry Dressing (see p. 162)
4 ripe papayas
    Lettuce leaves as needed
    Tomato slices for garnish

Curried Octopus Salad

I like eating simple salads in summer, but I also like my salads to have some substance. Octopus is the perfect ingredient for this kind of dish. You can buy it precooked, keep it in the refrigerator or freezer, and slice off just enough to use for a meal. Enjoy this dish with a well-chilled lager beer.

1. Combine octopus with chile, onion, celery, prunes, raisins, grapes, and melon. Toss with Curry Dressing. Mix well. Chill.
2. Cut papayas in half; seed. Spoon octopus salad into papaya cavities. Serve on lettuce garnished with tomato slices.

MAKES ABOUT 1½ CUPS

1 cup whipping cream
⅓ cup homemade mayonnaise
1 teaspoon curry powder
    (see p. 233)
    Salt and freshly ground
    black pepper to taste

SERVES 4

1 pound mantle meat from
    a 3-pound Juan de Fuca
    Strait flying squid or
    1½ pounds whole loligo
    squid
3 tablespoons olive oil
1 onion, finely chopped
2 shallots, finely minced
1 cup dry white wine or red
1 tablespoon finely minced
    garlic
1 sprig fresh Majorca
    rosemary, finely chopped
2½ cups fresh tomato pulp
½ cup squid ink (save while
    cleaning squid)
1 sprig lemon thyme
3 tablespoons chopped
    hazelnuts or pine nuts
    Fresh squid ink pasta

CURRY DRESSING

1. Combine all ingredients in blender or food processor
   bowl; blend until smooth.

Flying Squid in Rosemary Sauce on a Bed of Squid Ink Pasta

This dish, from the Sooke Harbour House on southern Vancouver Island, calls for the large "flying" squid of Juan de Fuca Strait, but other large, meaty squid may be used. Accompany this squid dish with a simple sauvignon blanc or a dry red country wine.

1. Cut squid mantle meat into julienne strips about 2 inches
   long. (If possible, complete this process the previous day.
   Leaving squid in the refrigerator overnight will improve
   its texture and flavor.)
2. Heat oil in heavy skillet; quickly sauté onion and
   shallots for about 30 seconds. Then stir in wine, garlic,
   rosemary, and tomatoes; simmer for 6 minutes.
3. Add squid, cover well, and simmer on low heat for
   55 minutes. After 45 minutes, add squid ink and lemon
   thyme. Stir in hazelnuts 2 or 3 minutes before serving.
   Remove rosemary and lemon thyme sprigs before
   serving.
4. Time pasta so it is just al dente when squid is done. Pour
   squid sauce over pasta and serve.

4 cups flour
1 tablespoon finely ground
    fresh rosemary
8 egg yolks
5 tablespoons squid ink,
    pressed through a sieve
    and collected in a bowl (if
    you have less available,
    add water)

FRESH SQUID INK PASTA★

1. Thoroughly mix together flour and rosemary. Arrange in a circle on a table. Pour egg yolks and squid ink into center and carefully mix.
2. Bit by bit, mix flour mixture with egg/squid ink mixture. Knead thoroughly to achieve a smooth consistency.
3. When firm, wrap pasta dough in a damp cloth and let stand for at least 1 hour.
4. When ready, flatten pasta into thin, crêpelike sheets, sprinkle with flour and let dry for 1 hour. The pasta dough is now ready to be cut (by hand or machine) into desired shape. Linguine or spaghetti shapes are fine for this recipe.

★ This pasta may be prepared in advance.

SERVES 4

¼ cup olive oil
1¾ cups cooked octopus meat,
    cut into 1-inch pieces
¼ cup dry white wine
2 cups skinned and chopped
    ripe Italian tomatoes
2 medium cloves garlic, peeled
    and chopped
    Salt and freshly ground
    black pepper to taste
1 tablespoon chopped fresh
    parsley or cilantro
    Cooked pasta for 4

Octopus in Tomato Sauce

The octopus used in this recipe needs to be slightly browned, but make sure to do this very quickly to avoid overcooking it. Accompany this dish with a light zinfandel, barbera, or other country wine.

1. Heat oil in heavy skillet. When oil just begins to smoke, add octopus and quickly sear for a few seconds on each side to brown lightly. Remove octopus; keep warm. Turn heat to medium.
2. Add wine; reduce until its liquid has evaporated and only an essence remains. Add tomatoes, garlic, salt, and pepper. Lower heat; simmer gently until tomatoes are cooked (about 20 to 45 minutes, depending on ripeness). Return octopus; toss; sprinkle with parsley; serve over pasta.

SERVES 4

2 pounds squid, cleaned, ink
    reserved
2 medium onions, chopped
1 clove garlic, minced
½ cup olive oil
    Salt and freshly ground
        black pepper to taste
    Pinch cayenne
½ cup dry red wine
½ cup water
    French bread or pasta for 4

Squid in Ink

Squid in ink is a favorite among Italians on the West Coast. It is based on the culinary principle that no part of an animal should be wasted — if it tastes good. Squid ink does indeed add a nice flavor to the dish. Accompany the squid with a light zinfandel, barbera, or other country wine.

1. Open squid mantle and lay out flat. Score with a sharp knife in a crisscross pattern (be sure not to cut all the way through). Cut squid into 1- to 2-inch pieces, leaving small tentacles whole.
2. Gently sauté onions and garlic in oil. Add squid. Season with salt, pepper, and cayenne. Sauté for 3 to 4 minutes. Remove squid and keep warm.
3. Add ink, wine, and water to pan. Cook briskly until reduced by ½. Return squid to pan. Heat through. Serve with French bread hot from the oven or ladle over freshly cooked pasta.

SERVES 6-8

2 pounds small squid mantles,
    cleaned and cut into ¼- to
    ½-inch rings
½ cup pickleweed joints,
    washed
    Salt and freshly ground
        black pepper to taste
¼ cup extra virgin olive oil
⅓ cup freshly squeezed lemon
    juice
1 teaspoon chopped fresh mint
1 tablespoon chopped parsley
1 clove garlic, minced

Marinated Squid Rings

Pickleweed is very common in our salt marshes. Its fleshy, jointed stems have a pleasantly tart taste that goes particularly well with the mild-flavored and crunchy-textured squid. A simple lemon/olive oil dressing turns this mixture of seaside vegetable and high seas mollusk into a sumptuous dish.

1. Drop squid into boiling water for about 30 seconds. Drain and let cool.
2. Toss squid with pickleweed joints. Season with salt and pepper.
3. Combine oil, lemon juice, mint, parsley, and garlic, and pour over squid. Marinate in refrigerator for several

Lettuce leaves as needed
2 ripe tomatoes, sliced for
   garnish
Lemon wedges for garnish

hours. Serve on a bed of lettuce leaves; garnish with tomato slices and lemon wedges.

SERVES 6

Seppie Con Piselli
(SQUID WITH GREEN PEAS)

I prefer fresh squid raw, or cooked two minutes at most, to keep it tender and crisp. But dishes such as this one from the Mona Lisa Deli call for cooking squid longer — and it works, though the texture is different. Accompany this dish with the wine you use for cooking the squid: a dry colombard, chenin blanc, or semillon.

3 pounds small squid (frozen
   or fresh)
4 tablespoons olive oil
1 clove garlic
   Sliver of hot red pepper pod,
   seeded
1 cup dry white wine
2 tablespoons freshly chopped
   Italian parsley
   Salt to taste
1 pound fresh peas

1. Clean squid (defrost frozen squid); save tentacles.
2. Cut squid mantles into small rings (or squares). Leave tentacles whole, unless they are bigger than a mouthful, in which case cut in half.
3. Heat oil in wide frying pan over medium heat; drop in garlic and pepper. When garlic is golden and pepper is deep brown, remove both.
4. Add squid to pan. When the squid has turned pink (about 3 minutes cooking time), add wine. When alcohol has evaporated, lower heat. Add parsley and salt, and continue cooking over low heat for about 20 minutes, or until the squid is tender. The smaller the squid are, the more quickly they cook.
5. Precook peas until they are tender. Add to squid. Adjust seasoning.

SERVES 4

Kalamarakia Tighanite

(DEEP-FRIED SQUID)

Deep-fried squid are the latest darling of the fast-food trade, but the delectable fritters have been around for a long time: they were introduced to the West Coast by Italian fishermen and Chinese cooks. Deep-fried squid go very well with all sorts of hot dips from a Mexican salsa fresca to a simple Chinese hot oil. Accompany this dish with a dark microbrewery lager beer or light ale.

1 pound cleaned fresh small
    squid
1 cup all-purpose flour
    Salt and freshly ground
        white pepper to taste
½ teaspoon paprika
    Almond or apricot oil
        as needed
    Lemon wedges as needed

1. Cut body of squid into strips or rings; leave tentacles whole.
2. Drain squid well. Shake in paper bag with seasoned flour to coat evenly. Let rest for about 4 to 6 minutes. Lightly toss in colander to shake off excess flour.
3. Heat oil to 375°. Deep fry squid until golden. Drain on paper towels.
4. Serve with lemon wedges.

SERVES 4

Octopus Fritters

Serve these fritters to those friends who must eat their seafood breaded and fried. Accompany this dish with a simple country wine or a microbrewery ale or lager beer.

1 egg, lightly beaten
1¼ cups iced water
1⅔ cups all-purpose flour
    Salt and freshly ground
        black pepper to taste
2½ cups sliced octopus arm
    (½-inch slices)
    Almond or apricot oil for
        deep frying

1. In a chilled bowl, blend together egg and water. Sift in flour. Season with salt and pepper. Do not worry about lumps, it is quite all right to have them in this batter.
2. Heat oil in wok to 340°.
3. Pat octopus slices with paper towel to dry. Dip into batter, one at a time, then immediately drop into oil. Deep fry until golden. Serve hot as snacks.

CRABS

DIPPING SAUCE FOR BOILED OR STEAMED CRAB

WEST COAST CRAB STEW

CIOPPINO DI GAMBERONI

SAN FRANCISCO CIOPPINO

CRAB BISQUE

CHATEAU STE. MICHELLE CRAB BISQUE

WILD RICE CRAB SALAD

FLORENCE FENNEL AND GALATHEID CRAB SALAD

DEVILED CRAB MEAT

CRAB AND OYSTER MUSHROOM CASSEROLE

PETRALE SOLE STUFFED WITH DUNGENESS CRAB
WITH CRAYFISH CREAM SAUCE

CRAB BAKED WITH ALMONDS AND CHEESE

STEAMED FRESH CRAB IN CURRY SAUCE

FRESH LINGUINE WITH CRAB SHELL SAUCE
AND LEMON THYME

DUNGENESS CRAB TASTEVIN

STIR-FRIED CRAB MEAT WITH FENNEL

DEEP-FRIED CRAB BALLS WITH VINEGAR DIP

CREAMED CRAB MEAT

CRAB LOUIS

COLD SHREDDED VEGETABLES WITH CRAB

CRAB AND VEGETABLES IN A CLEAR SAUCE

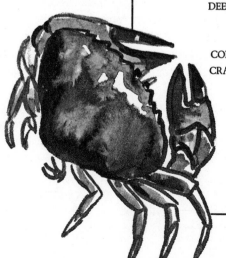

COMMON NAME	
Dungeness Crab *(Commercial Crab)* *(central California to Alaska)*	This large (to eight inches across) yellowish green crab is *the* commercial crab of the West Coast. It has become scarce in San Francisco Bay (agricultural pesticides washed down from the Central Valley are suspected), but it is still common in the north. It is a very meaty and very delicious crab. But it must be eaten absolutely fresh, since its meat will lose its flavor quickly after cooking.
Striped Shore Crab *(Baja California to* *British Columbia)*	A smaller version (to five inches across) of the Dungeness crab with red spots on its undersurface and large claws. It is quite common on rocky beaches of the outer coast and may be captured in tide pools.
Red Crab *(Baja California to Alaska)*	The red crab looks very much like a Dungeness, but it is chunkier and has a deep red coloration. It has a heavier shell (to eight inches across) and less meat than the Dungeness, but its flavor is exquisite. The red crab occupies much of the same habitat as the Dungeness — eelgrass beds and sandy bottoms — but it can often be found on rocky shores among cobbles or boulders or partly buried in sand. It is often taken with the Dungeness in crab pots or traps. Prepare like the Dungeness.
Red Rock Crab *(Baja California to Alaska)*	This brick red crab (two inches across) is common only in Puget Sound. It prefers holes in rocky bottoms. Its meat tastes superb. Prepare like a small Dungeness crab.
Lined Shore Crab *(Gulf of California to* *central Oregon)*	This small (about two to three inches across), dark red or green crab is ubiquitous on rocky beaches. It may hide in damp crevices and dart back and forth to examine bits of food dropped by picnickers. It is worth catching despite its small size, because it makes for a great addition to seafood stews.
Purple Shore Crab *(Gulf of California to* *southeastern Alaska)*	This small (one and one-half to two inches across) reddish crab lives in the tide pool zone one level below the lined shore crab. It is about the same size as the lined shore crab, just as hard to catch, and just as good to eat.
Mud Flat Crab *(southern California to* *British Columbia)*	This is the common shore crab of San Francisco Bay and Puget Sound. It is a small (one and one-half to two inches across), dull, pale green crab much like the previous two. It

prefers protected shores and rocky areas in bays and salt marshes. Like the two other shore crabs, it is a good cioppino crab.

Black-Clawed Crab
(California to British Columbia)

This tiny crab (one inch across) is common only in Puget Sound. In some places in the southern Sound, it can be collected by the shovelful. Here these crabs look much like mud-colored stones. Black-clawed crabs from the outer coast are much brighter and may be red, brown, and whitish. It is a good cioppino crab.

Porcelain Crab
(Gulf of California to British Columbia)

These tiny (one-half inch to about three-fourths inch across) cioppino crabs are very common on beaches where rocks rest on sand or gravel. They are blue or sometimes purplish red and make lovely garnishes on seafood dishes.

Fiddler Crab
(Baja California to southern California)

The small (one and one-half inches across) fiddler crab is almost terrestrial. It digs its burrows high above the high tide line. (It needs to dash down to the water only occasionally to moisten its gills.) Despite its small size, it is good to eat.

Puget Sound Box Crab
(Northwest waters, especially Puget Sound, Washington)

A very large (nine to twelve inches across), boxy and spiny crab common on rocky bottoms at a depth of five to eight fathoms. It can fold its legs underneath its body and turn itself into an armored "box." This delicious crab, which can weigh up to nine pounds, is too large and chunky to be boiled whole.

Puget Sound King Crab
(Juan de Fuca Strait, Washington, to Puget Sound, Washington)

This large (to ten inches across) chunky crab looks much like the Puget Sound box crab, but it cannot fold up its legs as neatly, and its bright orange shell is marked with purple bumps. Like the box crab it is very good to eat. It is unrelated to the "king" crab of Alaska.

Spider Crabs
(up and down the West Coast)

Spider crabs are more closely related to hermit crabs than to "true" *Cancer* crabs. (Their size varies from very small to very large.) Spider crabs have long meaty legs (the part commonly sold) and compact bodies that are small in relation to their overall size. A large spider crab (one of two species caught in Alaska and sold as "snow" crab) occurs as far south as Puget Sound and is sometimes caught in large crab pots set in deep water.

Kelp Crab
(Baja California to British Columbia)

Kelp crabs are small (to four inches across), angular spider crabs living on kelp and other seaweeds. They may be caught in crab traps. But watch out: their claws are small but deliver a vicious nip. Like other small crabs, kelp crabs are good cioppino crabs.

Hermit Crabs
(Gulf of California to Alaska)

Hermit crabs, which are more closely related to spider crabs than to *Cancer* crabs are also delicious to eat. (Their size varies greatly as with spider crabs.) They have large claws and shrimpy bodies with long, soft abdomens, which they prefer to hide in the abandoned shells of marine snails. Very large hermit crabs — some of a bright red color — live in the Sea of Cortez; the largest occupy the cast-off shells of conch.

Galatheid Crabs
(Mexico to British Columbia)

Large galatheid crabs look much like squat lobsters. (They come in a variety of sizes.) They are occasionally referred to as "lobsters" in areas where they are common. They share their Spanish name of *langosta* with all sorts of other marine creatures, some of which look remotely like a lobster — primarily because they possess claws — and some that do not look like lobster (spiny or otherwise) at all. Their only claim to the name lies in their lobsterlike taste.

Pea Crabs
(Mexico to Alaska; inside the shells of large clams, oysters, and mussels)

Pea crabs look very much like miniature Dungeness-type crabs, but I think they are tastier. The largest pea crabs, living in the largest clams, can reach a diameter of about one inch, but they rarely do. Pea crabs can be eaten steamed, sautéed, or stir fried, and they add a nice touch to seafood stews and appetizer trays. If you find pea crabs in your steamed clams, eat them — they should be cooked to perfection.

DESCRIPTION

Our crabs may be divided into three groups, based on their outward appearance — though there are some oddball crabs of very scurrilous appearance that do not look much like anything else but themselves. Representatives of the *Cancer* group (Dungeness, et al.) look more or less like the Dungeness. Swimming crabs can be told from walking crabs by the different shape of the last pair of legs: the pointed "feet" of walking crabs have been modified into flat, paddlelike "swimmerets." Needless to say, "swimming" crabs commonly walk, and "walking" crabs can swim. Try to classify the crab you catch by the way it looks, not by what you see it do.

The Dungeness crab's much smaller cousins are very common on the coast. Several species range all the way from British Columbia to Baja California. They look very similar. At least enough so that cooks can easily recognize them. All are edible and very tasty. Some species have little body meat but more than make up for this with copious amounts of meat in the claws. These crabs can sometimes be taken by hand in tide pools (watch those claws).

Spider crabs look like, but are not, marine spiders. To avoid upsetting consumers with references to their peculiar appearance, seafood processors have given them "trade" names, such as "king" crab. When properly handled they are very good to eat. Just make sure you really get "snow" or "king" crab when you order crab legs in a restaurant, and not fake crablike *surimi*.

Great numbers of small crabs occupy our intertidal zones by the millions (a few even burrow in sand above the tide line); there are edible species too numerous to recount here. Sometimes they can be found by the thousands on exposed tideflats. Their flavors vary quite a bit, but all add interesting touches to seafood stews.

HABITAT

Crabs are ubiquitous on our coast. They scuttle across beaches, crawl about rocks and kelp, and hide in eelgrass beds or salt marshes. Some even climb high up into the wildflower margin above the upper shore. Wherever you look in the intertidal zone, you will discover at least one kind of crab. The larger crabs live in deeper water; usually, the larger the crab is, the deeper down it will live.

METHODS OF CATCHING

If you are fast, you can catch small beach crabs by hand or with a hand-held net. You may find Dungeness and other large crabs by wading through eelgrass beds at low tide. Or look under rocks and in intertidal crevices. All crabs respond eagerly to bait. You should be successful, whether you use a simple crab ring or a fancy trap. I have had the best luck when

I have set my crab pots a few hundred feet offshore (all you need is a small rowboat to get you out there). Be sure to cook crabs as soon as possible after capture. Crabs should not be cooked if they have died en route to the cooking pot.

AVAILABILITY IN FISH MARKETS AND RESTAURANTS

Dungeness crabs are landed off the northern California, Oregon, and Washington coasts primarily in late fall and early winter; most Alaskan Dungeness are caught in summer and early fall. This would indicate that most of the "fresh" crab encountered at San Francisco's Fisherman's Wharf during the height of the tourist season probably comes all the way from Alaska. Since the Alaska crabbing grounds are almost as far from San Francisco as New Orleans, one frequently encounters crab that is not as fresh as it should be (interestingly enough, several San Francisco fishmongers specialize in selling Gulf of Mexico crabs and oysters). You should experience no problems, of course, with the freshness and quality of the crab served in the city's better restaurants, like the venerable Tadich Grill. But you may have to pay a lot for the pleasure.

For a real crab feast you may get greater pleasure out of driving north along the coast to Noyo and eating the delectable Dungeness at the source.

Commercial landings in both Oregon and Washington are often lower than California catches, but there are fewer people to share in the bounty. Good, fresh Dungeness crab is both more common in Northwest seafood markets, and less expensive.

Other local crabs, particularly the red crab, are occasionally for sale in seafood stores. Your best bet for buying fresh crab on the West Coast is to shop for fresh, live crab in the Chinese or Japanese markets (and seafood markets) of our larger cities. It will be hard to do better, unless you catch the crabs yourself.

Never buy precooked crab, unless it has been removed from the shell: cooked whole crab spoils very rapidly.

SEASONS

Year-round, except where seasons set by fish and game departments apply. Female Dungeness crabs (broad belly flap) may never be taken.

HOW TO CLEAN

Crab may also be cleaned before it is cooked. Clean small crabs by breaking them apart and rinsing them under cold running water. There are two easy ways of cleaning live large crabs (large beach crabs to Dungeness or box crabs):

Turn crab upside down and set the cutting edge of a sharp heavy-bladed knife along the center of the narrow triangular flap on the crab's belly. Strike the back of the knife blade with a mallet or your fist. The blow should be heavy enough to cut through the abdomen, but not strong enough to break through the back shell. This will kill the crab instantly. Once the crab has been killed, hold the shell down with your knife, grasp first one set of legs and then the other; twist away the body meat with the legs. Rinse off the remaining bits of innards under cold running water.

Or, prop up a spade or other edged tool. Grab the crab firmly by the legs and face it away from you. Strike the narrow triangular belly flap against the edge. This should break the crab into three parts. The carapace with the intestines will fall away, and you will hold the legs with the attached body meat. Rinse off the few bits of entrails clinging to the meat under cold running water. You are now ready to cook the crab.

When cleaning a female crab (other than a Dungeness, which must be thrown back), never throw away the yellow pâté (the gonads), clinging to the inside of the carapace. I consider them the best part of these crustaceans. If you are lucky enough to find a (legal) female crab with roe clapped under its broad tail, carefully remove it and serve it on sushi, topped with a raw quail egg.

Hermit crabs are also easy to clean. If you cannot pull them from their shell—beware of the pincers—break the shell with a hammer and remove the crab from its hiding place.

Pea crabs are too small to be cleaned; eat them whole.

HOW TO PREPARE

In a large cooking pot, heat salt water to a boil. Quickly drop the crabs into the seething water one by one, the largest ones first. Crabs can be cooked in fresh water, but the salt will firm the meat and improve the flavor. Cover the pot and cook the crabs for about ten or fifteen minutes, then take them from the pot and quickly cool them in ice water. When the crabs have cooled enough to be handled, clean them by lifting the top shells from the rear and pulling them off. Break the carcass in half. It is customary to wash out the intestines, gills, and other internal organs, but many of these can be eaten and are quite flavorful. The gut should be discarded, but just about everything else can be eaten—even the gills can be sucked. Do not eat any of these internal organs when a "red tide" warning is out—crabs eat clams (see Index). Cleaning out the halves of the crab's body will leave you with the body meat and the leg meat. The body meat can be loosened by smacking the body halves with the palm of your hand (or the blade of a Chinese cleaver), and it can then be shaken out. The legs and claws can be cracked with pliers or with a nut-cracker and the long pieces of meat shaken, pulled, or sucked from the cavities.

Small beach crabs and hermit crabs can be added whole to stews; larger ones may be stir fried, boiled, or steamed, then cracked, picked or sucked clean (depending on their size). Large claws are especially rewarding.

Small shore, tideflat, or seaweed crabs are ideally suited for cioppinos and other seafood stews. (Crabs with plant or animal growth on their carapaces should be scrubbed clean before cooking—not all of these hitchhikers are palatable.) Too small to give much meat, these lesser crabs can be boiled to flavor bisques. The body meat should fall out during the cooking, and the legs can be picked clean with toothpicks. Prolonged stewing will just about dissolve the crab meat, but the delicious flavor will linger in the stew.

Pea crabs are so small they can be served on sushi in small clusters. I like dipping them into a lemon butter or a Japanese (rice vinegar) sweet and sour sauce. Pea crabs are found in the mantle cavities of large clams, sea and horse mussels, and sometimes oysters. They can be eaten whole. But you will need a lot of crabs to make a meal—most are smaller than a dime.

½ cup freshly squeezed lemon
  juice
½ cup freshly squeezed lime
  juice
⅓ cup plus 2 tablespoons rice
  vinegar
1 cup dark soy sauce
2 tablespoons tamari sauce
3 tablespoons hon-mirin★
  (sweetened Japanese
  cooking wine), heated to
  burn off alcohol
2 tablespoons (a small handful)
  dried bonito flakes
  (hana-katsuo)★
1 2-inch square of giant kelp
  (konbu)★
½–1 teaspoon finely minced fresh
  gingerroot (optional)

Dipping Sauce for
Boiled or Steamed Crab

Dipping sauces like this do more than merely add flavor; they also have antiseptic properties. This makes them particularly suitable for foods consumed at beach picnics. If you do not have the time to create such an elaborate sauce, simply bring some light soy sauce and a few teaspoons of prepared Japanese horseradish (wasabi) and perhaps some minced fresh gingerroot. Mix them together to taste just before you get ready to dip your crab.

1. Mix all ingredients in ceramic container and let stand, covered, 24 hours in a cool place. Strain through cheesecloth and mature 3 months in a cool dark place or refrigerate. Keeps indefinitely, but should be used within 1 year for best flavor.

★ Available in Oriental markets or in the gourmet food section of your supermarket.

SERVES 4–6

6 large, live red rock crabs
1 cup chopped red onion
4 medium cloves garlic,
      smashed with side of
      cleaver
3 large chiles poblanos or
      chiles verdes, peeled,
      seeded, and chopped
      (see p. 25)
1 cup chopped cilantro or
      parsley
1 cup olive oil
6 cups coarsely chopped meaty
      tomatoes, roasted, peeled,
      and seeded
2 teaspoons chopped fresh basil
      (or more to taste)
   Salt and freshly ground
      black pepper to taste
¼ teaspoon freshly ground
      cumin (optional)
   Fresh garlic bread as needed

West Coast Crab Stew

Any kind of crab will go well in this stew: large rock crabs, small rock crabs, or whatever you are fast enough and lucky enough to catch. Drink an unpretentious country wine or good lager beer with this dish.

1. To kill crabs, lay each crab on its back, place the cutting edge of a sharp knife along the center of the narrow flap on the crab's belly and strike the back of the knife with a mallet. The blow should be hard enough to cut through the abdomen, but not so hard as to cut through the top shell. Once the crab has been killed, hold the top shell down with your knife, grasp first one set of legs and then the other, and twist away the body meat with them. Rinse off the remaining bits of intestinal matter under cold running water. Scrape off the crab "butter" inside shell and set aside.
2. When all crabs have been killed and cleaned, crack legs and claws by tapping with back of Chinese cleaver or chef's knife.
3. Place crabs in a large Dutch oven or other heavy kettle. Add onion, garlic, chiles, cilantro, and olive oil. Cover and simmer over low to medium heat for 15 to 20 minutes.
4. In the meantime, gently stew tomatoes in a saucepan.
5. Pour over crabs. (If this tomato sauce seems a bit on the thin side, you may add up to 2 tablespoons tomato paste to thicken it and give it flavor.)
6. Stir crabs and tomatoes well. Sprinkle with basil. Season with salt and pepper. Cover and simmer for 30 minutes. About 5 minutes before serving, stir in cumin.
7. Serve with thick slices of garlic bread (made by spreading French bread slices with olive oil and finely chopped garlic and toasting it under the broiler).

SERVES 6

Cioppino di Gamberoni
(CRAB STEW)

¼ cup vegetable oil
1 medium onion, chopped
5 medium cloves garlic,
    chopped
6 small ripe tomatoes, chopped
2 tablespoons chopped fresh
    parsley
1 cup water
8 small potatoes, peeled and
    quartered or 6 medium
    potatoes
3 fresh medium-sized crabs,
    cooked and cracked
    Salt and freshly ground
    black pepper to taste

This recipe comes from the Mona Lisa Deli, a lusty Italian delight in the culinary wilderness of Bellingham, Washington. Somehow Vince Zizzo, the chef, always seems to be able to get the best and freshest crab, or in fact the best of everything. Accompany the stew with a tossed green salad, lots of bread for dunking into the sauce, and a nicely aged Martini barbera.

1. Heat oil over medium heat in large pot. Add onion and garlic and cook to a golden brown. Add tomatoes and parsley. Stir well. Cook for 15 minutes over medium heat.
2. Add water and potatoes. Cook until potatoes are almost done.
3. Add cracked crabs. Cook, covered, for another 20 to 30 minutes, or until potatoes are cooked. Stir gently from time to time.
4. Season with salt and pepper. Serve immediately.

SERVES 4

San Francisco Cioppino

½ medium red onion, chopped
1 cup olive oil
½ stalk celery, chopped or
    1 stalk lovage
1 medium carrot, peeled and
    chopped
1 tablespoon fresh fennel,
    chopped
1 chile poblano or chile
    verde, peeled, seeded, and
    chopped (see p. 25)
½ stalk leek (white part only),
    chopped
3½ cups chopped, cooked meaty
    (ripe) tomatoes
1 tablespoon tomato paste
    (optional) or 1–2
    sun-dried tomatoes,
    chopped
3½ cups water
    Salt and freshly ground
    black pepper to taste
½ teaspoon oregano
2 teaspoons fresh chopped basil
½ teaspoon fresh thyme or
    ¼ teaspoon dried
4 whole bay leaves
    (California laurel)
    Dash cayenne
½ pound halibut
½ pound swordfish
8 large scallops, shucked
2 tablespoons all-purpose flour
2 large crabs or 4–6 small
    crabs or 12 or more very
    small crabs, left whole,
    or ½ pound crab meat

Almost anything goes in a cioppino, but to be good, the seafood stew must meet certain requirements. The seafood must be impeccably fresh. The sauce must be light, not strong and overpowering. There should be an aroma of herbs, and you must be able to taste the fish. You can accompany this dish with just about any of the lighter country red wines, or you may wish to match a sauvignon blanc to it. Anything goes, just make sure it tastes good to you.

1. In a heavy saucepan, sauté onion in ½ cup olive oil over medium heat. Lightly cook for about 1 minute (do not brown). Add celery, carrot, fennel, chile, and leek. Cook 5 minutes more. Add tomatoes, tomato paste, water, herbs, and spices (except chervil). Simmer for at least 2 hours, stirring regularly.
2. Cut halibut and swordfish into ½- by 2-inch cubes. Lightly dust fish and scallops with flour. Set aside.
3. If using larger crabs, clean and break in half. Set aside.
4. In a large, heavy skillet, sauté garlic in remaining ½ cup olive oil over high heat for a few seconds. Add all of the seafood, except clams. Sauté about 2 minutes until fish and scallops have turned golden. Add wine and stir; cook for 1 minute.
5. Add sauce and clams, cover pot, cook 5 minutes over low heat. Cioppino will be done when clams have opened. Transfer to soup tureen. Sprinkle with chervil. Serve hot with toasted garlic bread spread with olive oil, garlic, and oregano. Provide ample napkins and bibs for your guests.

8 large shrimp, deveined, but
    not shelled
½ cup small shrimp, shelled
    and deveined
24 (or more) steamer clams
1 tablespoon finely chopped
    garlic
½ cup dry white wine
1 tablespoon chopped chervil
    or parsley
    Toasted garlic bread for 4

SERVES 6

1 tablespoon minced shallot
2 tablespoons unsalted butter
2 tablespoons all-purpose flour
2 cups unsalted chicken stock
2 cups light cream or
    half-and-half
1 pound freshly cooked crab
    meat
    Salt and freshly ground
    white pepper to taste
6 teaspoons finely chopped
    chervil
6 teaspoons crème fraîche
3 teaspoons salmon caviar or
    golden whitefish caviar,
    drained

Crab Bisque

This is a more delicate soup than the crab stews. It makes a perfect soup course for a fancy dinner, yet it is simple enough to serve as a luncheon dish as well. Accompany it with a crisp white wine or a fino sherry.

1. Sauté shallot in butter until soft and translucent. Add flour, cook and stir 1 minute.
2. Slowly stir in stock, then cream. Cook for 5 minutes, stirring regularly.
3. Shred crab meat by hand; add to soup. Season with salt and pepper. Heat crab through.
4. Pour soup into individual serving bowls. Sprinkle each serving with chervil. Place a dollop of crème fraîche in center of each serving. Top with a dollop of salmon caviar.

SERVES 4-6

6 tablespoons unsalted butter
2 tablespoons finely chopped
    green onion
2 shallots, finely chopped
1 small clove garlic, minced
2 cups chicken broth
2 cups Chateau Ste. Michelle
    chardonnay
⅛ teaspoon freshly ground
    white pepper
2 cups half-and-half
1½–2 cups fresh Dungeness crab
    meat, cooked
4 tablespoons Chateau Ste.
    Michelle Johannisberg
    riesling
    Chopped fresh parsley for
    garnish

Chateau Ste. Michelle Crab Bisque

Dungeness crab bisque is one of the dishes for which Washington State is becoming justly famous. This version, from western Washington's Chateau Ste. Michelle winery is particularly delectable. Accompany this bisque with a Chateau Ste. Michelle Johannisberg riesling.

1. Combine butter, green onion, shallots, garlic, broth, chardonnay, and pepper. Simmer until liquid is reduced by ⅓.
2. Add half-and-half. Simmer, stirring constantly, until liquid reduces just enough to thicken slightly.
3. Reduce heat and stir in crab meat. Cook only until crab meat heats through. Remove from heat.
4. Just before serving, stir in riesling. Sprinkle with parsley.

SERVES 4-6

⅓ cup homemade mayonnaise
⅓ cup sour cream or thick
    crème fraîche
¼ cup chile salsa
2 teaspoons freshly squeezed
    lemon juice
1 teaspoon freshly squeezed
    lime juice
1 teaspoon Dijon mustard
4–6 large radicchio leaves (use
    several if you can only
    find small ones)
3 cups cooked wild rice

Wild Rice Crab Salad

Wild rice is now grown on the West Coast, from California to Idaho. It is of an excellent quality and should be used more widely in our cookery. This dish calls for a fruity rosé wine.

1. In a bowl, blend together mayonnaise, sour cream, salsa, citrus juice, and mustard to make the dressing. Refrigerate.
2. Chill radicchio leaves.
3. Combine rice, crab, onion, tomato, and celery. Season with salt and pepper.
4. Place each radicchio leaf in a bowl, hollow side up. Divide salad into serving portions and heap onto

½ pound freshly cooked crab
   meat, chilled
½ cup thinly sliced green onions
1 large ripe tomato, peeled,
   seeded, and diced
1 cup thinly sliced celery or
   ¾ cup chopped lovage
Salt and freshly ground
   black pepper to taste
4–6 tablespoons chopped chervil
   or cilantro
4–6 teaspoons salmon caviar,
   drained

radicchio leaves. Sprinkle with chopped chervil. Top
each serving with 1 teaspoon salmon caviar. Serve
dressing on the side.

SERVES 4

Water for boiling
½ pound galatheid crab meat
1 small fennel bulb, washed,
   stems and outside leaf
   bases removed, cut into
   julienne strips
½ cup cracked hazelnuts
¼ pound snow peas, washed,
   ends removed, and cut
   into bite-sized pieces
1 small kohlrabi, peeled, cut
   into small cubes
5 tablespoons olive oil
2 tablespoons freshly squeezed
   lemon juice
1 clove garlic, finely chopped
¼ teaspoon dry mustard or
   Dijon mustard

Florence Fennel and Galatheid Crab Salad

*This recipe is from the Sooke Harbour House. Sinclair Philip
says that it is possible to catch these squat little lobsters by hand,
but you are more likely to get significant numbers as an incidental
catch in shrimp traps where they prey on trapped crustaceans. Their
flavor is a little richer and stronger than that of prawns, somewhat
like European "langoustines."*

1. Bring water to boil, drop in galatheid crabs; reduce heat
   and cook about 2 minutes. Keep larger specimens intact
   to use as garnish.
2. Peel galatheid crab tails; mix with fennel, hazelnuts,
   snow peas, and kohlrabi in bowl.
3. Make dressing by blending together oil, lemon juice,
   garlic, and mustard. Blend until mustard is well incorporated. Pour over salad.
4. Form a ring around outside of serving platter with
   large whole cooked galatheid crabs, claws facing inward.
   Serve.

SERVES 4

Deviled Crab Meat

This is one of those standard American dishes that seemingly has been around forever and will survive any multitude of fancy food movements. Accompany it with lots of lager beer or hard cider.

1 pound crab meat
¼ teaspoon dry mustard
¼ teaspoon mace
  Dash cayenne
1 tablespoon chopped parsley
1 teaspoon Worcestershire
  sauce
3 tablespoons melted butter
  (salted or not, according
  to taste)
1 tablespoon freshly squeezed
  lemon juice
1 egg, beaten
¼ cup dry bread crumbs

1. Mix crab meat with mustard, mace, cayenne, parsley, and Worcestershire sauce.
2. Stir in butter, lemon juice, and egg.
3. Place in 4 well-buttered scallop shells or ramekins. Sprinkle with bread crumbs.
4. Bake in a preheated 350° oven for 15 minutes or until golden.

SERVES 6

Crab and Oyster Mushroom Casserole

Oyster mushrooms have a delicate, yet pronounced, flavor that makes them a perfect ingredient for seafood dishes. I love using them with oysters, scallops, clams, and other mollusks, but I feel they do a lot for crab as well. This casserole recipe is not your standard middle America, mid-fifties casserole, but something special. It was given to me by a little old lady from Pasadena who knew what was cooking.

1 cup oyster mushrooms,
  chopped
2 tablespoons unsalted butter
½ cup cream
1 pound cooked crab meat
  Freshly squeezed lemon
  juice from ½ lemon
1 teaspoon capers
1 teaspoon chopped chervil
2 egg whites, beaten into soft
  peaks

1. Sauté mushrooms in butter until tender. Add cream and cook until reduced to quite a thick consistency.
2. Stir in crab meat, lemon juice, capers, chervil, and egg whites.
3. Pour into a buttered casserole dish and bake in a preheated 350° oven for about 20 minutes.

Petrale Sole Stuffed with Dungeness Crab with Crayfish Cream Sauce

SERVES 6

½ cup unsalted butter
6 tablespoons diced shallots
1¼ teaspoons finely diced garlic
2 cups sliced mushrooms
3 teaspoons chopped parsley
3 cups Dungeness crab meat, drained
¾ cup grated Parmesan cheese
  Salt and freshly ground black pepper to taste
6 petrale sole fillets
  White wine as needed
  Crayfish Cream Sauce

¼ cup brandy
2 cups dry white wine
1½ cups fish fumet
1 cup Crayfish Stock (see p. 184)
¾ cup cream

The Shelburne Inn is such a lovely place and serves such gorgeous food, it is sometimes hard to believe it is actually in the middle of nowhere just north of the mouth of the Columbia River. It is certainly worth a special trip, for the quality of the fresh shellfish alone. Accompany this dish with a California chardonnay.

1. Melt butter in sauté pan over moderate heat. Add shallots and garlic; sauté 1 minute. Add mushrooms and parsley; sauté 2 to 3 minutes. Add crab meat; sauté for 2 minutes.
2. Transfer to a bowl and toss with cheese. Salt and pepper to taste. Set in refrigerator to cool.
3. Lay sole fillets flat on cutting board; salt and pepper lightly. Spread filling evenly along fillets and roll up carefully. Place in buttered baking dish; dot each fillet with butter. Pour white wine into baking dish. Bake in preheated 450° oven for about 10 minutes. Remove fish from baking dish; drain on a rack and keep warm. Serve with Crayfish Cream Sauce.

CRAYFISH CREAM SAUCE

1. Deglaze baking pan with brandy; flame to burn off alcohol. Add wine and fish fumet; reduce by ½ over medium heat. Add stock and reduce for 3 minutes. Stir in cream and reduce until sauce has thickened.

1 pound crayfish bodies
1 chopped onion
1 celery stalk, chopped
¼ cup chopped parsley
1 tablespoon black peppercorns
1 tablespoon thyme
8 cups water
2 cups dry white wine

CRAYFISH STOCK

1. In blender or food processor, coarsely chop crayfish bodies. Combine with remaining ingredients in stock pot. Quickly bring to boil; then simmer 1 hour. Strain and cool.

SERVES 3-4

1 small green pepper, chopped
¼ cup butter
4 teaspoons arrowroot
1 cup evaporated milk
⅓ cup water
½ teaspoon salt
½ teaspoon chervil
1 cup sliced celery
2 tablespoons chopped pimiento
1 pound fresh crab meat
2 hard-cooked eggs, coarsely
    chopped
½ cup buttered bread crumbs
½ cup shredded Cheddar cheese
½ cup toasted slivered almonds

Crab Baked with Almonds and Cheese

This recipe comes from Lila Gault's The Northwest Cookbook. *"This variation of crab au gratin comes from a kitchen regularly supplied with fresh crab from a pot set out just beyond the beach in front of the house."*

1. Sauté green pepper in butter melted in large frying pan. Remove from heat and stir in arrowroot.
2. Combine evaporated milk with water. Add to butter, green pepper, and arrowroot. Return all to low heat and cook slowly, stirring constantly until sauce is thick and smooth.
3. Stir in salt, chervil, celery, pimiento, and crab meat.
4. Add eggs.
5. Pour into greased long baking pan. Top with buttered crumbs, shredded cheese, and almonds. Bake in 350° oven for 30 minutes.

SERVES 4

Steamed Fresh Crab in Curry Sauce

2 teaspoons almond oil
2 cloves garlic, minced
1 teaspoon curry powder
    (see p. 233)
1 cup unsalted chicken stock
¼ teaspoon salt (or to taste)
½ teaspoon sugar
1 teaspoon gingerroot, minced
1 chile poblano or chile verde,
    coarsely diced into ¼-inch
    squares or ½ bell pepper
    Cornstarch paste as needed
    (see p. 37)
1 large whole fresh
    Dungeness crab
2 tablespoons dry sherry or
    Shaoxing wine
6 slices gingerroot
2 green onions, roots removed;
    cut into 2-inch shreds
3 sprigs cilantro for garnish

Like the French, Chinese chefs tend to favor a milder curry sauce, as compared to the cooks of India and southeast Asia. Still, even a mild curry like this has its effect on wine. I would accompany this dish with either a dry gewürztraminer or muscat.

1. Heat oil in saucepan to medium-high. Sauté garlic until fragrant. Add curry powder. Reduce heat to medium and stir for about 1 minute (avoid burning curry). Add stock, salt, sugar, and minced gingerroot; bring to boil and cook for 1 minute. Add chile; stir in enough thin cornstarch paste to make a light sauce. As soon as sauce thickens, remove from heat and reserve. This sauce can be made ahead of time and reheated just before serving.
2. Remove top shell from crab in 1 piece (use bottle opener to pry it off). Cut or break off legs; crack legs and claws with side of cleaver. Rinse all parts under running water. Clean out gills and intestines (save crab "butter" for another recipe, or spread on a slice of French bread and eat right away).
3. Reassemble crab on an oval platter. Before putting on the top shell, sprinkle meat with sherry, lay gingerroot slices on top, then put on top shell.
4. Bring water in steamer to rolling boil. Steam crab for about 15 to 20 minutes, depending on size.
5. In the meantime, reheat curry sauce (or keep hot in double boiler).
6. Remove steamed crab from steamer; drain excess water. Lift top shell off crab; pour curry sauce over crab; sprinkle with onion shreds; return top shell. Garnish with cilantro. Serve.

SERVES 4

Fresh Linguine with Crab Shell Sauce and Lemon Thyme

2 live crabs
¼ cup olive oil
   Cayenne to taste
   Freshly ground black pepper
     to taste
4 tablespoons brandy
1½ cups dry white wine
3 carrots, chopped
3 stalks celery, chopped
6 cloves garlic, peeled
1 medium onion, peeled and
   chopped
3 tablespoons tomato paste
6 cups fish stock (water may
   be substituted, but the
   stock adds more flavor)
   Bouquet garni
   Cooked linguine for 4
1 cup whipping cream
   Claws and the 4 largest legs
   of each crab for garnish
2 tablespoons finely chopped
   lemon thyme

Here is another recipe from the most creative of seafood restaurants, the Sooke Harbour House. Drink a well-chilled first-rate chardonnay with this dish.

1. One at a time, place crabs, shell side down, on a sturdy cutting board. Let crab relax, then aim for the center of the crab with a heavy cleaver and give it a decisive whack to split it. Throw away the gills. Remove the top shell and crack it into small pieces with the heavy cleaver. Set aside claws and the 4 largest legs for the garnish. Break body and remaining legs into small pieces with the cleaver. Repeat process with second crab.
2. Heat olive oil in large saucepan. Add all of the broken up crab pieces. Cook for 5 minutes, stirring frequently. Season with cayenne and pepper. Flambé the crab with brandy. Turn to high heat, add wine and cook until wine is reduced by ½. Add vegetables, garlic, and tomato paste; sauté together. Then add stock and bouquet garni (attach the string to the handle of the saucepan for easy removal).
3. Bring to a boil. Gently simmer for 1 to 1½ hours.
4. Remove bouquet garni.
5. In small batches, put crab and vegetable mixture into the bowl of a food processor (steel blade attached) or into a blender and process until pulverized. Strain sauce, first through a coarse strainer, then through a fine one.
6. Return sauce to stove over medium heat and reduce to 2 cups.
7. Place crab legs and claws in a steamer and heat.
8. At the same time, bring the whipping cream to a boil. (Watch it! This is a touchy step. Don't burn it.) Slowly stir in crab shell sauce. As the sauce begins to thicken, add the cooked linguine and toss well until hot.
9. Transfer to serving bowl. Decorate with steamed crab legs and claws. Sprinkle with lemon thyme.

A few sprigs fresh thyme or
   1 teaspoon dried
A few sprigs fresh (French)
   tarragon or *1 teaspoon*
   dried
A few sprigs parsley
A few sprigs fresh basil or
   1 teaspoon dried
2 *bay leaves*
   Stems from a small bunch of
   parsley

BOUQUET GARNI

1. Tie in a small cheesecloth bag with a string.

SERVES 6

1 *shallot, chopped*
1 *pound fresh morel*
   mushrooms (in season),
   chopped
¼ *cup unsalted butter*
1¼ *pounds Dungeness crab*
   meat and legs
¼ *cup capers*
¼ *cup Pernod*
1 *cup heavy cream*
2 *cups Hollandaise Sauce*
   (see p. 19)
6 *sprigs fresh cilantro for*
   garnish

Dungeness Crab Tastevin

I have always enjoyed the meals at Le Tastevin in Seattle,
my favorite French restaurant in the Northwest. Chef Jacques
Boiroux has a nice touch with fresh local seafood. For one of his
dishes Jacques won an award at the San Francisco Crab Cooking
Olympics in March of 1984. Prepared by the hand of the master,
it is sublime. I talked Jacques out of the recipe and discovered that
the dish is surprisingly easy to prepare.

1. Sauté shallot and morels in butter for 2 minutes. When
   butter is hot, add crab, capers, and Pernod; mix
   together.
2. Arrange the crab/mushroom mixture in an oven-proof
   gratin dish or individual gratin dishes.
3. Carefully blend cream into Hollandaise Sauce. Pour over
   crab.
4. Place under broiler until golden brown. Garnish with
   cilantro.

SERVES 6

1/3 cup daikon, sliced lengthwise
      with a potato peeler, then
      cut into thin strips
1 carrot, peeled and sliced
      lengthwise with a potato
      peeler, then cut into thin
      strips
1/2 cup fennel bulb (finocchio),
      cut into thin strips
1/2 green onion (green part
      only), cut into thin strips
2 tablespoons vegetable oil
1 clove garlic, chopped
2 shallots, chopped
1/2 pound fresh crab meat
2 teaspoons nuoc mam
1/2 teaspoon freshly ground
      black pepper
   Steamed rice for 6

Stir-Fried Crab Meat with Fennel

This dish was inspired by a recipe in Bach Ngo's excellent book on Vietnamese cooking. The original calls for cellophane noodles, but I like the fennel better. I also added the strips of daikon, green onion, and carrot. The vegetables made the dish go better with the wine I had at hand, a 1983 Kiona semillon.

1. Place daikon, carrot, fennel, and green onion on a platter; set aside.
2. Heat oil in a frying pan over high heat. Drop in garlic and shallots and fry until golden brown, stirring constantly.
3. Add crab meat and continue to stir fry, still using high heat to remove moisture and dry the crab meat. When the meat is brown, add the vegetables; stir to combine and heat. Add nuoc mam and pepper; stir. Serve immediately with steamed rice.

SERVES 4

1/2 pound fresh cooked crab
      meat, finely chopped
2 ounces pork loin fat, chopped
6 fresh water chestnuts, peeled
      and finely chopped
1 green onion, finely chopped
2 eggs (preferably duck eggs,
      but chicken eggs will do),
      beaten
2 tablespoons dry sherry or
      Shaoxing wine

Deep-Fried Crab Balls with Vinegar Dip

You can serve this dish hot or cold. We prefer the crab balls hot, when their exterior is crisp and the meat hot and moist. They also go better with the vinegar dip when hot. If you prefer to serve them cold or at room temperature, use a Mexican salsa fresca as dip.

1. Using a blender or food processor, mix together crab meat, pork fat, water chestnuts, and green onion. Add eggs, sherry, salt, cornstarch, and gingerroot. Do not puree.
2. In wok, heat oil until bubbles form around a bamboo

2 tablespoons cornstarch
½ teaspoon minced gingerroot
2 cups almond oil
2 tablespoons black
    Chinjiang vinegar
1 tablespoon yellow rice
    vinegar
2 teaspoons light soy sauce
½ teaspoon sugar

chopstick held upright in oil. With a teaspoon, form a small ball of crab mixture. Check 1 crab ball to test cooking temperature; it should brown and cook through in about 5 minutes. Raise heat if necessary. Cook about 6 balls at a time; avoid crowding them. Drain on bamboo strainer or paper towel. Avoid overcooking.

3. Make dip by mixing black vinegar, rice vinegar, soy sauce, and sugar in a shallow bowl; pour onto serving platter and surround with crab balls.

SERVES 4

Creamed Crab Meat

2 tablespoons all-purpose flour
2 tablespoons unsalted butter
1 cup cream
2 hard-cooked eggs (preferably
    duck eggs), chopped
    Salt and freshly ground
    black pepper to taste
1 teaspoon California paprika
    Dash cayenne
1 pound cooked crab meat
1 teaspoon dry sherry or
    Shaoxing wine
    Toast, or toasted lefse
    triangles as needed

Some dishes are timeless. Here is one of them. Try it for lunch with a light chardonnay or pinot blanc. Fill out the meal with freshly baked bread and a tossed green salad.

1. Make a roux by stirring flour into the butter melted over low heat.
2. Add cream, eggs, seasonings; cook until smooth and thick. Do not let boil, or cream may curdle.
3. Add crab meat; cook for a minute or so to heat through, then stir in the sherry.
4. Serve on toast points.

SERVES 4

Crab Louis

1 cup homemade mayonnaise
½ teaspoon nuoc mam
2 tablespoons chile sauce
    (preferably homemade
    salsa)
¼ cup chopped chile poblano
    or chile verde
¼ cup chopped green onions
2 tablespoons chopped green
    olives
    Salt and freshly ground
    black pepper to taste
4 large lettuce leaves
    (preferably radicchio)
1 pound cooked crab meat,
    picked over for fragments
    of shell and cartilage
4 teaspoons salmon caviar,
    drained

This is a true West Coast dish. The recipe spread from San Francisco up and down the coast, and that is about all that is known. It is not even certain at which San Francisco restaurant it originated, though it was most likely the St. Francis (others claim it came out of the now defunct Solari's). In any case, no one seems to have a copy of the original recipe. It may or may not have contained Worcestershire sauce. I like the subtle flavor of nuoc mam better. Just make sure your crab is fresh, or your Crab Louis will not be enjoyable.

1. Combine mayonnaise, nuoc mam, sauce, chile, onions, and olives. Season with salt and pepper.
2. Wash and dry lettuce leaves. Place in serving bowls, 1 per bowl.
3. Mix crab meat with ½ the sauce. Divide crab into 4 equal parts; spoon onto lettuce leaves. Pour remaining sauce onto crab. Top with 1 teaspoon salmon caviar each.

Cold Shredded Vegetables with Crab

SERVES 4

1 teaspoon dry mustard
1 teaspoon sugar
1½ tablespoons light soy sauce
1 teaspoon ginger juice (made by squeezing peeled gingerroot in a garlic press)
1 tablespoon freshly squeezed tomato juice
1½ tablespoons Chinese sesame oil
1½ teaspoons Chinjiang vinegar*
2 wood ear black mushrooms
3 cups warm water
1 tablespoon almond oil
1 egg (preferably a duck egg)
2 large leeks
3 green onions, cut diagonally into ½-inch pieces
2 small zucchini
2 small carrots
1 long daikon
2 long Japanese kyuri cucumbers
2 medium tomatoes
½ cup cooked crab meat

This crisply textured raw vegetable salad, with its tangy mustard-based dressing, is great as a luncheon or picnic salad. Accompany it with a good imported lager beer.

1. In mixing bowl, combine mustard and sugar; gradually add soy sauce and stir to prevent lumps. Stir in ginger juice and tomato juice. Add sesame oil and vinegar; stir this dressing well and set aside.
2. Wash and soak mushrooms in 3 cups warm water for 1 hour.
3. Heat oil in large pan. Beat egg; pour into pan; make into a very thin omelet. Gently fry on both sides. Set aside to cool.
4. Trim leeks, green onions, zucchini, carrots, and daikon. Cut ends off cucumbers, but do not peel. Peel carrots and daikon. Shred vegetables with shredder or cut into fine shreds with Chinese cleaver. Wash tomatoes and cut each into 8 wedges. Shred crab meat with fingers. Thinly slice omelet into strips. Pour boiling water over mushrooms and drain. Cut out hard center and cut floppy "ears" into thin strips.
5. Arrange shredded vegetables in center of serving plate, mounding lightly as you build layers of cucumber, carrot, crab, mushrooms, zucchini, leeks, daikon, green onion, and so on, ending with cucumber shreds. Arrange tomato wedges around outer edge. Working from center of vegetable mound, arrange omelet strips like spokes of a wheel. Add dressing and serve.

* Available in Oriental markets.

SERVES 4

Crab and Vegetables in a Clear Sauce

This recipe calls for very fresh crab (live and lively) and can be used with any firm, mild-flavored vegetables in season. Serve it with a big California chardonnay or with one of the more exotic microbrewery ales.

2 medium turnips, peeled
2 small carrots, peeled and
    sliced into ½-inch pieces
2 cups unsalted chicken stock
½ teaspoon minced fresh
    gingerroot
1 tablespoon Tientsin
    Preserved Vegetable★
1 tablespoon chicken fat
2 tablespoons almond oil
½ cup cooked crab meat
½ cup cooked tiny shrimp
3 fresh asparagus spears, cut
    into ½-inch pieces
½ cup fresh button mushrooms
½ cup straw mushrooms, peeled
8 fresh water chestnuts, peeled
4 green onions cut diagonally
    into ½-inch pieces
1 teaspoon salt (or to taste)
    Pinch sugar
    Cornstarch paste (see p. 37)

1. Use melon baller to cut turnips into large balls. With a Chinese cleaver (or chef knife), cut 4 evenly spaced notches into rim of each carrot slice (do not cut into center core). Carrot slices should look like little flowers.
2. Parboil turnips and carrots in stock until barely tender. Remove from stock and plunge into cold water; drain.
3. Mince together gingerroot and Tientsin Preserved Vegetable; set aside.
4. In small pot over medium heat, render pieces of chicken fat.
5. Pour oil into hot wok. When it begins to smoke, briskly fry crab meat and shrimp for 1 minute. Add asparagus, mushrooms, and water chestnuts, stir frying until they are hot. Add gingerroot mixture, then onions. Stir fry another 30 seconds. Add ½ stock, salt, and sugar; bring to boil. Add turnips, carrots, and remaining stock. Cover and reduce heat; simmer for 5 minutes. Uncover, push ingredients up side of wok out of liquid, and slowly pour in cornstarch paste. Stir liquid to prevent lumps as it thickens. Recombine, then mix in melted chicken fat. Remove to serving platter.

★ Available in Oriental markets.

CRAYFISH

CRAYFISH RAGOUT
CRAYFISH SOUP
CRAYFISH IN APPLE CIDER
STEAMED CRAYFISH IN MUSTARD SAUCE
CRAYFISH NABEMONO
BLOOMING FLOWERS BRING WEALTH
SAUTÉED CRAYFISH
CRAYFISH IN LEMON BUTTER
CRAYFISH-STUFFED CHILES VERDES
STIR-FRIED CRAYFISH CURLS

COMMON NAME
Crayfish
(California to British Columbia)

Crayfish are basically small freshwater lobsters with reddish brown bodies and large red or bluish claws. Ours reach a maximum length of about six inches; exceptionally large individuals may reach eight inches. Only experts can tell the various species apart. But they are all very good to eat, so why worry about the exact scientific name.

DESCRIPTION

Our western crayfish are larger than the crayfish of the Midwest and the South (and tastier). According to seafood authority A. J. McClane, they more closely resemble the European crayfish than crayfish from east of the Rocky Mountains. Not only are they good to eat, but they are also very high in protein and in all sorts of beneficial minerals.

HABITAT

Crayfish are very plentiful in lowland rivers, lakes, and sloughs, and in mountain lakes. They are delicious wherever you can get them.

On the West Coast, crayfish are most common and tastiest in the lowland waters and sloughs of Oregon's Willamette Valley and in the valley rivers of central California. In really cold waters, they may grow very slowly and not develop their full flavor; in waters that are too warm, their meat and flavor become coarse (in which case they must be boiled longer, and with spices). I have tasted crayfish from a great number of rivers, ponds, and lakes up and down the West Coast, and I like them all.

METHODS OF
CATCHING

All you need for catching these freshwater lobsters is a good crayfish (or shrimp) pot and some bait — basically the same kind of equipment, though on a smaller scale, that you use for catching crabs. Check your traps about once a day. This should easily give you enough of the tasty crustaceans for a meal. If your catch is too small, or if you are expecting a crowd, hold the captured crayfish in a burlap sack or in a fine-meshed cage suspended in fresh water until you are ready to use them. Do not hold them in a bucket, unless you have a strong aerator: crayfish need a lot of oxygen, and they will die in no time at all if left to sit in stagnant water. I learned that the hard way, when I lost several dozen crayfish just before an important dinner party.

SEASONS

Year-round in the lowlands of California. May to about October or November in Washington. Crayfish withdraw into holes and wait out cold water in a state of torpor. They are edible in the early spring, but they need a few weeks of warm weather to feed and fatten up.

HOW TO CLEAN

Clean crayfish after cooking. Break or cut them in half where the tail and carapace join; shell the tail as you would a shrimp tail. Save fat and coral from the head as well as any roe.

HOW TO PREPARE

Once crayfish have been removed from the water, they must be cooked as quickly as possible to retain a fresh taste. For the same reason, they should be eaten as quickly as possible once they have been cooked. Cooking crayfish is really very simple. Ignore instructions that call for cooking the delicate crustaceans in a highly spiced *court bouillon* (water flavored with spices, herbs and/or vegetables). Cook the crayfish in just plain boiling water, without adornments. *Never* overcook crayfish. Drop them into water that is at a full rolling boil and cook them only until the shells turn bright red (from one to three minutes), *no* longer or they will become tough. I frequently encounter recipes that call for cooking these tender morsels for twenty minutes or more. Do not do it. You will hopelessly overcook them.

Many recipes use only crayfish tails. But do not throw out the bodies: break them open to scoop out their insides and use these to flavor soups and salads; mix them with plain rice if their taste is too strong for you. Or, grind the entire cephalothorax (the fused head and trunk) *very fine* and use it as a thickener for seafood bisques. Its flavor is quite different from that of the tails, but you will be surprised how tasty this neglected part of the crayfish is. Use only the *very freshest* crayfish for this. As with all crustaceans, the delicate insides spoil quickly.

Traditional recipes for this delectable crustacean keep preparation simple so that none of the delicate flavor is lost. Even the classic *buisson d'écrevisses* or "crayfish bush" consists of nothing more than several dozen crayfish — cooked simply — arranged in a vase with meadow wildflowers.

SERVES 6

2 tablespoons olive oil
2 cups cubed chicken meat
1 large red onion, chopped
2 Italian sausages, pricked
1½ cups uncooked long grain rice
4 cups unsalted chicken stock
   Salt and freshly ground
      black pepper to taste
½ teaspoon California paprika
   to taste
1 pound crayfish tails
1 cup freshly shucked peas

Crayfish Ragout

I like free-for-all seafood stews. They are so versatile: as long as you follow the basic recipe it seems to matter little what goes into the pot. Try a simple country red or white wine with this ragout.

1. Heat oil in large skillet; add chicken and cook for about 5 minutes or until cubes are lightly browned on all sides. Remove from pan to platter.
2. Sauté onion until golden. Remove from pan to chicken platter.
3. Add sausage; sauté until lightly browned. Add rice; sauté until lightly browned. Return chicken and onion to pan. Add stock. Stir well to blend. Season with salt, pepper, and paprika.
4. Simmer, covered, for 30 minutes.
5. Add crayfish and peas. Cover and cook for about 5 minutes, or until crayfish meat has turned opaque.

SERVES 4

12 very large crayfish or
      2–3 dozen smaller ones
1½ quarts boiling water
½ pound ripe tomatoes, chopped
1 medium onion, chopped
1 fresh chile jalapeño, sliced
¼ cup olive oil
1 sprig of epazote
   Salt to taste

Crayfish Soup

We do not know for sure how the mission padres of California cooked their crayfish bounty, but we can assume that they followed recipes well tested by their Mexican compadres. The most simple of these calls for boiling the crustaceans in the meatless Friday pozole. This soup is a lot tastier (though perhaps not as nourishing) when you leave out the pozole's lentils or chick-peas.

1. Drop crayfish into boiling water (salted, if you must). Cook only until shells turn red. Remove immediately. Reserve cooking water for soup broth.
2. Cut crayfish crosswise in half. Set aside tails. Crack open heads. Scrape out fat and coral; mash together in mortar. Crush shell. Return all to broth. Cook for 5 minutes

more. Strain broth through cheesecloth. Discard shell fragments.

3. Fry tomatoes, onion, and pepper in oil over high heat until the liquid has sufficiently evaporated.

4. Add epazote and season with salt. Cook mixture until it thickens a little. Shell tails and cut in half down the center; crack large claws. Add to soup; heat through and serve hot.

SERVES 4–6

Crayfish in Apple Cider

If you want to spice up the crayfish a little bit, try cooking them in apple cider (or applejack). This is one of my all-time favorites. Use a dry cider made from tart apples. Serve with mashed potatoes, crisp-cooked vegetables, and a chilled sauvignon blanc, pinot blanc, or semillon.

1½ pounds cooked, peeled
    crayfish tails, preferably
    same size
3 tablespoons unsalted butter
2 tablespoons shallots, finely
    chopped
2 tablespoons cider
    concentrate* or applejack
¾ cup heavy whipping cream
    Salt and freshly ground
    black pepper to taste

1. Rinse tails under cold running water, remove vein running down back, and pat dry.

2. Melt butter in heavy skillet and add crayfish tails and shallots. Add cider and stir.

3. Remove crayfish tails with slotted spoon. Keep warm.

4. Add cream to skillet and cook over high heat for 1 minute (no longer, sauce may curdle). Add salt and pepper. Return crayfish tails to skillet and cook just long enough to heat through.

* To make concentrate boil 1 cup of dry cider down to 2 tablespoons of concentrate. If you like a stronger flavor, boil down 2 cups. If using a sweet cider, add a little vinegar before boiling down to balance the sugar.

SERVES 2-4

Steamed Crayfish in Mustard Sauce

1½ pounds small crayfish tails
   (the ones that are too
   small to use in other
   dishes)
4 green onions, flattened
   with the side of a cleaver
4 pieces of gingerroot, sliced
   the size of a quarter and
   smashed with the side of
   a cleaver
1 tablespoon Shaoxing wine,
   dry sherry, or sake
½ teaspoon salt
2 tablespoons dry mustard
3 tablespoons warm water
2 tablespoons light soy sauce
1 tablespoon Shaoxing wine,
   dry sherry, or sake
1 tablespoon Chinese sesame
   oil
½ teaspoon sugar
1 tablespoon finely chopped
   fresh coriander for garnish

*Here is one you might want to prepare when friends come for
dinner. The natural sweetness of fresh crayfish is emphasized by
the spicy mustard sauce. This dish may be presented hot or cold.*

1. Cut the crayfish tails along the backs about ½ inch into
   the tails. Remove the black vein; pat tails dry. Mix green
   onions, gingerroot, wine, and salt. Marinate crayfish
   tails in mixture 30 minutes. Discard green onions and
   gingerroot.
2. Mix mustard with water; add soy sauce, wine, oil, and
   sugar. Combine and set aside.
3. Arrange crayfish tails on a heat-proof plate and steam
   for 3 minutes in a steamer. (A Chinese bamboo steamer
   works best.) Remove steamer from heat and let the crayfish stand covered for 30 seconds. Stir the sauce mixture
   until well blended. Pour over crayfish, tossing gently
   to mix well. Sprinkle with coriander and serve.

SERVES 4

Crayfish Nabemono

2 pounds fresh crayfish tails, shelled
4 cups unsalted chicken stock
1 cup sake (a first-rate brand only, the quality of the sake will make a major difference in the taste of the dish)
1 cup water
1 slice gingerroot, peeled
1 zucchini, sliced diagonally
3 carrots, sliced into julienne strips and blanched in boiling water
2 chiles anchos or chiles verdes, cut into cubes
2 green onions, cut diagonally into ½-inch pieces
¼ teaspoon salt to taste
Soy Dipping Sauce
(see p. 80)

This do-it-yourself dish is great for parties and informal get-togethers. Supply your guests with lots of napkins and plenty of well-chilled porter.

1. Rinse crayfish under cool water. Set aside.
2. Combine stock, sake, water, and gingerroot. Bring to a boil. Transfer to a fondue dish. Keep hot.
3. Using chopsticks (or fondue forks), let each diner cook his own crayfish and vegetables in the broth. Serve with Soy Dipping Sauce.

SERVES 4

4 cups chopped broccoli
¾ pound medium-sized
    crayfish tails in shell
½ teaspoon salt
1 tablespoon Shaoxing wine,
    dry sherry, or sake
4 teaspoons cornstarch
½ egg white
¼ teaspoon sugar
1 tablespoon oyster sauce
    Dash freshly ground white
    pepper
½ cup unsalted chicken stock
1 teaspoon sesame oil
1 cup almond or apricot oil
3 green onions, cut into 1-inch
    pieces
1 teaspoon minced gingerroot

Blooming Flowers Bring Wealth

*The Chinese, who are eternal optimists, connect beauty with
wealth. This extends even to food: if you cannot have real flowers
in the house, food made to look like flowers will do just fine.
Drink a dry gewürztraminer, muscat, or well-chilled lager beer
with this dish.*

1. Wash broccoli and shake off excess water. Using a sharp
   paring knife peel off the tough skin from the stems.
   Cut the florets into pieces 2 inches long by ⅔ inch
   wide. Slice stems diagonally into 2- by ½-inch pieces.
2. Shell crayfish tails and remove sand vein. In a bowl, mix
   crayfish with ⅛ teaspoon salt, wine, 2 teaspoons cornstarch, and egg white. Set aside.
3. In a small bowl, combine ¼ teaspoon salt, sugar, oyster
   sauce, pepper, 2 teaspoons cornstarch, 2 teaspoons stock,
   and sesame oil. Mix well and set aside.
4. Set wok over high heat and add 1 tablespoon almond
   oil. When oil is hot, add broccoli and ½ teaspoon salt;
   toss for 1 minute. Add remaining stock and cover pan.
   Cook for 2 minutes over high heat. Remove lid and
   transfer broccoli to a plate.
5. Heat remaining almond oil in wok over high heat
   (about 350°). Add marinated crayfish. Separate crayfish
   in oil (do not let them stick together) and cook for
   1 minute; remove from oil with strainer and drain.
6. Empty all but 1 tablespoon oil from wok; add green
   onion and minced gingerroot; stir green onion and
   gingerroot for 15 seconds, then add shrimp and sauce
   mixture from bowl. As soon as sauce has thickened,
   blend in broccoli. Transfer entire contents of wok
   to warmed serving plate and serve at once.

SERVES 10–12
AS AN APPETIZER;
2–4 AS A MAIN COURSE

Sautéed Crayfish

4–5 cups raw crayfish tails
    in the shell, well washed
3 cups sliced oyster mushrooms
    or fresh shiitake
½ cup sliced green onions
½ cup olive oil or ¼ cup
    clarified butter and ¼ cup
    olive oil
    Salt and freshly ground
    black pepper to taste
2 tablespoons finely chopped
    basil
½ cup chardonnay*

This recipe originated as an impromptu rendition of one of my favorite shellfish. Clean crayfish just as you would prawns by pulling shell segments off the tail meat. Drink a dry northwest riesling with this dish.

1. Sauté crayfish tails, mushrooms, and onions in oil over medium-high heat until crayfish tails begin to change color. Drain off ½ the oil. Sprinkle crayfish tails with salt, pepper, and basil.
2. Add chardonnay; cook over high heat until tails have turned bright red and meat is opaque. Serve hot.

* Be sure to use a wine that is not overoaked—a nice Guenoc or Parducci from California, a Shafer Vineyards from Oregon, or a Chateau Ste. Michelle from Washington will all work nicely.

SERVES 6

Crayfish in Lemon Butter

3 cups crayfish meat, cooked
   and cleaned (pull meat
   from tails and remove
   dark vein running down
   back of tail)
¼ cup fresh unsalted butter
   (do not use margarine,
   it will spoil the taste)
1 tablespoon freshly squeezed
   lemon juice (do not use
   bottled juice)
   Salt and freshly ground
   pepper to taste
2 tablespoons capers
   Baked rice for 6

This is a very delicate dish. It is best when made with absolutely fresh crayfish (they should be alive when you cook them). Accompany the crayfish with a delicate dry riesling, sylvaner or müller-thurgau.

1. Gently sauté crayfish in butter, stirring frequently. Cook until lightly browned. Remove and place on warm platter.
2. Add lemon juice, salt, and pepper to browned butter. Pour over crayfish and garnish with capers. Serve with baked rice.

SERVES 4-6

Crayfish-Stuffed Chiles Verdes

12 crayfish
¼ cup cold-pressed olive oil
    (more or less, as needed)
3 ripe tomatoes, chopped
1 large red onion, chopped
3 cloves garlic, chopped
2 tablespoons chopped parsley
1 tablespoon vinegar
   Freshly ground black pepper
      to taste
   Pickled olives to taste
   Capers as needed
12 large chiles verdes, roasted
      and peeled (see p. 25)
   Tortillas as needed
   Salsa picante

The flavor of cold-pressed olive oil goes very well with crayfish. I like to use a lot of olive oil in my cookery, especially after I learned that recent medical research may prove what some of us have maintained all along: that olive oil is good for your circulatory system because it fights bad cholesterol and encourages good cholesterol. Do keep in mind, however, that olive oil is fattening, and rather nicely so. Enjoy this dish with a rich California sauvignon blanc.

1. Kill crayfish by inserting sharp knife between body and tail; cook in hot olive oil until shells turn red. Remove from skillet and let cool.
2. Break crayfish in half. Shell tails and finely chop meat. Scrape fat and coral from body; add to tail meat, mix well.
3. Fry tomatoes, onion, and garlic in oil until most of the liquid has evaporated; add to crayfish with parsley, vinegar, pepper, olives, and capers; blend well.
4. Stuff chiles with mixture. Bake in moderate oven until heated through. Serve with hot flour tortillas and salsa picante.

SERVES 2-4

1 pound crayfish tails with
    shells, scrubbed
½ gallon cold water
1 teaspoon salt
½ teaspoon baking soda
½ teaspoon freshly ground
    black pepper
3 tablespoons hoisin sauce
2 tablespoons sugar (optional)
1 teaspoon salt (optional)
1 tablespoon rice vinegar
    (if not using sugar, you
    may use a Chinese
    sweetened vinegar)
    Cooking oil as needed
6 green onions, chopped into
    1-inch pieces
1 piece fresh gingerroot the
    size of a hazelnut, minced
1 clove garlic, minced
1 teaspoon cornstarch
½ teaspoon soy sauce

Stir-Fried Crayfish Curls

This is a quick dish to enjoy when you have just pulled up your crayfish trap full of the delectable freshwater lobsters. Accompany it with well-chilled (preferably microbrewery or Mexican) lager beer.

1. Wash crayfish tails in cold water, in which salt and baking soda have been dissolved. Drain and pat dry. Place tails in bowl and sprinkle with pepper.
2. Make sauce of hoisin, sugar, ½ teaspoon salt, and vinegar.
3. Heat a little oil in wok (or heavy frying pan), fry crayfish 1 minute on each side, sprinkle with remaining salt and add green onions, gingerroot, garlic, and sauce.
4. Fry and stir to blend; then add a mixture of cornstarch dissolved in soy sauce and a little water. Braise crayfish for 2 minutes more and serve.

SPINY LOBSTER

SHELLFISH STEW
SPINY LOBSTER STEW
POACHED WHOLE SPINY LOBSTER
STIR-FRIED SPINY LOBSTER
HOT AND SOUR LOBSTER
LANGOSTINO FETTUCINE

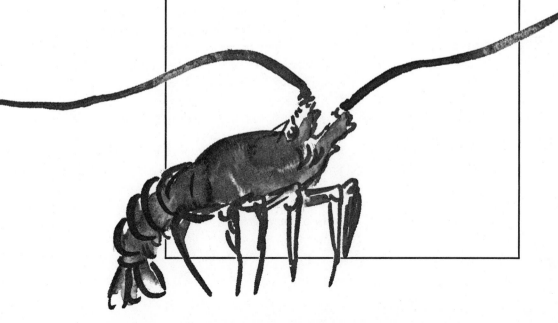

COMMON NAME
Spiny Lobster
(Mexico to southern California)

This large clawless lobsterlike crustacean of southern waters is the only species of spiny lobster found on the West Coast. It weighs an average of one to five pounds. Exceptionally large ones may weigh from seven to fifteen pounds. Females under ten and one-half inches long may not be harvested to assure strong breeding populations. Spiny lobsters are every bit as delicious as their clawed cousins. They should be very fresh and must be alive until just before they are cooked.

DESCRIPTION

Spiny lobsters lack large claws. They rely instead on sharp body spines to discourage predators. They appear formidable, indeed. Looking at these large stalk-eyed marine crustaceans as they multileggedly crawl about, their antennae probing, stirring, and tasting the environment, it is easy to understand why these lobsters are called "bugs" in southern California. They are so tasty, however, that a nickname like that has made no dent in their popularity.

HABITAT

The spiny lobster is a denizen of southern waters — it is rarely found north of Point Conception. It is omnivorous (its eating habits do not affect the flavor of its meat) and occupies more or less the same habitat occupied by the large Dungeness crab, which is common farther north.

METHODS OF CATCHING

Spiny lobsters may be caught in lobster traps, but many are brought up by divers. Very rarely, spiny lobsters get themselves entrapped in tide pools, an opportunity not to be missed by the hungry connoisseur.

AVAILABILITY IN FISH MARKETS AND RESTAURANTS

There is a lot of fresh spiny lobster available in restaurants and seafood markets in southern California. Even greater quantities of spiny lobsters are caught in Baja California. Most lobsters are trapped in Magdalena Bay, a huge saltwater lagoon on the Pacific Coast northwest of La Paz. Spiny lobsters are trapped, killed, and frozen at Magdalena Bay and then transported to market by land or air. Due to government regulations very little — if any — fresh lobster is sold. This means that most, if not all, lobster eaten in Baja California reaches the consumer frozen. Here, as elsewhere, quality varies. But it also means that there is always good frozen lobster available, especially in restaurants.

SEASONS

Year-round. Check local regulations for limits and closures.

HOW TO CLEAN

Cooking preparations are simple. Lay the lobster on its back on a cutting board and sever its spinal cord by driving the sharp point of a knife into the mouth between the bases of the heavy-set antennae. Then split the lobster in half by cutting downward with a heavy knife, tapping the knife blade with a wooden mallet to force it through the hard shell.

Most of the animal is edible. You only need to remove the stomach or "sand sac" from the head, pull out the large intestinal "vein" that runs from the head to the tail, and wash away the spongy gills. Save the green liver or "tomalley."

HOW TO PREPARE

It is essential to cook spiny lobster quickly, or the meat will toughen hopelessly. Brush the lobster halves with olive oil, lay a few laurel leaves onto the meat, and place the lobster on the barbecue grill shell side down. As the lobster cooks, liberally baste the meat with olive oil. In a few minutes the meat will turn opaque; the lobster is done. Spiny lobster may also be boiled like crab and cleaned afterward.

Crack the shells by hand and moisten the pieces of meat with plain olive oil, with olive oil into which lobster's tomalley has been blended, or with a simple lemon butter. Some people eat only the lobster's tail, but that is wasteful: the head (cephalothorax) holds large lumps of excellent meat as well. Eating lobster is a messy affair; wipe the juices from your hands with pieces of bread.

Save the shells of lobsters for thickening bisques. After lengthy roasting in an oven they may be ground and used to add color and flavor to soups or *sauce nantua.*

SERVES 8–10

1 cup coarsely chopped red
    onion
4 cloves garlic, finely minced
¼ cup mission olive oil
1 cup tomato juice (preferably
    homemade)
3½ cups peeled and chopped
    meaty tomatoes (red or
    yellow)
½ cup dry sauvignon blanc or
    semillon
    Salt and freshly ground
    black pepper to taste
1–2 teaspoons fresh basil or
    ¾ teaspoon dried
1–2 teaspoons fresh thyme or
    ¾ teaspoon dried
1–2 teaspoons fresh marjoram or
    ¾ teaspoon dried
2 teaspoons dried oregano
1 bay leaf (California laurel
    or Oregon myrtle)
¼ teaspoon freshly ground
    pepper to taste
12 steamer clams or mussels
1½ pounds spiny lobster meat,
    cut into ½-inch chunks
    (or cooked gooseneck
    barnacle stalks, peeled)
1 cup tiny shrimp, cooked
4 tablespoons finely chopped
    chervil
¼ cup chopped flat Italian
    parsley or cilantro
8–10 teaspoons crème fraîche
5 teaspoons shrimp roe, lobster
    roe, uni (sea urchin roe)
    or golden whitefish caviar
8–10 borage flowers

Shellfish Stew

This is one of those seafood stews in which almost anything goes. I like it with chunks of firm spiny lobster meat, but you can use anything that strikes your fancy. Crab meat, small crabs, and mud shrimp all go well. Let your taste buds and your purse rule the stew.

1. Sauté onion and garlic in oil until onion is tender, but not brown.
2. Add tomato juice, tomatoes, wine, and all seasonings except parsley. Let simmer for 20 to 30 minutes, or until it has thickened to desired consistency. (It should be quite thick.)
3. Add scrubbed steamer clams in shell, cook until clams open. Add lobster chunks; heat through. Just before serving, add shrimp. Sprinkle with parsley and chervil. Place a dollop of crème fraîche in the center of each serving. Top with ½ teaspoon of roe. Lay a borage flower onto each.

SERVES 6

2 pounds freshly cooked spiny
    lobster, in the shell
½ gallon milk
½ cup unsalted butter
    Lobster tomalley and coral
    (liver and gonads) if
    available
¼ teaspoon very finely minced
    fresh thyme
1 cup heavy cream
    Salt and freshly ground
    white pepper to taste
6 toasted lefse triangles
6 teaspoons sturgeon caviar

Spiny Lobster Stew

*Lefse, a traditional Norwegian flat bread, look like tortillas but
are made from potato dough. Lefse go very well with seafood dishes
and, when they are crisp toasted, with caviar. Accompany this stew
with lefse triangles on the side and a nice fino sherry or perhaps
a well-chilled aquavit.*

1. Remove meat from lobster body. Cut into small cubes.
   Save tomalley and coral.
2. Place milk in saucepan or double boiler. Break up
   lobster shells into small pieces. Stir pieces into milk.
   Scald milk. Strain out lobster shell.
3. In heavy saucepan, sauté lobster pieces lightly in
   butter. Add milk and stir in lobster, coral, and thyme.
   Blend until integrated. Bring back to a boil. Immediately
   remove from heat. Stir in cream. Season with salt and
   pepper.
4. Float 1 toasted lefse triangle atop each serving. Drop
   1 teaspoon of sturgeon caviar onto each lefse triangle.

Poached Whole Spiny Lobster

Salted water (1 tablespoon
salt per quart of water)
as needed
1–1½ pounds lobster per serving
or 1 small lobster per
person

Serve this lobster with lemon butter or lemon wedges and a dry sauvignon blanc. It makes for great picnic fare when cold, just be sure to keep it chilled; or remove the meat and use it in recipes calling for cooked lobster.

1. Bring water to a rolling boil.
2. Cut off the lobster's long antennae close to head. Grasp lobster behind head and plunge it head first into boiling water (watch those spines). Cover pot. Bring water to a simmer; do not boil. After water reaches simmer, begin timing and cook 7 to 10 minutes per pound of lobster. Do not overcook. Test for doneness by pulling off a leg to check body meat. (If the meat separates from the shell and is white/opaque, the lobster is done.) Remove lobster from pot and drain.
3. To serve split lobster down the back with a heavy knife (use a wooden mallet, if necessary, to break shell). Remove and discard both the black intestinal (sand) vein running down the tail and the small stomach (sand sac) located near the eyes. Save the green liver and the coral-colored roe (female lobsters only). Both are delicious and may be ground with butter and made into a dipping sauce, or they may be added to sauces.

SERVES 4–6

2 pounds spiny lobster tails
2 cloves garlic, minced
1 teaspoon fermented black
    beans, washed and drained
2 tablespoons almond oil
¼ pound finely chopped
    (or ground) pork
1½ cups hot water
1½ tablespoons Chinese soy
    sauce
2 green onions, cut into slivers
2 tablespoons cornstarch
3 tablespoons Shaoxing wine
    or dry sherry
3 tablespoons cool water
    Chopped cilantro leaves for
    garnish
3 tablespoons salmon caviar,
    drained for garnish
    Cooked rice for 6

Stir-Fried Spiny Lobster

I first had this dish in the small Sacramento River town of Locke, a weather-beaten wooden place between the river and the Mokelumne sloughs, inhabited by artists and retiring Chinese. I brought the lobster and a friend provided the green onion and cilantro from his garden. We bought the other ingredients at the local grocery. Accompany it with a good Chinese lager beer.

1. Pry lobster from shell with an oyster knife (or other stiff-bladed knife). Cut on the bias into ⅛-inch-thick slices.
2. Mince together garlic and black beans.
3. Heat wok until it smokes. Add oil. When oil is hot, add garlic/bean mixture. Cook and stir for a few seconds. Add pork and cook about 10 minutes, stirring to break up meat. Stir in hot water and soy sauce. Add lobster slices and cook for 2 minutes. Add green onion.
4. Reduce heat. Mix cornstarch, wine, and cool water and stir into wok. Cook over low heat for 30 seconds, stirring constantly. Sauce should not be too heavy. Spoon sauce into center of platter. Arrange lobster slices in center in an appealing pattern. Sprinkle with cilantro. Loosely scatter salmon caviar over the arrangement. Serve with bowls of steaming rice.

SERVES 4

8 *Chinese dried black mushrooms*
1 *pound cooked spiny lobster tail*
¼ *cup Chinese sesame oil*
2 *tablespoons almond or apricot oil*
2–3 *dried red Oriental peppers*
1 *teaspoon ground Sichuan peppers*
2–3 *red Fresno chiles, seeded and shredded*
½ *cup red wine vinegar*
¼ *cup sugar*
   Salt to taste
1 *Japanese* kyuri *cucumber, thinly sliced or 1 small English cucumber*

Hot and Sour Lobster

When done right, this dish is composed of very attractive color contrasts: white lobster meat, red chile, cucumber, and black mushrooms. It may be prepared in advance and served cold as an appetizer. Accompany it with a fino sherry or well-chilled sparkling wine.

1. Soak black mushrooms in hot water until spongy. Remove tough stems and shred.
2. Cut lobster meat into ¼-inch-thick slices; refrigerate.
3. Heat sesame oil and almond oil in wok. Add dried Oriental peppers and Sichuan pepper. Cook, stirring constantly, until peppers turn black. Remove wok from heat. Strain out seasoned oil. Wipe wok clean.
4. Return seasoned oil to wok. Combine vinegar and sugar. Add to wok. Add salt. Heat to boiling and let bubble, stirring until the sugar is entirely dissolved. Let mixture cool. Pour into a measuring cup. Set aside.
5. Decoratively arrange cucumber slices on serving platter. Place lobster meat in overlapping slices in center of platter, on top of cucumber. Sprinkle shredded black mushrooms and red chiles around edge of platter. Cover and chill in refrigerator until ready to serve.
6. Just before serving, pour sauce over dish. Toss at table.

SERVES 4

½ pound cooked spiny lobster
   meat
2 cloves garlic, minced
2 shallots, minced
½ cup butter or olive oil
½ cup grated dry Sonoma Jack
   cheese or Parmesan
¾ cup whipping cream
½ teaspoon freshly ground
   white pepper to taste
¾ pound fettucine, cooked and
   drained
½ teaspoon salt to taste
1 tablespoon fresh cilantro,
   chopped

Langostino Fettucine

Other cooked seafood, clams, shrimps, barnacle meat, scallops, or the tiny pea crabs may be used instead of the lobster. Accompany this dish with a California pinot blanc or sauvignon blanc.

1. Cut spiny lobster meat into bite-sized pieces.
2. Sauté garlic and shallots in butter until translucent. Stir in cheese, cream, lobster, and pepper. Cook while stirring until thoroughly heated. Add to hot fettucine; toss lightly. Salt to taste. Sprinkle with cilantro.

SHRIMPS

SHRIMP COCKTAIL

GARLIC SHRIMP

MARINATED SHRIMP

SHRIMP SOUP

SHRIMP AND WATER CHESTNUT SOUP

PUDDLE DUCKS

ASPARAGUS SHRIMP SALAD WITH PICKLED RED GINGER

SHRIMP-STUFFED SANDWICHES

RISO CON GAMBERI

SHRIMP WITH LOBSTER SAUCE

CAMARÓNES SAN FELIPE EN CERVEZA

MUD SHRIMP IN BEER

SHRIMP IN BLANC DE NOIR

MUD SHRIMP IN GARLIC BUTTER

COLD SPICY SHRIMP

HOT SHRIMP

SHRIMP CURRY

COLD SHRIMP CURRY WITH NECTARINES

SPICY STEAMED SHRIMP

SICHUAN SHRIMP DUMPLINGS

BARBECUED MEXICAN SHRIMP

BROILED SHRIMP WITH GARLIC BUTTER

CHICKEN LIVERS WITH FRESH SHRIMP
AND CHINESE BROCCOLI

SHRIMP WITH SNOW PEAS

TWICE-COOKED SHRIMP

PAN-FRIED SHRIMP

BAKED PRAWNS

STUFFED PRAWNS I

STUFFED PRAWNS II

PRAWN SAUTÉ

BROILED PRAWNS

SMOKED PRAWNS

CAMARÓNES EN FRIO

COMMON NAME
Shrimps and Prawns
(Gulf of California to Alaska)

These are small crustaceans with a large head and a large, vertically flattened tail. Some species have large claws. There is no difference in common American usage between the terms "shrimp" and "prawn." Large shrimp are commonly called prawns. Like crayfish, but unlike such other crustaceans as crabs or lobsters, little distinction is made in the species of the shrimp harvested commercially. The only classification is based on size (so many per pound). Many fishmongers would be hard put to say what species they are selling at a given time, much less tell where they come from.

Tide Pool Shrimp
(California to Alaska)

Green grass shrimp, small brokenback shrimp, long-fingered shrimp, pistol shrimp, and all sorts of other small hard-to-see transparent shrimp may be found hiding under rocks or trapped in tide pools or shallow embayments. They can be caught with a fine-meshed net. Small ones can be cooked and eaten whole.

Mud Shrimp and
Burrowing Ghost Shrimp
(Baja California to
British Columbia)

Mud shrimps and burrowing ghost shrimps dig extensive, multibranched, labyrinthine burrows, marked on the outside by small, conical mounds. Burrowing ghost shrimps grow to an average length of about four inches but may reach six. They are of a pale pink or pastel color. They burrow at the mid- to upper-tide levels where the sand is heavily intermixed with mud. The somewhat smaller mud shrimp often occurs in the same habitat, but it may live in very muddy tide-flats, and likes it deeper down in the tidal zone. The farther down in the tidal zone these crustaceans live, by the way, the larger they will be. Both can be prepared like other shrimp.

DESCRIPTION

Live shrimp have translucent, almost gelatinous flesh, which turns firm and white on cooking, and their see-through shells are marked with colorful lines, streaks, and dots (most of which disappear on cooking when the shells turn more or less red).

To the amateur and commercial shrimper all shrimp look more or less the same, and all taste good. Commercial classification of shrimp is more by size than by species. The size rules are not uniform, but generally, any count up to fifteen per pound are considered as "jumbo" prawns; a count of sixteen to twenty are "extra large," twenty-one to thirty per pound are "large," thirty-one to forty per pound are "medium." In the small sizes almost anything goes.

Adding to the jumble of species and sizes is the fact that a store or restaurant selling local shrimp today may sell exotic ones tomorrow, and vice versa. It all depends on availability. Currently, shrimp from some fifty countries are imported into the United States.

A few things should be kept in mind:

Two pounds of uncooked shrimp in the shell will yield slightly more than one pound of meat after shelling and deveining.

Gray, that is, clear-colored shrimp taste better than reddish ones, for the pinkness comes from iodine stored in their bodies. Very pink shrimp can have an almost medicinal taste; good for goiter, not for your palate.

Iodine taste in shrimp has nothing to do with spoilage; learn to distinguish between the smell of iodine and that of ammonia — if it smells of ammonia, it has gone bad.

Shrimp caught in the brackish water of bays and estuaries have very little iodine since the food they eat comes from water with a low level of salinity and minerals. The so-called river shrimp contain almost no iodine and are thus consistently sweet. Unfortunately, they do not commonly occur in commercially viable quantities.

HABITAT

Shrimp live on the bottom of saltwater bays, estuaries, inlets, and in the open ocean. They wander back and forth in great congregations as they feed. Most of our shrimp occur in both very deep and quite shallow water. At times, they may even be trapped in tide pools. There are a number of other small shrimp that regularly occur in bays, eelgrass beds, and tide pools. All of these are edible and may be caught with a dip net.

Tiny pink shrimp are caught commercially from Alaska as far south as Oregon. Spot shrimp are caught off the California coast, particularly off Monterey. Large sidestripe, coonstripe, brokenback, and smooth shrimp are caught in Northwest waters.

The most commonly sought after shrimp in the Sea of Cortez are the blue shrimp, *camarón azul*; the white shrimp, *camarón blanco*; and the brown shrimp, *camarón café*. These shrimp have made up the bulk of the "jumbo prawns" served in California restaurants.

METHODS OF CATCHING

The most fun way of getting fresh shrimp is to catch your own, with either a trap, a dip net, or by hand (if you are quick enough). Shrimp are quite easy to catch in traps; so easy that strict seasons have been imposed by fisheries departments.

The best candidate for dipnetting is the blacktail shrimp, which occurs in both Puget Sound and San Francisco Bay but is most commonly encountered in shallow water in the south of its range (though it actually prefers deeper water). It is one of the commercial deep-water shrimps of California, but it does enter bays with sandy bottoms. If you are quick and in the right spot at the right time, you can catch your limit. There are also several free-swimming species in shallow water over mud flats. Try dipnetting these as well. If they are large enough and catchable, eat 'em.

Intertidal or subtidal shrimp can sometimes be shaken from kelp (it is possible to trap them on bunches of kelp suspended in the water). Collect them with a fine-meshed fishnet or butterfly net. You may have to look very carefully: subtidal shrimp often take on the coloration of the seaweed to which they cling.

Dig cautiously when looking for mud or ghost shrimp; their fragile tunnels may cave in before the animals are found. A stealthy approach and a quick stroke with a long shovel blade a foot or so below the surface often spell success. These crustaceans are quite flabby and helpless once they lie exposed on the beach (beware the ghost shrimp's large claws). You are very likely to come up with a goodly mess of these burrowing shrimp as you dig for clams. Prepare them like other crustaceans. Commercial operators catch burrowing shrimp with the aid of pumps which use pressure to force the shrimp from their burrows.

AVAILABILITY IN FISH MARKETS AND RESTAURANTS

Shrimp and prawns are perhaps our most widely available seafoods. It is difficult to find a market not carrying at least frozen (or canned) shrimp. Finding good fresh shrimp is not always easy. Your chances of getting perfectly fresh shrimp are best in large metropolitan areas where the turnover is high, and in proximity to shrimping ports.

When buying fresh shrimp, make sure they are translucent, without spots and blotches. On frozen shrimp, look especially for black splotches on the shell. These are signs of spoilage. One black spot on the shell, and you can be certain that the meat is spoiled. Your greatest ally is your nose. Smell the shrimp before you buy them. If there is even a whiff of ammonia, reject them. One bad shrimp can impart its off-flavors to the whole batch.

You can enjoy fresh prawns, of a high enough quality to be served raw, in Vancouver, mostly because British Columbia fishermen catch excellent prawns in Howe Sound (just a half an hour north of Vancouver by car). Here, there also is a sufficient number of Japanese fishermen who know how to properly handle such delicacies.

SEASONS

Year-round for commercial shrimp. Check local fisheries regulations for recreational shrimping seasons, which vary widely from year to year, depending on the size of shrimp stocks.

HOW TO CLEAN

Break or cut the tail off the carapace (head). Place your left thumb on the underside of the tail at head end. Place your right thumb on the underside of the tail at the tail end. Grasp the tail firmly between your fingers. Twist thumbs in opposite directions. The shell should twist off. If the shell is too sturdy, make a shallow lengthwise incision along the underside or back to ease removal.

HOW TO PREPARE

Start with first-rate fresh shrimp. If you cannot find good fresh shrimp, you are much better off cooking with first-rate frozen shrimp. There is nothing wrong with good frozen shrimp—if it has been handled and defrosted properly. It is just that really fresh shrimp is so much better.

Do not overcook shrimp. If the shrimp are boiled, they should be cooked only until the shells change color—two or three minutes at the most. Or you can steam them for ten to fifteen minutes. Grilling shrimp takes about six to eight minutes, depending on size; stir frying raw shrimp takes only a couple of minutes. Just remember that fresh shrimp can be eaten raw, so there is no sense in boiling them to death.

After cooking shrimp, use the heads to flavor seafood stews, or grind them up to thicken bisques. Just inside the carapace, you can often find a patélike mass, the coral (gonads), which is very good to eat spread on crackers, toast, or sushi. I prefer it on sushi, because the taste and texture of the paté go better with the acidulated sushi rice than with crunchy crackers or baked bread. If your shrimp come laden with eggs, prepare them the same way.

SERVES 4 AS AN APPETIZER

2 cups tiny pink shrimp
¼ cup cold-pressed, virgin olive oil
¼ cup freshly squeezed lemon juice
¼ cup finely diced red onion
1 teaspoon minced fresh basil or ½ teaspoon dried
½ teaspoon crushed dried oregano
½ cup finely cubed celery or chopped lovage
Shredded lettuce
Salmon caviar or golden whitefish caviar for garnish

Shrimp Cocktail

Here is my version of the great American classic. Serve it with a well-chilled pleasantly dry white wine as an appetizer.

1. Combine shrimp, oil, lemon juice, onion, basil, and oregano. Toss and mix well.
2. Cover and marinate in refrigerator for a minimum of 4 to 6 hours, but preferably overnight.
3. Drain. Save marinade. Toss celery with shrimp mixture.
4. Place lettuce in 4 cocktail cups. Top with shrimp mixture. Garnish with whitefish or salmon caviar. Serve marinade as dressing.

2 tablespoons almond or
    apricot oil
5–6 medium cloves garlic,
    coarsely chopped
1 pound mud or ghost
    shrimp, shelled, deveined,
    and cut into ¾-inch pieces
2 green onions, cut diagonally
    into ½-inch pieces
4 teaspoons cornstarch
2 tablespoons light soy sauce
2 tablespoons dry sherry or
    sake

Garlic Shrimp

Here is a variation on the theme of garlic and mud shrimp. The trick is to cook them very quickly in your hot wok. Serve them as an appetizer accompanied by fino sherry or warmed sake.

1. Heat wok until it begins to smoke. Add oil and heat. When oil is hot, add garlic and stir fry for a few seconds. Do not brown.
2. Add mud shrimp. Stir fry for about 30 seconds. Stir in green onion. Toss.
3. Combine cornstarch, soy sauce, and wine. Add to wok. Toss and stir until sauce thickens and clears. Do not overcook. Serve at once.

1 pound tiny pink shrimp
¼ cup olive oil
¼ cup white wine vinegar
1 tablespoon finely chopped
    chives (or to taste)
2 teaspoons hot Dijon or
    Düsseldorf-style mustard*
3 medium cloves garlic,
    crushed (or to taste)
2 tablespoons chopped
    chiles jalapeños or
    serranos (or to taste)
½ teaspoon California paprika
    (or to taste)
¼ teaspoon salt (or to taste)
    Chopped cilantro or parsley
    for garnish

Marinated Shrimp

Despite the addition of hot mustard to the ingredients, this is a surprisingly delicate appetizer. It goes well with chardonnay or with very dry riesling.

1. Cook shrimp. Drain and cool.
2. Combine oil, vinegar, chives, mustard, garlic, chiles, and paprika. Add cooled shrimp. Toss well.
3. Cover and refrigerate at least 3 hours, tossing occasionally.
4. To serve, drain, sprinkle lightly with salt (optional) and cilantro or parsley.

* Or use the delightful mustard made by the sisters at Our Lady of the Rock convent on Shaw Island, Washington.

SERVES 4

Shrimp Soup

This is a good soup for a light lunch, or it may be served as an appetizer course at dinner. Enjoy it with a well-chilled sauvignon blanc or semillon.

1 red onion, diced
1 potato, diced
2 tablespoons olive oil
2 tablespoons all-purpose flour
1 cup water
2 cups milk
½ cup cream
2½ cups tiny pink shrimp
¾ cup shelled fresh peas
2 tablespoons minced chervil
   or parsley
   Salt and freshly ground
   black pepper to taste
4 teaspoons thick crème fraîche
4 teaspoons salmon caviar for
   garnish

1. Sauté onion and potato in olive oil for about 5 minutes, or until onion is tender. Stir in flour; cook 1 minute. Gradually stir in water (be sure no lumps form). Simmer gently until potatoes are barely tender.
2. Stir in milk and heat. Add cream.
3. Add shrimp, peas, chervil, salt, and pepper. Heat thoroughly, but do not bring to a boil (or cream may curdle).
4. Pour into 4 serving bowls. Place 1 dollop of crème fraîche in center of each serving. Top with salmon caviar.

SERVES 4

Shrimp and Water Chestnut Soup

Simple soups like this play an important role in Chinese cuisine, because they refresh the palate without neutralizing food flavors. Like Japanese miso shiru, *they are served throughout the meal as a beverage.*

5 cups light, clear unsalted
   chicken stock
2 green onions, minced
8 fresh water chestnuts, peeled
   and thinly sliced
¼ pound small pink shrimp,
   cooked, shelled, and
   deveined
1 teaspoon salt (or to taste)

1. Bring stock to boil. Add onions and water chestnuts. Add shrimp and salt. Return soup to boil. Cook only long enough to reheat shrimp. Serve hot.

SERVES 4

4 Nami black mushrooms*
3 egg whites (preferably
    duck eggs)
6 cups rich unsalted
    chicken stock
1 teaspoon minced
    gingerroot
2 green onions, cut into
    very fine slivers
½ cup green peas, shelled
12 small shrimp, cooked and
    shelled
1 tablespoon light soy sauce
    Salt and freshly ground
    white pepper to taste
2 tablespoons Shaoxing wine
    or dry sherry

Puddle Ducks

This soup looks complicated at first sight, but it is really quite easy to prepare. Do not worry much about the shape of the ducklings, anything goes! Serve it as an appetizer soup, accompanied with dry sherry.

1. Wash and soak mushrooms in warm water for 1 hour. Slice mushrooms into thin strips; set aside.
2. Make the ducklings within an hour or less of serving. Have a steamer ready. Eggs and mixing bowl should be at room temperature. Beat egg whites, starting slowly, then progressively faster after eggs begin to foam. Beat to soft peaks. (If whites are too stiff, they tend to break apart during the shaping process.)
3. From egg whites, form 2 ducklings per serving. Use a tablespoon to form duckling body. Flatten egg white in spoon; turn over onto steaming plate. To make body, add blob of egg white for neck and head, another piece for tail. Use a toothpick to carefully shape head and tail. (Once you have practiced, this is a lot easier to do than it sounds.)
4. Steam 1 duckling as a test. Steaming should take 30 to 60 seconds to set surface of egg. (You may dab on yellow food coloring or egg yolk to mark bill and eyes of ducklings.)
5. Thirty minutes before serving, heat stock to just below a boil; add mushrooms, gingerroot, green onions, and peas.
6. Five minutes before serving, add shrimp and soy sauce. Season with salt and pepper. Pour soup into 4 warm serving bowls. Stir a little Shaoxing wine into each bowl. Float 2 ducklings on each bowl of soup. Serve.

* Available in Oriental markets.

Asparagus Shrimp Salad with Pickled Red Ginger

SERVES 4

This versatile salad may be served while the asparagus is still warm, or it can be chilled. Salads made with steamed vegetables are typical Chinese fare. Serve this salad with a dry sherry or country white or red wine. Or try it with a good porter.

1 tablespoon light soy sauce
¼ teaspoon ginger juice (made by pressing peeled gingerroot in garlic press)
Pinch sugar
1 tablespoon sesame oil
12 medium-sized asparagus stalks, cooked and sliced into 2-inch pieces
1 cup tiny shrimp, cooked
4 pieces pickled red ginger, thinly sliced and cut into thin slivers
2 teaspoons finely chopped cilantro
2 teaspoons golden whitefish caviar for garnish

1. Mix soy sauce, ginger juice, sugar, and oil in small bowl.
2. Toss together asparagus, shrimp, and ginger.
3. Divide onto 4 plates. Pour dressing over asparagus, add shrimp, and let it permeate the salad. Serve at room temperature. Sprinkle with cilantro and top with whitefish caviar.

Shrimp-Stuffed Sandwiches

SERVES 4

Add a touch of gourmet to your picnic lunch. This sandwich is light and refreshing. I enjoy it with a chilled lager beer or room temperature ale.

4 pieces pita bread
Cold-pressed, virgin olive oil as needed
4–6 lettuce leaves (preferably radicchio)
2 tomatoes, peeled, seeded, and diced
½ cup diced fresh shiitake or oyster mushrooms
½ cup alfalfa sprouts
⅓ cup pickled ripe olives*
1 small ripe avocado, peeled and diced
1½ cups tiny pink shrimp
Lemon or lime wedges

1. Slit open pita bread along one side. Brush insides with olive oil.
2. Toss remaining ingredients. Stuff ¼ of filling into each pocket. Serve with lemon or lime wedges.

Riso con Gamberi
(SHRIMP WITH RICE)

SERVES 6

2 pounds medium shrimp
¼ cup vegetable oil
1 small onion, chopped
4 small cloves garlic, finely
    chopped
1 tablespoon chopped fresh
    parsley
1 small tomato, chopped or
    1 teaspoon tomato paste
3¾ cups water
1½ cups rice
    Salt and freshly ground
        black pepper to taste
    Parmesan cheese to taste

This recipe comes from a small Italian deli that cooks up some marvelous dishes with fresh local ingredients. The Mona Lisa Deli started out in San Diego and moved to — of all places — Bellingham, Washington. This dish calls for a nice barbera or light zinfandel.

1. Wash shrimp, leaving shell intact. Set aside in a colander.
2. Pour oil into medium saucepan. Add onion and garlic; cook until onion and garlic turn a light golden color. Add parsley. Reduce heat to a light simmer and add tomato. Stir until onion and garlic are mixed well with tomato.
3. In the meantime, cook shrimp in water about 3 to 5 minutes. When they turn pink, remove with a slotted spoon. Peel shrimp; set aside. Return shells to water and boil for another 5 minutes.
4. Strain water; return to high heat. Cook for about 10 minutes.
5. Add rice, salt, and pepper. When mixture returns to boil, reduce heat and simmer over very low heat for 20 minutes more. Adjust seasoning. Add more salt to taste. Coarsely chop shrimp; stir into rice mixture and heat through. Remove from heat. Let stand for 1 minute. Grate Parmesan over top. Serve hot.

SERVES 4

Shrimp with Lobster Sauce

16 medium-sized raw shrimp, unshelled
2 tablespoons almond oil for stir frying
  Lobster Sauce

Contrary to popular belief, Chinese lobster sauce (unlike French lobster sauce) does not contain lobster. It is a delicious egg and pork sauce traditionally served over lobster or shrimp. Also contrary to popular belief, almond oil (like apricot oil, but unlike hazelnut or walnut oil) has much less flavor and smell than peanut oil, and it interferes little with the flavors of the food. It is excellent for stir frying.

1. Shell, devein, and butterfly shrimp. To butterfly, slice along the back about ¾ of the way through the flesh with a small paring knife. Spread shrimp open and remove sand vein. Cover and set into a cool place, but do not refrigerate.
2. Heat wok to medium-high. When hot, slowly pour in oil around side of pan to heat evenly.
3. Drop shrimp into wok all at once and toss. Keep tossing shrimp so they cook uniformly. As soon as they begin to curl, remove them to a serving dish.
4. Make Lobster Sauce.
5. Add shrimp to hot Lobster Sauce. Cook briefly. Mix and serve.

2 teaspoons salted black beans
1 large clove garlic, minced
1 large egg (preferably a duck egg)
1 tablespoon water
2 teaspoons almond oil
½ pound coarsely ground pork (not sausage)
½ cup unsalted chicken stock
2 green onions, sliced in ½-inch pieces
½ tablespoon light soy sauce
1 teaspoon sugar
  Cornstarch paste (see p. 37)

LOBSTER SAUCE

1. Soak beans for 10 minutes; rinse and drain. Mash with garlic. In small bowl, beat egg with water. Set aside.
2. Heat wok to medium heat; add oil. When oil is hot (not smoking) add garlic/bean mixture. Briskly stir until aroma of beans and garlic is strong, but do not overcook. Add pork in small pieces; stir fry until cooked, about 4 minutes. Add stock, green onions, soy sauce, and sugar, stirring as mixture comes to a boil. Thicken mixture with cornstarch paste to create a light creamlike sauce (not too thick). Slowly stir in beaten egg, creating swirls of egg in the sauce. Cook briefly.

Camarónes San Felipe en Cerveza
(SHRIMP IN BEER, SAN FELIPE-STYLE)

SERVES 6-8

Beer as needed to cover
    shrimp
1 cup salt water (We used
    water from the bay
    without ill effect.)
1 bay leaf or 10–12 juniper
    berries or to taste (We
    used a sprig of wild sage.)
6 garlic cloves, lightly crushed
1 large dried chile mulato or
    several small chiles
    piquins to taste (or level
    of endurance)
1 lemon or lime, sliced
    Quartered lemons as needed
5-6 pounds freshly caught
    shrimp, unpeeled,
    heads on
    Spicy Dipping Sauce
    Salsa Chile Verde
    (see p. 228)

½ onion, finely minced
2 very ripe tomatoes, peeled
    and mashed
2 pods red chile pulp
¼ teaspoon salt
3 tablespoons vinegar
1 tablespoon olive oil

This recipe is very simple and can be reproduced on any beach. But you might want to prepare the dipping sauce ahead of time and bring it to the party. Or, for a special treat, if you can find fresh green chiles in the fishing port wilderness (this is easier done in Baja than along the Oregon coast), serve the shrimp with a chile verde dipping sauce. If you can take the heat, serve them with plenty of well-chilled Mexican beer. Otherwise, serve a simple white country wine.

1. Combine first 6 ingredients in medium stock pot and bring to a rolling boil. Drop live shrimp into pot. Cook until shrimp turn bright red; take pot off heat and let shrimp rest in beer 5 minutes.
2. Shell freshly cooked shrimp and eat them as they are or dip them into Spicy Dipping Sauce or Salsa Chile Verde. Suck fat from heads. Garnish with quartered lemons.

SPICY DIPPING SAUCE

1. Blend all ingredients until smooth.

1 pound tomatillos
6 chiles serranos, chopped
  Water
4 tablespoons vegetable oil
¼ medium onion
  Salt to taste

SALSA CHILE VERDE

1. Remove papery husks from tomatillos, chop coarsely, place in pot with just enough water to cook them; add chiles, and simmer until tender. Carefully strain off excess water (if any). Mash and blend until smooth.
2. Heat oil in heavy skillet; add onion and fry until translucent (do not brown). Add tomatillo/chile mixture and cook over high heat until sauce has reduced a little; about 5 minutes. Be careful not to burn. When sauce seems thick enough, add salt and serve.

SERVES 4–6

5–6 pounds unpeeled mud
       shrimp, left to soak in
       clean salt water for 1 hour
    Clean salt water to cook
       shrimp as needed
    Beer to cover
 1 cup clean salt water
 1 bay leaf (plucked from a
       California laurel tree) or
       a few berries from a
       bluff-side juniper
 6 lightly crushed cloves garlic
       (you may use wild garlic
       or wild onion bulbs)
12 black peppercorns
 1 piece fresh gingerroot the
       size of a hazelnut, crushed

Mud Shrimp in Beer

You are on the beach. You have just dug a mess of clams and as an incidental catch, you have a bucketful of mud and ghost shrimp. While the clams hang in a burlap sack suspended in salt water to clean, you might as well cook up the shrimp. Since beer and clamming go so well together, cook your shrimp in beer.

1. Quickly immerse shrimp in boiling salt water to kill. Remove as soon as they turn red.
2. Combine remaining ingredients except shrimp; bring to a boil. Add shrimp; cook 5 minutes. Turn off heat and let shrimp sit in beer for 5 minutes. Serve.

SERVES 4–6

1 pound large shrimp, cleaned,
    deveined, split down the
    center, but left in shell
Chateau Ste. Michelle
    blanc de noir to cover
    shrimp
½ cup freshly grated Parmesan
    cheese
½ cup bread crumbs
1 tablespoon minced fresh
    parsley
1 tablespoon minced garlic
2 tablespoons Chateau Ste.
    Michelle blanc de noir
1 tablespoon olive oil

Shrimp in Blanc de Noir

The blanc de noir called for in this recipe is a delightfully crisp Washington State sparkling wine from the Chateau Ste. Michelle winery. It does marvelous things to the shrimp.

1. Cover shrimp with blanc de noir and marinate in refrigerator for at least 2 hours.
2. Combine cheese, bread crumbs, parsley, and garlic.
3. Beat together blanc de noir and olive oil.
4. Remove shrimp from marinade and drain. Brush with wine/oil mixture. Sprinkle heavily with cheese/crumb mixture.
5. Broil 6 to 8 inches from heat for 5 to 8 minutes, depending on size. Serve immediately.

SERVES 4–6

½ cup unsalted butter
½ cup very fruity olive oil
2 tablespoons finely chopped
    garlic (or more, to taste)
1 red chile California
    (colorado), seeded and cut
    into thin strips or 2 red
    chiles Fresnos (select chile
    according to your tolerance
    of hot spices)
Salt and freshly ground
    black pepper to taste
1½ pounds mud shrimp or
    ghost shrimp, shelled and
    deveined
½ cup finely minced fresh
    cilantro

Mud Shrimp in Garlic Butter

If you ever get a batch of mud shrimp that taste too much of the substrate, cook them in lots of garlic. That will fix them. Accompany this dish with lots of French bread for sopping up the juices and a weedy sauvignon blanc.

1. Heat 1 tablespoon butter and 2 tablespoons olive oil in large heavy skillet. Add garlic and sauté until soft.
2. Add chile, salt, pepper, and shrimp. Sauté until shrimp turn opaque.
3. Add remaining butter and olive oil; heat through.
4. Place shrimp on warm plates; spoon butter over; sprinkle with cilantro. Serve hot.

SERVES 6

3 cups unsalted chicken stock
    (1½ cups if only shrimp
    tails are used)
½ cup red wine vinegar
1 red onion, cut into small
    cubes
2 teaspoons dry mustard
1 teaspoon Tabasco sauce or
    other bottled hot sauce
1 teaspoon chopped fresh thyme
    Salt and freshly ground
    black pepper to taste
3 pounds whole fresh raw
    shrimp or 1½ pounds
    tails
1 ripe avocado, sliced
    Freshly squeezed lime juice
    as needed
6 teaspoons thick crème fraîche
3 teaspoons finely chopped
    cilantro
    Salmon caviar for garnish

Cold Spicy Shrimp

Despite the spiciness of this dish, the delicate taste of the shrimp comes through very well. So, be sure to use only the best and freshest shrimp you can find. A simple dry country wine without pretensions, a sylvaner perhaps or a grenache rosé, should go well with the spice.

1. Pour stock into saucepan. Stir in vinegar, onion, mustard, Tabasco, thyme, salt, and pepper (be sure mustard does not form lumps).
2. Bring to a boil. Add shrimp. Simmer until shrimp turn pink.
3. Remove from heat; allow to cool, then chill. Drain off liquids.
4. Arrange on 6 plates with avocado slices. Sprinkle lime juice over avocado slices. Place 1 dollop of thick crème fraîche on each mound of shrimp; sprinkle with chopped cilantro; top with salmon caviar.

SERVES 4

4 tablespoons olive oil
2 tablespoons all-purpose flour
2 red onions, finely chopped
1 chile poblano or chile verde,
    peeled, seeded, and finely
    chopped (see p. 25)
2 ripe tomatoes, peeled, seeded,
    and coarsely chopped
2 teaspoons chopped fresh
    cilantro
  Salt and freshly ground
    black pepper to taste
  Pinch cayenne
  Dash nuoc mam or light soy
    sauce
1½ pounds raw shrimp, shelled
2 teaspoons chopped fresh dill
    weed

Hot Shrimp

This dish calls for a hot summer day, impeccably fresh shrimp, and lots of chilled beer. It is just perfect for patio parties.

1. Heat oil in saucepan over low heat. Stir in flour; cook for 1 to 2 minutes. Do not brown.
2. Add onions, chile, tomatoes, cilantro, salt, pepper, cayenne, and nuoc mam. Simmer for a couple of minutes, until onion is tender.
3. Add shrimp. Cover and simmer for 10 minutes or until shrimp have turned pink.
4. Serve hot. Garnish with dill.

SERVES 6

¼ cup butter
¼ cup all-purpose flour
1 teaspoon curry powder (or to
    taste)
½ teaspoon chopped fresh dill
    weed
  Salt and freshly ground
    white pepper to taste
2 cups milk
3 cups cooked shrimp
1¼ cups cubed apple
  Cooked rice for 6
  Chopped cilantro for garnish

Shrimp Curry

This traditional shrimp dish is excellent when served over California rice. Accompany it with a stout porter or a hearty ale. Or try a rough red country wine.

1. Melt butter in saucepan. Stir in flour and seasonings (be sure no lumps form). Gradually stir in milk. Cook over low heat and stir until mixture thickens. Do not brown.
2. Add shrimp and apple; heat through. Spoon over rice. Sprinkle with chopped cilantro.

SERVES 4

Cold Shrimp Curry with Nectarines

Butter lettuce, escarole, or
other frilly lettuce as
needed
4 medium-ripe nectarines
½ pound medium prawns,
cooked and shelled
3–4 large ripe purple plums
(such as Santa Rosa)
½ ripe pineapple cut into short
spears (discard core)
2 tablespoons thinly sliced
green onion
Curry Dressing

*Shrimp are still plentiful in the waters of the Sea of Cortez,
though they have declined in numbers since 1940, when Ed Ricketts
described the ocean waters at Guaymas as "soupy with shrimp."
Shrimp from the Gulf of California generally reach southern
California markets quite fresh. This subtropical dish makes good
use of them. It is superb when made with the delectable pineapples
grown at San José del Cabo or Todos Santos. Accompany it with
a muscat de frontignan, a muscat alexandria, or an off-dry
gewürztraminer.*

1. Line large platter or shallow bowl with lettuce leaves.
2. Cut 2 nectarines into large chunks and combine with
   prawns and plums in large bowl.
3. Mound mixture in center of platter.
4. Cut remaining 2 nectarines into slices. Arrange nectarine
   slices and pineapple spears around edge of prawn mixture.
   Sprinkle with green onion.
5. Serve Curry Dressing on the side.

1 cup sour cream (do not use a
sour cream substitute)
2 tablespoons freshly squeezed
lemon juice
2 teaspoons sugar
1¼ teaspoons curry powder of
your choice (see below)
¼ teaspoon salt (or to taste)

CURRY DRESSING

1. Combine ingredients and blend well.

MAKES ABOUT
3 TABLESPOONS

1 tablespoon peeled cardamom
   seeds
1 stick cinnamon, crushed*
1 teaspoon whole cloves
1 teaspoon whole black
   Tellicherry peppercorns
½ teaspoon freshly grated
   nutmeg
1 teaspoon cumin seeds
1 teaspoon ground turmeric
¼ teaspoon mace

CURRY POWDER

1. Combine all ingredients in a spice grinder, pepper mill
   (set to fine), or a small, clean coffee grinder; grind
   thoroughly.

* Use real cinnamon bark; not the cassia bark commonly
sold as cinnamon in the United States.

Note: May be kept for weeks if tightly sealed and
refrigerated.

SERVES 4

1 bay leaf (California laurel
   or Oregon myrtle)
1 teaspoon juniper berries
4 medium cloves garlic,
   quartered
1 chile serrano, coarsely
   chopped
  Salt and freshly ground
   black pepper to taste
½ cup dry white wine
½ cup water
1½ pounds raw shrimp in the
   shell
½ cup melted unsalted butter
   (or more, to taste)

Spicy Steamed Shrimp

*I like to prepare this dish with very hot peppers. If your palate
is tender, use a milder pepper, such as a poblano or an Anaheim.
Accompany the shrimp with a well-chilled lager beer.*

1. Combine first 8 ingredients in a saucepan. Cover and
   simmer for 10 minutes.
2. Add shrimp, cover, and simmer 5 minutes longer.
   Remove shrimp. Strain stock and save for use in other
   shrimp recipes.
3. Serve shrimp in the shell with melted butter for
   dipping (the shells are edible, but you may remove
   them just before dipping the shrimp).

Sichuan Shrimp Dumplings

1 slice (about ⅛ inch thick)
  fresh gingerroot, peeled
  and finely chopped
2 medium green onions,
  trimmed and finely
  minced
½ cup fresh water chestnuts,
  finely chopped
1 large egg white
1 pound medium raw shrimp,
  shelled, deveined, and
  finely chopped
1 tablespoon cornstarch
1 tablespoon light soy sauce
½ teaspoon salt
¼ teaspoon sugar
½ teaspoon chili oil (optional)
1 package (14 ounces) round
  won ton skins (or square
  ones with edges trimmed)
2 tablespoons sesame seeds
  Green Onion and Cilantro
  Sauce

This most delectable recipe comes from the kitchens of Janet Trefethen, Hugh Carpenter, and Sarah Scott at Trefethen Vineyards in the Napa Valley. If you like more spice and fire, add more gingerroot and some red chile flakes. Accompany this dish with a Trefethen white riesling or with any dry riesling of your choice.

1. Place gingerroot, green onions, and water chestnuts in a 2-quart mixing bowl and set aside.
2. In a small bowl beat the egg white until just foamy. In blender or food processor, process ½ the shrimp with ½ the egg white until the shrimp is finely chopped. Add to the water chestnut mixture. Repeat with the remaining shrimp and egg white. Place all of the shrimp and water chestnut mixture in blender or food processor bowl. Add cornstarch, soy sauce, salt, sugar, and chili oil (if used) and mix. Set aside.
3. Line a baking sheet with wax paper and dust the paper lightly with cornstarch. Set aside.
4. Place a heaping teaspoon of the shrimp mixture in the center of a won ton skin. With your finger, moisten the edge of the skin with water and fold it in half. Pinch the edges firmly together to seal them. Then moisten the ends and pinch them together. Place on the prepared baking sheet and cover with a dry kitchen towel. Continue with the remaining shrimp mixture and won ton skins. The dumplings may be refrigerated for up to 1 hour. Or you may freeze them on the baking sheet, transfer them to a double plastic bag, seal well, and freeze for up to 1 month. Do not thaw before cooking.
5. In a small skillet over medium-high heat, toast the sesame seeds (stirring all the while) until they turn a light golden color, about 30 seconds. Remove to a small bowl and set aside.
6. A few minutes before serving, bring 4 or 5 quarts of lightly salted water to a boil over high heat. Add the fresh or frozen dumplings and stir once. After all dump-

lings have floated to the surface (1 to 1½ minutes), cook for 30 seconds more. Drain and transfer to a 3-quart bowl. Pour the Green Onion and Cilantro Sauce over the top and toss until the dumplings are coated. Slide the dumplings onto a serving dish, sprinkle with the toasted sesame seeds and serve immediately.

3 tablespoons fresh cilantro
    leaves
1 slice (about ⅛ inch thick)
    peeled, fresh gingerroot
1 large green onion, trimmed
    and cut into 1-inch pieces
1 tablespoon light soy sauce
1 tablespoon sesame oil
2 tablespoons red wine vinegar
1 teaspoon chili oil
½ teaspoon sugar

GREEN ONION AND CILANTRO SAUCE

1. Mince gingerroot and green onion with Chinese cleaver, or process in a blender or food processor. Mix with remaining ingredients.

SERVES 4

24 large fresh Gulf of
    California shrimp tails,
    shelled and deveined
    (tails intact)
½ cup lemon/lime juice (well
    mixed)
¾ cup olive oil
4 medium cloves garlic,
    chopped
3 chiles jalapeños or serranos,
    chopped
    Minced cilantro as needed

Barbecued Mexican Shrimp

This dish is best consumed on the beach, when the shrimp are fresh off the boat. It should be served with salsa fresca, lots of fresh tortillas, and a good Mexican lager beer.

1. Mix citrus juice, ½ cup olive oil, garlic, and chiles in a shallow glass or ceramic dish. Add shrimp and marinate overnight.
2. Remove shrimp from marinade; dip in remaining olive oil. Thread onto skewers and barbecue over hot mesquite coals for about 5 minutes on each side. Sprinkle with cilantro and serve hot.

SERVES 6

Broiled Shrimp with Garlic Butter

2 pounds large fresh shrimp
   in shells
8 tablespoons unsalted butter
½ cup olive oil
1 tablespoon freshly squeezed
   lemon juice
¼ cup finely chopped shallots
1 tablespoon finely chopped
   garlic
   Salt and freshly ground
   black pepper to taste
4 tablespoons finely chopped
   fresh cilantro or
   flat-leaved parsley
   Lemon wedges for garnish

Garlic and shrimp have a surprising affinity for each other. Besides, I like lots of garlic in just about any dish. Accompany these shrimp with a big California sauvignon blanc.

1. Shell shrimp, but do not remove last shell segment and tail fins. Cut through back of shrimp to lift out sand vein. Rinse shrimp quickly under cold running water; pat dry with paper towels.
2. Preheat broiler to its highest temperature.
3. In a shallow flameproof baking dish just large enough to hold shrimp in 1 layer, melt butter over low heat (do not let it brown); stir in oil, lemon juice, shallots, garlic, salt, and pepper. Add shrimp, turning them in the butter/oil mixture until they are covered on both sides.
4. Place pan under broiler, 3 to 4 inches from source of heat. Broil shrimp for 5 minutes, then turn them over and broil them for another 5 minutes (or more) until they are lightly browned. (Do not burn them, if they turn dark too fast, set them farther away from broiler unit.) Do not overcook shrimp, they taste better undercooked than overcooked.
5. Transfer shrimp to heated serving platter, pour pan juices over them, and sprinkle them with cilantro.
6. Garnish with lemon wedges and serve.

SERVES 2 HUNGRY PICNICKERS

½ pound chicken livers
2 tablespoons cornstarch
2 tablespoons almond or
   apricot oil
1 green onion, finely chopped
1 cup fresh mushrooms
   (2 cupped handfuls of
   wild mushrooms), chopped
   Salt and freshly ground
   black pepper to taste
¾ pound Chinese broccoli
   (or regular broccoli)
¼ pound shrimp, peeled
1 teaspoon cornstarch
1 tablespoon soy sauce
   Cold water as needed

Chicken Livers with Fresh Shrimp and Chinese Broccoli

To get an idea of how Chinese fishermen in China Camp and other fishing villages along San Francisco Bay ate in the nineteenth century, bring your picnic wok with you and some food (try to buy shrimp locally) and cook up this simple country dish. You may use commercial mushrooms or fresh shiitake, or you can pick wild mushrooms in season in the Marin woods (look for old cottonwood logs covered with oyster mushrooms). This dish may be eaten straight from the pan with chopsticks. You will need, besides your wok, cooking tools and a source of heat.

1. Wash and dry chicken livers, then thinly slice; toss in 2 tablespoons cornstarch. (This may be done ahead of time.)
2. Heat oil in wok; fry livers for 1 minute. Add onion, mushrooms, salt, and pepper. Mix well. Cook broccoli in boiling water 3 to 5 minutes or until just tender. Drain and add to wok. (You may precook broccoli for picnic.) Add shrimp.
3. Blend 1 teaspoon cornstarch, soy sauce, and water to a smooth paste. Add to wok. Bring to boil, stirring until slightly thickened. Cook for 3 minutes. Take wok off the fire and dig in.

SERVES 4

⅓ pound fresh snow peas
¼ pound fresh medium-sized
    shrimp
½ cup unsalted chicken stock
2 teaspoons light soy sauce
1 teaspoon dry sherry or
    Shaoxing rice wine
Salt and freshly ground
    black pepper to taste
Pinch sugar
3 teaspoons almond oil
½ cup unpeeled straw
    mushrooms
1 large clove garlic, minced
2 teaspoons gingerroot, cut
    into slivers
8 large fresh water chestnuts,
    peeled and thinly sliced
    crosswise
2 green onions, sliced on the
    bias into 2-inch pieces
Cornstarch paste as needed
    (see p. 37)

Shrimp with Snow Peas

This dish has proved to be very popular with our friends. There is something very appealing about the combination of shrimp and crunchy snow peas. We serve it with well-chilled Japanese lager beer.

1. Soak snow peas in cold water for 2 hours to crisp; then break off ends.
2. Soak shrimp in salted cold water for 1 hour. Shell shrimp, keeping tail intact. Deeply slit shrimp along back (do not cut all the way through). Devein and spread shrimp almost flat.
3. In small bowl, mix stock, soy sauce, sherry, sugar, salt, and pepper.
4. Swirl oil into very hot wok. When oil begins to smoke, add shrimp and stir fry about 20 seconds, or until they curl. Using a slotted spoon, remove shrimp to serving platter.
5. Stir fry mushrooms for 30 seconds; add garlic and gingerroot; stir fry another 30 seconds. Add snow peas, green onions, and water chestnuts; briskly stir fry for 1 minute. Add stock mixture; bring to boil, tossing until snow peas are bright green. Push ingredients up the sides of the wok out of liquid. Slowly pour in cornstarch paste to slightly thicken sauce. Push all ingredients, including shrimp, back down into the sauce. Toss briefly. Serve immediately.

SERVES 2-4

1 pound medium-sized shrimp
1 teaspoon Shaoxing rice wine
   or dry sherry
2½ teaspoons coarse salt
½ teaspoon whole Sichuan
   peppercorns
1 tablespoon minced garlic
1 teaspoon minced gingerroot
¼ teaspoon crushed dried chiles
¼ cup minced green onions
4 cups vegetable oil
2 teaspoons cornstarch
   Shrimp roe or salmon caviar
   (drained) for garnish

Twice-Cooked Shrimp

This is one of those dishes that seems to be made for Chinese Shaoxing rice wine. But it also goes very well with warmed sake. Be careful how much you imbibe: the stuff is powerful.

1. Cut open shrimp to last tail segment, cutting ⅔ into flesh with a sharp knife (or scissors). Remove the sand vein. Rinse shrimp in cold running water; pat dry with paper towels. Place in bowl and sprinkle with wine and 2 teaspoons salt. Mix well; let stand for 10 minutes.
2. Place peppercorns in small, heavy skillet. Shake over medium heat until they just begin to smoke. Remove from skillet and coarsely grind in a mortar.
3. Mix garlic, gingerroot, peppercorns, chiles, and ⅛ cup green onion in a small bowl; set aside.
4. Heat the oil in wok to 375°.
5. Sprinkle cornstarch over shrimp and mix well.
6. Cook shrimp in hot oil in 2 batches; 2 minutes each. Check oil for proper temperature before cooking second batch. Remove each batch with strainer to paper towels to drain; then transfer to platter.
7. Remove all but 2 tablespoons oil from wok. Reheat oil and add the bowl of minced ingredients; stir fry for 10 seconds. Add shrimp. Toss for 30 seconds, then add ½ teaspoon salt. Stir for another 15 seconds. Remove contents of wok to platter; sprinkle with remaining green onions. Garnish with shrimp roe or salmon caviar.

SERVES 4

Pan-Fried Shrimp

4 tablespoons olive oil
    (or more, as needed)
4–6 cloves garlic, crushed
    (or to taste)
1 pound large raw shrimp
1 beaten egg
½ cup dry white wine
    (preferably sauvignon
    blanc)
    Salt and freshly ground
    black pepper to taste
    Chopped parsley or chives
    for garnish
    Shrimp roe or salmon caviar
    for garnish

Many of the shrimp we get fresh from fishermen up north are laden with an additional treat: delectable roe. The roe may be cooked with the shrimp and stripped from the legs afterwards, or it may be salted and eaten raw. Accompany this dish with a rich California fumé blanc.

1. In large, heavy skillet, heat olive oil and garlic until hot.
2. Dip shrimp in egg and drop into skillet, one by one. Sauté quickly over high heat 2 to 4 minutes.
3. Remove shrimp and garlic. Add wine, salt, and pepper to pan. Reduce by ½. Pour over shrimp. Garnish with parsley and shrimp roe.

SERVES 4

Baked Prawns

16 large prawns
¼ cup freshly squeezed lemon
    juice
¼ cup freshly squeezed lime
    juice
1 cup unsalted butter
½ cup chopped chervil or
    parsley
6–8 cloves garlic, minced
1 cup bread crumbs
2 teaspoons California paprika
    Shrimp roe or salmon caviar
    for garnish
    Lemon wedges for garnish

Caviar turns this into a very festive dish for special dinners. The shrimp roe comes free with the shrimp, and salmon caviar is inexpensive. If you ever want to have caviar with lunch, here is your chance. Serve the prawns with sparkling wine or a first-class chardonnay for dinner and chilled lager beer for lunch.

1. Shell prawns. Make deep lengthwise incision in tails, but do not cut all the way through. Remove sand veins.
2. Spread and flatten tails. Place prawns — 4 to a serving — in individual buttered ramekins. Sprinkle each serving with ½ the lemon juice and ½ the lime juice.
3. Combine butter, ¼ cup chervil, and garlic in bowl. Blend well. Place a little of the mixture on each prawn.
4. Combine crumbs, remaining chervil, and paprika and

place a little of this mixture on each prawn as well.

5. Bake in 400° oven for 15 minutes. Garnish with shrimp roe and lemon wedges.

SERVES 4

Stuffed Prawns I

With a little imagination, these stuffed prawns take on the drama of a miniature Viking fleet, stuffed higher than the gunwales with tasty loot. I serve it with a simple chardonnay, pinot blanc, or sauvignon blanc.

16 jumbo prawns
¾ cup butter
¼ cup chopped parsley
2 cups bread crumbs
½ cup crab meat
½ cup dry sherry
½ cup chopped almonds
   Shrimp roe or salmon caviar
      (drained) for garnish
   Melted butter for dipping
   Lemon wedges for garnish

1. Shell prawns leaving final tail segment. Cut tails down back and open to make a cavity. Remove sand veins. Place prawns in buttered baking dish.
2. Melt butter. Combine remaining ingredients. Mound stuffing in cavity of each shrimp.
3. Bake in preheated 350° oven for about 20 minutes, or until tails curl up and shrimp meat is bright white.
4. Garnish each prawn with a dab of shrimp roe or salmon caviar. Serve with melted butter and lemon wedges.

SERVES 6-8

1 pound prawns (about
    14–16), peeled (leave on
    final tail segment)
1 cup chopped oyster
    mushrooms
⅓ cup chopped shallots
1 clove garlic, minced
1 teaspoon nuoc mam, oyster
    sauce, or light soy sauce
¼ cup butter
1½ cups soft bread crumbs
1 tablespoon chopped red
    (ripe) chile or bell pepper
    Melted butter
    Chopped parsley or cilantro
    for garnish

Stuffed Prawns II

This is a spicier version of stuffed shrimp. You can make it as hot as you want to. Drink well-chilled lager beer with it.

1. In large skillet cook mushrooms, shallots, garlic, and nuoc mam in butter until shallots and garlic are soft. Remove from heat; stir in bread crumbs and chile. Set aside.
2. Cut a slit along underside of each shrimp; do not cut all the way through. Remove sand vein. Brush entire shrimp with melted butter. Mound stuffing in cavity of each shrimp.
3. Place shrimp in buttered shallow baking dish. Bake in preheated 400° oven 10 to 12 minutes or until heated through. Garnish with parsley or cilantro.

SERVES 4

4 tablespoons butter
¼ cup dry sherry
⅛ teaspoon powdered ginger
1 medium clove garlic, mashed
32 medium prawns, peeled and
    cleaned
    Juice of ½ lemon

Prawn Sauté

This recipe comes from Lila Gault's The Northwest Cookbook. *"This simple prawn sauté is an elegant main dish. It should be served with long-grain or brown rice."*

1. In large saucepan melt butter and allow it to brown lightly.
2. Add sherry, ginger, and garlic. Stir and simmer for 2 minutes, then add prawns.
3. Simmer over medium heat for 4 minutes more, then sprinkle with lemon juice. Stir twice and remove from heat.

SERVES 4

16 raw prawns, peeled and
   deveined
½ cup light soy sauce
½ cup dry sherry or
   Shaoxing wine
1 tablespoon freshly squeezed
   lemon juice
4 cloves garlic, crushed
¼ cup almond oil

Broiled Prawns

This tasty dish is very easy to prepare and, once the prawns have marinated, it cooks up quickly. Serve it with fino sherry as an appetizer course, or with porter or ale for lunch.

1. Rinse prawns and blot dry with paper towels.
2. Mix remaining ingredients well; pour over prawns. Refrigerate, tightly covered, 4 to 6 hours.
3. Remove prawns from marinade. Drain.
4. Broil about 3 minutes on each side. Serve hot.

SERVES 4–6

24 large prawns, cooked
   and peeled
   Muscat de frontignan or
   other sweet wine to cover
1 tablespoon coarse noniodized
   salt (or to taste)
   Apple or alder wood chips

Smoked Prawns

I use a Little Chief Smoker made by Luhr Jensen in Hood River, Oregon, a great little smoker.

1. Place prawns in flat glass or ceramic dish; cover with wine and sprinkle with salt. Marinate for a minimum of 2 hours (or overnight).
2. Rinse under cold water and lay onto oiled smoker racks for drying. Air dry for about 40 minutes.
3. Smoke for 2 hours, using 2 pans of apple or alder wood chips.

SERVES 4–6

2 pounds very fresh prawns
4 large onions
3 cloves garlic
1 cup olive oil
  Salt and freshly ground
    black pepper to taste
  Lime and/or lemon juice
    as needed
3 large ripe tomatoes
½ cup vinegar
  Dijon mustard to taste*
½–1 cup pickled chiles jalapeños,
    sliced (reserve pickling
    juice)

Camarónes en Frio
(COLD SPICY PRAWNS)

This dish comes from the people who discovered San Francisco Bay and established its first towns, the Mexicans. It is delicious and, if kept cool, it makes for great picnic fare. If you plan to take this dish on a picnic, make all parts ahead of time, place them in tightly covered plastic containers, but do not assemble them until you are ready to eat. Make sure to bring lots to drink, the more jalapeños you use, the more liquids you will need. Choose your drink according to your taste and with care. Beer, or any other carbonated beverage, will not go well with chiles, unless you can stand the extra heat generated by the bubbles. An inexpensive red wine will do fine; freshly squeezed fruit juices are best. And be sure to bring lots of freshly made flour tortillas.

1. Thoroughly scrub prawns. Pat dry. Chop 1 onion with garlic cloves; cook in ½ cup oil over medium heat until translucent. Add prawns to onions and garlic; fry until opaque. Remove from heat; toss. Tightly cover and set in refrigerator to chill for 2 hours.
2. Slice remaining onions, sprinkle with salt and cover with lime juice. Cover and marinate for 2 hours in refrigerator.
3. Slice tomatoes. Sprinkle with salt and pepper. Cover and chill.
4. To make dressing, blend remaining oil with the vinegar; season to taste with mustard, juice from chiles, salt, and pepper.
6. Arrange chilled prawns on platter. Decorate with marinated onion, seasoned tomato, and jalapeños.
7. Pour dressing over prawns. Serve.

* Or use the excellent mustard made by the sisters of Our Lady of the Rock convent on Shaw Island, Washington.

BARNACLES

BARNACLE COCKTAIL
BAKED BARNACLE
GIANT BARNACLE
MARINATED GOOSENECK BARNACLES AND CHEESE
SAUTÉED GIANT ACORN BARNACLES

COMMON NAME
Acorn Barnacle
(several very similar species occur
all along the West Coast)

This grayish white barnacle has a squat to very pointed shell (one-half inch across and larger). Only large acorn barnacles of at least an inch or more across should be collected; the smaller ones are not worth the labor. This is a very tasty barnacle.

Giant Barnacle
(northern Baja California to
southeastern Alaska)

The giant barnacle is our largest barnacle (two and one-half to three inches high and longer across) and one of the largest in the world. Look for it in subtidal areas. It makes very good eating.

Gooseneck Barnacle
(central Baja California to
Bering Strait)
DESCRIPTION

This stalked barnacle is common on the outer coast (to six inches across). The stalks are superb to eat.

Acorn barnacles have dense "volcano-shaped" grayish white shells. The shells are rough with sharp projections and form dense clusters and mats on intertidal rocks, often on the high tide line.

The giant barnacle is the largest of our West Coast barnacles. It prefers deep water, below the low-tide level and is best collected by divers. Giant barnacles regularly grow to two or three inches in diameter. When crowded, they may reach four or five inches in height. A beaklike protuberance projects above the edge of the shell. The giant barnacle is one of the nicest seafoods in the Pacific Northwest, because it has the consistency of crab meat and scallop and a crablike flavor. Others have described its taste as unique, but with similarities to both crab and scallops.

The gooseneck barnacle lacks the hard external shell of the acorn barnacle. It is sheathed in a tough, leathery skin, which is studded with a white, tightly fitted calcareous plate on the pointed crown of its body. This barnacle protects itself from aggression by living in such tight clusters on exposed rocks that only the armed crowns rise above the communal mass. Gooseneck barnacles living on the margins of these colonies are very short; those in the middle may have stalks up to half a foot long.

HABITAT

Barnacles are found in tidal and subtidal areas. They

attach themselves to rocks, pilings, and holdfasts of kelp. They cluster together in dense colonies. When crowded, barnacle shells grow into long, somewhat fragile tubes, which may stretch to a length of six inches. These tubes often can be broken off in large chunks (new barnacles will quickly colonize the bared spot). Where barnacles assume a squat form, they are almost impossible to remove from rocks. They should be collected from a soft support instead, such as wooden pilings or the holdfasts of kelp.

METHODS OF CATCHING

Acorn barnacles can be pried off the rocks with the tip of a stout knife (or a screwdriver blade).

Giant barnacles can be removed from rocks with a very stout knife blade or crowbar. They are easily pried off soft supports such as kelp or wood.

Gooseneck barnacles are easy to gather—just separate them from their support by inserting a sharp knife between the stalk and the rock they sit on. They should be cooked as soon as possible after they are collected.

AVAILABILITY IN FISH MARKETS AND RESTAURANTS

Only occasionally can barnacles be found in Oriental seafood markets. They occur even more rarely in restaurants. Only one restaurant, the Sooke Harbour House on southern Vancouver Island, British Columbia, regularly serves barnacles.

SEASONS

Barnacles can be collected year-round.

HOW TO CLEAN

Barnacle shells may be cracked with a hammer, and the meat removed by hand or with a crab pick.

HOW TO PREPARE

Barnacles are rather peculiar animals, because they have no hearts or circulatory systems. But they do have tasty pink depressor muscles inside their shells, and they carry delicately flavored roe in their mantle cavities. These are the edible parts; the rest of the animal is discarded. But this still leaves you with a lot of meat from a four- or five-inch barnacle.

Small barnacles may be boiled or steamed whole; the meat can be pushed out with a skewer or toothpick after it is done. Crack the shell of acorn barnacle before or after cooking with a hammer or fish club. Remove the meat (and roe) and rinse well.

Once you have obtained your giant barnacle it is really quite easy to prepare. Boil whole giant barnacle in salted water for fifteen to twenty minutes. Pry off beak/trapdoor. (Caution: the beak is very sharp.) Remove and discard legs and upper body. Carefully spoon out roe. Rinse the shell and pull out pink muscle meat.

Or, break the shell with a hammer and remove meat. Separate the roe from the flesh. Rinse the meat. Cook the meat for a few seconds in butter over medium heat.

Gooseneck barnacles are an easily prepared gourmet treat. Wash them carefully in fresh water (you may have to vigorously scrub the base of the stalk with a small, stiff-bristled brush). Cook, then peel off the stalk.

SERVES 6–8 AS
AN APPETIZER

Barnacle Cocktail

1 lemon
1 lime
2 cups cooked barnacle meat
½ cup chile salsa
¼ cup chopped fresh cilantro
Barnacle roe (if available)
Crackers, small toast rounds,
 or toasted lefse triangles
 as needed

This quickly made appetizer may be prepared with either a red or green salsa. If you have access to fresh Mexican limónes, use these instead of the lemon and lime. Accompany this dish with Margaritas.

1. Squeeze juice from lemon and lime over barnacle meat. Toss well. Let marinate in a cool spot for 15 minutes. Drain off excess citrus juice.
2. Spoon salsa over barnacle meat. Toss. Sprinkle with cilantro. Garnish with roe. Serve with crackers, small toast rounds, or toasted lefse triangles.

SERVES 4

2 cups cooked gooseneck
    barnacle meat
4 slices dry (day old) French
    bread, crusts removed
¼ cup unsalted butter, melted
½ teaspoon mace
    Salt and freshly ground
    black pepper to taste
2 cups Béchamel Sauce
    (see p. 18)

Baked Barnacle

*Accompany this dish with a hearty microbrewery porter
or a simple pink wine.*

1. Grind barnacle meat into paste in food processor
   or blender.
2. Soak bread slices in water, squeeze dry, and crumble
   into barnacle paste.
3. Mix butter with mace, salt, and pepper; blend into
   barnacle mixture.
4. Place in a buttered pan and bake in a preheated 275°
   oven for 15 minutes or until lightly browned on top.
5. Serve hot with Béchamel Sauce.

2–4 giant barnacles per serving
    Salt to taste
    Water for boiling

Giant Barnacle

*The giant barnacle is the largest West Coast barnacle. It grows to
two or three inches in diameter and four to five inches in height.
The pink depressor muscles inside the shell and the delicately
flavored roe carried inside the mantle cavity are the edible parts.
I think the meat tastes somewhat like a cross between scallop and
crab, though really with a flavor of its own. Accompany this
simple dish with a Guenoc sauvignon blanc or a dry northwest
riesling and eat it without condiments to get the full pleasure
of their delicate flavor.*

1. Boil barnacles for 15 to 20 minutes in salted water.
2. Remove from water; cool. Pull off beak/trapdoor;
   remove legs and upper body. Carefully spoon out roe
   (eat on toast or use as garnish). Rinse shell and remove
   pink muscle meat. Bon appetit!

SERVES 6

1 pound Teleme Jack, Pleasant
   Valley gouda, or other
   mild white cheese
1 pound cooked (pink stalk)
   gooseneck barnacle meat
1 cup olive oil
¼ cup red wine vinegar
½ teaspoon sweet basil
¼ teaspoon dry mustard
¼ teaspoon oregano
¼ teaspoon salt to taste
1 teaspoon minced garlic
   Pinch freshly ground black
   pepper to taste
1 Japanese kyuri cucumber,
   thinly sliced or English
   cucumber

Marinated Gooseneck Barnacles and Cheese

This is a country dish that calls for plenty of freshly baked bread, raw, fresh vegetables for munching, and a dry white country wine (sauvignon blanc, pinot blanc, semillon, or a blended wine) or a first-rate lager beer.

1. Cut cheese into thin slices about 2 inches square. Arrange a simple layer of overlapping slices in a shallow serving dish. Spread barnacle meat on top.
2. In jar, combine remaining ingredients except cucumber. Shake to blend. Pour over barnacle meat and cheese.
3. Cover and refrigerate at least 4 hours or overnight.
4. Garnish with cucumber rounds. Serve from platter with slotted spoon.

SERVES 2

2 tablespoons unsalted butter
⅛ teaspoon finely minced
   garlic
⅛ teaspoon finely minced
   shallot
1 teaspoon dry white wine
4 giant barnacles, cleaned and
   picked over (for shell
   pieces)
½ teaspoon finely chopped
   parsley

Sautéed Giant Acorn Barnacle

I know of only one restaurant that regularly serves giant barnacles: the Sooke Harbour House on southern Vancouver Island. Owner Sinclair Philip calls the giant barnacle one of the nicest of seafoods, because it has the consistency of crab meat and scallops and a crablike flavor. Accompany barnacles with a nice, dry chardonnay, fumè blanc (like the McDowell Valley from California), or northwest riesling.

1. In a small pan, melt butter over medium heat. Add garlic, shallot, and wine. Cook for a few seconds. Add barnacle meat and cook on both sides for approximately 5 seconds each. Add parsley and serve.

INDEX

COOKBOOKS FROM
PACIFIC SEARCH PRESS

American Wood Heat Cookery (2d Ed. Revised & Enlarged)
    by Margaret Byrd Adams
The Apple Cookbook by Kyle D. Fulwiler
The Bean Cookbook: Dry Legume Cookery
    by Norma S. Upson
The Berry Cookbook (2d Ed. Revised & Enlarged)
    by Kyle D. Fulwiler
Canning and Preserving without Sugar
    by Norma M. MacRae, R.D.
The Eating Well Cookbook by John Doerper
Eating Well: A Guide to Foods of the Pacific Northwest
    by John Doerper
The Eggplant Cookbook by Norma S. Upson
A Fish Feast by Charlotte Wright
Food 101: A Student Guide to Quick and Easy Cooking
    by Cathy Smith
One Potato, Two Potato: A Cookbook by Constance Bollen
    and Marlene Blessing
River Runners' Recipes by Patricia Chambers
The Salmon Cookbook by Jerry Dennon
Starchild & Holahan's Seafood Cookbook by Adam Starchild
    and James Holahan
Wild Mushroom Recipes by the Puget Sound Mycological
    Society
The Zucchini Cookbook (3d Ed. Revised & Enlarged)
    by Paula Simmons